Theology and Film

Theology and Film
Challenging the
Sacred/Secular Divide

Christopher Deacy

Gaye Williams Ortiz

Blackwell
Publishing

© 2008 by Christopher Deacy and Gaye Williams Ortiz

BLACKWELL PUBLISHING
350 Main Street, Malden, MA 02148-5020, USA
9600 Garsington Road, Oxford OX4 2DQ, UK
550 Swanston Street, Carlton, Victoria 3053, Australia

The right of Christopher Deacy and Gaye Williams Ortiz to be identified as the authors of this work has been asserted in accordance with the UK Copyright, Designs, and Patents Act 1988.

First published 2008 by Blackwell Publishing Ltd

1   2008

Library of Congress Cataloging-in-Publication Data

Deacy, Christopher.
    Theology and film : challenging the sacred/secular divide/Christopher Deacy, Gaye Williams Ortiz.
        p. cm.
    Includes bibliographical references and index.
    ISBN 978-1-4051-4437-7 (hardcover : alk. paper)—ISBN 978-1-4051-4438-4 (pbk. : alk. paper)
    1. Motion pictures—Religious aspects—Christianity. I. Ortiz, Gaye Williams. II. Title.

    PN1995.5.D44 2007
    261.5′7—dc22

                                                    2007019134

A catalogue record for this title is available from the British Library.

Set in 10/13pt MPhotina
by SPi Publisher Services, Pondicherry, India.
Printed and bound in Singapore
by Markono Print Media Pte Ltd

The publisher's policy is to use permanent paper from mills that operate a sustainable forestry policy, and which has been manufactured from pulp processed using acid-free and elementary chlorine-free practices. Furthermore, the publisher ensures that the text paper and cover board used have met acceptable environmental accreditation standards.

For further information on
Blackwell Publishing, visit our website at
www.blackwellpublishing.com

Picture credits: film countdown pictures © Antonio Jorge Nunes/Shutterstock
3D media icon © Stelian Ion/Shutterstock.

Contents

Contents

Note on the Text

Although the book as a whole has been a joint enterprise, we split the task of writing each individual chapter as follows:

Part I:
- Theology and Film – Chris Deacy

Part II:
- Introduction – Chris Deacy
- Woman as Spectacle: Theological Perspectives on Women and Film – Gaye Ortiz
- The Green Screen: Theological Perspectives on the Environment and Film – Gaye Ortiz
- A Time to Kill? Theological Perspectives on Violence and Film – Chris Deacy
- The Final Verdict: Theological Perspectives on Justice and Film – Chris Deacy
- Dark Beauty: Theological Perspectives on War as Cinematic Mythology – Gaye Ortiz
- Heaven, Hell, and the Sweet Hereafter: Theological Perspectives on Eschatology and Film – Chris Deacy
- Conclusion: Theological Perspectives on Cinematic Storytelling – initiated by Gaye Ortiz with added material from Chris Deacy

Preface

How possible is it to develop theological perspectives on film without sacrificing theological integrity? How does film appreciation enrich theological inquiry and assist in the understanding of, and dialogue between, contemporary culture and theology? These questions underpin what has been a most fruitful collaboration between us, crossing the transatlantic divide, over the last three years. Although it is by no means a formal "sequel," this book is in many ways a continuation of the exploration that was initiated by the publication a decade ago by Blackwell of *Explorations in Theology and Film* (eds. Clive Marsh & Gaye Ortiz). Just as that text was concerned with popular film and how it lends itself to exploring theological themes, so this book is designed to further the conversation by means of stimulating awareness of a range of methodological and theoretical issues and to aid discussion about certain filmic "texts." In the context of theology and culture, we maintain that film is a necessary and vital element and so have sought to continue the academic dialogue between film and theology in a positive (even enthusiastic) but critical manner.

In particular, this book will revisit the penultimate chapter in the *Explorations* volume – David Jasper's "On Systematizing the Unsystematic: A Response" (Jasper, 1997) – in which Jasper questioned how the "serious" business of theology could by definition be compatible with what amounts to Hollywood's propensity for dabbling in a world of illusions and fantasy. Not surprisingly, Jasper's argument has prompted much theological speculation in subsequent years (see e.g. Deacy, 2001, pp. 9, 105; Marsh, 2004, pp. 83–7; Loughlin, 2005, pp. 1–2), and it is our intention, here, to further the discussion by suggesting that, despite the danger that conflating theology and film can cause "when used in the wrong hands" (Jasper, 1997, p. 236), we can do nothing else but bring culture and theology into serious dialogue in an effort to understand the post-9/11 world in which we live, where we have indeed seen "wrong hands" wreak havoc.

What makes *Theology and Film* distinctive is our emphasis upon the sea-change in theological, religious, and cultural concerns of the new millennium and especially post-9/11. Whether we are speaking of religious fanaticism and fundamentalism or the media's trivialization of cultural values and moral standards, there is much work to be done in continuing mutual conversation instead of resorting to authoritarian edict, censorship, or even hostilities as remedies for the cultural crisis of the new millennium. It may sound a grand claim that this book can avert catastrophic and even eschatological confrontation! What we advocate, however, is that the microcosm of everyday cultural activity, namely watching films and developing theological perspectives, requires careful and serious attention on the part of the theologian.

"Culture" is, of course, a heterogeneous term, and it is not our intention to suggest, here, that there is only one cultural standard or expression in relation to which a conversation with theology may be conducted (nor, indeed, is it our intention to suggest that theology can in any sense be separated from culture – a theme which we will come back to in chapter 1). As the material on Iranian filmmaking in chapter 3 illustrates, there is much in the way of cultural diversity, and in a different pair of hands there is no reason why a similarly themed book could not have been written from the perspective of, say, Bollywood and Indian religion. For the most part, however, the "culture" being referred to in this book tends to pertain to that of a contemporary Western (and in many cases more specifically American) culture, while the "theology" we refer to denotes (though by no means exclusively) areas of Christian beliefs, values, and themes, in accordance with the interests and expertise of the authors.

Rather than simply comprise an unqualified celebration of the way in which theology and film might be thought to feed into each other, this book will take stock of the many nuanced ways in which, throughout history, film and religion have managed (or not, in many cases) to relate. To this end, the first chapter will address in detail the work of H. Richard Niebuhr, whose 1952 publication *Christ and Culture* remains an important benchmark against which contemporary developments in the modern theology and film interchange should be viewed. For those of us who teach modules in theology and film, it is all too easy, sometimes, to lay emphasis on those occasions where some form of dialogue or accommodation between theology and film can be fathomed – as the plethora of literature on the cinematic pursuit of Christ-figures has rather wearingly, and disconcertingly, demonstrated – at the expense of a more critical dissection of the degree to which theology and film are still often seen to comprise discrete and even incompatible subject areas.

As one of us recently discovered when teaching a module on biblical hermeneutics to a class of divinity students training for the priesthood, work undertaken at the interface between the Bible and popular culture, along the lines of Robert Jewett's *Saint Paul at the Movies* (1993) or Adele Reinhartz's *Scripture on the Silver Screen* (2003), is often met with derision and disdain within theology. Even though, in this particular instance, the ostensible topic for discussion was the dangers of uncritically appropriating Christ-figure motifs, the mere mention of *Edward Scissorhands* (Tim Burton, 1990) or *Mystic River* (Clint Eastwood, 2003) led to at least one cry of "blasphemy," and a general consensus among the students that the "serious" business of theology was being dumbed down. Appropriately, therefore, the aim of this book is to accord serious consideration to the limitations of, as well as the potential for, dialogue, and the fact that all five of Niebuhr's models of how Christians can converse with culture require (albeit for different reasons) caution on the part of the theologian will hopefully go some way toward insuring that this book will be of use to anyone interested in the intersection between theology and culture, irrespective of their particular ideological or denominational affiliations.

The text is structured so that there are two clear parts. Following the emphasis in the first part on theoretical and methodological questions that arise in the area of theology and film, the second part of this book will consist of an application of many of these insights to a range of theological perspectives and filmic themes. Focusing on six areas – feminism, the environment, violence, justice, war, and eschatology – together with a final chapter which examines a number of theological perspectives on cinematic storytelling, we will explore whether (and to what extent) a two-way dialogical process exists between theology and film. Can a film challenge our reading of theology in a no less incisive and critical manner than theology can be used to challenge our reading of films? Specific questions to be examined in this book include:

- Have contemporary female characters in films transcended or simply confirmed sexism in society? What are the ramifications of gender identity and a culturally inscribed objectifying portrayal of women for the pursuit of theology? Can any parallels be drawn between feminist critiques of theology and that of the film industry? How do (to cite one specific example) Iranian filmmakers address the limitations imposed upon the representation of women in film as well as the religious values within which they operate?

- In light of creation care ethics, to what extent are environmental films capable of warning us of the dangers that humanity faces when it ignores the power of nature or subverts the natural world for its own convenience and financial gain? Are such pictures a sign of the times, able to prompt the film industry to assume the (perhaps unwilling) role of prophet?

- Can violence be redemptive? Are there grounds for interpreting violence not merely as a destructive and disruptive force, but as something potentially efficacious and even liberating? If so, where does this lead those conservative media critics for whom there is a disjuncture between the ostensibly peaceful values of Christianity and the alleged glorification of violence in TV and films? In light of the controversy surrounding *The Passion of the Christ* (Mel Gibson, 2004), can one condemn violence in one context but condone it in another?

- What are the compromises and limitations of justice? How is the dichotomy between earthly and heavenly justice, as expounded by St. Augustine, reflected – if at all – in "secular" courtroom dramas? Is there a barrier, in cinematic depictions of the law, between the celestial and terrestrial? Does conscience have a role in justice and law-making?

- What religious baggage do we bring with us when we watch war films? In light of the recent emphasis on the "war on terror," particularly in documentary films, do films reflect a shift in the Christian "just war" tradition? How do films about war (and for that matter peace) affect the ability of theologians to respond to questions about the morality and necessity of warfare?

- How have films depicted traditional eschatological ideas concerning life and death, heaven and hell? To what extent have cinematic portrayals of the afterlife tended to use earthly realities as the point of departure and visualized the transcendent through the lens of this-worldly phenomena? How does this impact upon debates in modern theology about mind-dependent worlds and the desacralization of the apocalypse with its emphasis on human, rather than divine, agency?

Theology and Film has been written to appeal to an international market, and with our own different continental perspectives informing the content of the text, this has been a genuinely cross-cultural collaboration. Although it is principally aimed at second year undergraduate students and upward, we hope that our book will be of interest to anyone who wishes to explore the interface between theology and film in the modern (and, indeed, postmodern) world.

This book also has an accompanying website, at www.blackwell publishing.com/theologyandfilm, where the theological explorations conducted in this book can be extended. We strongly encourage you to visit our site, which is a regularly updated resource for further research into the study of theology and film by students, teachers, and other readers.

Acknowledgments

We both wish to thank Wiley-Blackwell, and especially Rebecca Harkin and Andy Humphries along with Fiona Sewell, for their help during the writing of this project. There are also a number of people we wish to thank separately for their support and guidance.

The Department of Communications and Professional Writing of Augusta State University has offered a flexible teaching schedule for the past three years, allowing for time to research and write these chapters. I value my continued contact with fellow scholars in theology and film, especially Rob Johnston, Peter Malone, Sara Anson Vaux, and Clive Marsh, who offer more food for thought than I could possibly ever consume! I am grateful to the community of the Unitarian Universalist Church of Augusta for liberating and challenging me personally in the integration of intellectual inquiry and spiritual journey. As always, I thank my family and, in particular, Wilfred for supporting my work and enriching my life.

Gaye Ortiz
Augusta, Georgia

I am grateful to my colleagues at the University of Kent who have supported me over the last three years. In particular, my thanks go to Robin Gill and Jeremy Carrette, who read the first draft of the manuscript and offered, as ever, constructive and valuable guidance. I also wish to thank Karl Leydecker and Laurence Goldstein in the School of European Culture and Languages for arranging teaching relief for me from one of my first year modules in order that I could concentrate on putting the finishing touches to the manuscript. As ever, I am indebted to my parents, Gerald and Jennifer Deacy, my grandfather, A. Philip Stokes, my mother-in-law, Barbara Hazell (who always used to ask how the book was progressing, but sadly passed away in September 2006 before the writing was finished), and my beautiful wife, Caroline, whose constant love and support have been unceasing.

Chris Deacy
Canterbury, Kent

Part I

Methodological Considerations

Theology and Film

No serious theological activity can take place without a consideration of the social, economic, political, and cultural matrix within which it is practiced. The distrust of human judgment that permeates Karl Barth's *The Humanity of God*, for instance – with the concomitant understanding that God is Wholly Other, we can only know God through God's own revelation, and theology should thus be self-validating (cf. Barth, 1967, pp. 39, 47) – cannot be dissociated from what Barth witnessed at first hand as the folly of World War I, and the sincerely held belief that humanity was utterly lost before God. For Dietrich Bonhoeffer, similarly, the rise of Nazi Germany played an instrumental role in the formation of his program of theological ethics, whereby just "as Christ bears our burdens, so ought we to bear the burdens of other human beings" (in Floyd, 2005, p. 51). Bonhoeffer believed that the Church had forgotten the "costliness" of God's bearing our flesh, and his own experiences in a German prison camp, where he died in 1945, led to the writing of his *Letters and Papers from Prison*, where he argued, in correspondence with his friend Eberhard Bethge, that in order to respond authentically to the challenge of the Gospel one must be a person for other persons – "It is not some religious act which makes a Christian what he is, but participation in the suffering of God in the life of the world" (Bonhoeffer, 1963, p. 123). For Jürgen Moltmann, also, the concept of hope for the coming Kingdom of God that permeates his theology, based on the Cross and Resurrection of Jesus Christ, was, paradoxically, rooted in his experience as a German prisoner of war during World War II. When an American military chaplain gave him a copy of the New Testament, the 19-year-old Moltmann found that his eyes were opened to the reality

 Chris Deacy

of God whose empathy lies with the broken-hearted, and that God was present even behind the barbed-wire fence of his Belgian prison camp. His subsequent attempt to reconstruct key Christian doctrines in light of God's promises for the future was inextricably linked to his exposure to the time when "I saw men in the camp who lost hope. They simply took ill, and died" (in Miller & Grenz, 1998, pp. 104–5). This chapter aims to suggest that, when it comes to continuing our explorations in theology and film (to paraphrase the title of Marsh & Ortiz's 1997 volume), it is no less vital to take stock of the historical and cultural context within which such a dialogue might proceed. No theology – indeed, for that matter, no film – is ever produced in a cultural vacuum, and not even those theologians, like Barth, who feel that it is neither possible nor desirable for human culture to be able to contribute to a theological discussion (Barth, 1967, pp. 51–2) can claim total immunity from the cultural environment within which they work. Was it not Barth, after all, who enjoined Christians to "hold the Bible in one hand and the newspaper in the other" (see, e.g., Miller & Grenz, 1998, p. 9)?

Although the remit of this book is to specifically examine the interaction between theology and film, it is envisaged that the fruits of the theology–film exchange will have much wider repercussions. On a pedagogical level, it is surprising just how many opportunities tend to arise in the course of teaching a theology module that is not specifically film-based to engage with film and other cultural agencies. In a module on science and theology, for example, it can be extremely fruitful to examine the interface between Christianity and physics in light of Robert Zemeckis's *Contact* (1997), where Matthew McConaughey's Father Joss and Jodie Foster's Ellie Arroway raise – not least through their divergent interpretations of Occam's razor – theologically sophisticated questions pertaining to the relationship between science and faith, rationality and superstition, and, ultimately, whether a personal and beneficent creative force can be thought to sustain the universe in the absence of empirical verification. Similarly, *The Butterfly Effect* (Eric Bress & J. Mackye Gruber, 2004) can be a fruitful entry-point into a discussion of Einstein's theory of relativity and the death of the Newtonian mechanistic account of the universe. There is also the case of Neil Jordan's 1999 adaptation of Graham Greene's novel *The End of the Affair*, which may be found to provide a more subtle and challenging slant to the science–religion debate, in its careful study of the emotional consequences of a loss of belief in inherited faith-based assumptions concerning the design and intelligibility of the universe, than the polarized debate that is represented by the

Creationists on the one hand and Richard Dawkins on the other might suggest. There is a downside here, however. No matter how beneficial it may be to motivate students by utilizing a medium in the classroom with which they happen to be familiar, the rationale for appropriating films in this manner needs to be addressed. Conrad Ostwalt rightly noted in a 1998 article that students are "stimulated by the auditory and visual experience of movie watching in ways that reading fails to achieve," and "not intimidated by it ... they are empowered, confident, and bold" (Ostwalt, 1998, ¶4). But it is less clear that his subsequent claim that "With film as part of their curriculum, students seem more willing to take imaginative risks and to think critically" (ibid.) is entirely accurate and can be sustained.

For a start, there is too often a tendency to assume that, because a theological motif or parallel has been located in a film, this comprises a legitimate – and even objective and normative – reading of that film. In Robert Johnston's words, "There is a danger, as anyone teaching in the field of Christianity and the arts knows, in having overenthusiastic viewers find Christ-figures in and behind every crossbar or mysterious origin" (R. Johnston, 2000, p. 53). John Lyden similarly argues that "If every bloodied hero becomes a Christ figure ... it will seem that we can find Christianity in every action film," the net result of this being that this may "stretch the interpretation of such films to the breaking point and do an injustice both to Christianity and to the films in question" (Lyden, 2003, p. 24). To give one recent example, the fact that, upon a superficial rendering, in Clint Eastwood's Oscar-winning film *Mystic River* (2003) the protagonist, Jimmy Markum (Sean Penn), has tattooed on his skin a large Christian cross might suggest that he qualifies as a Christ-figure. After all, to further the correlation, he is, in Charlene Burns's words, "a suffering man with a cross on his back, albeit made of ink rather than wood" (Burns, 2004, ¶11). However, when one considers that Jimmy is a vengeful murderer and thief who certainly suffers for the death of his daughter but is, by the film's denouement, far from racked with guilt for having killed his best friend, Dave Boyle (Tim Robbins), whom Jimmy had wrongly supposed to be responsible for his daughter's murder, it is very far from obvious that Jimmy comprises a Christ-figure. If, as Burns indicates, "A Christ-figure is an innocent victim for whose suffering we are responsible and through whose suffering we are redeemed" (ibid.), then it is apparent that none of the characters in this film meets this criterion. If we simply impose Christian symbolism on to such films, then we fail to hear what these motion pictures are saying *in their own right.* To call a film character a Christ-figure is, above all, dishonest if that identification is made without regard for the *context* within which the alleged Christ-figure appears, and, at the very least, it "borders on triteness" (Marsh, 2004, p. 51). As Robert Pope asserts with respect to the animated movie *Chicken Run* (Peter Lord & Nick Park, 2000), it is not impossible to discern a Christ-figure motif even here in that Rocky the Rooster comes from a realm beyond (the chicken farm) and, through him, the chickens hope to fly (or ascend) to freedom. But, Pope wisely counsels, this "pushes the analogy further than it really ought to go if we are to regard an animated chicken as a 'Christ-figure,' " and he continues that "to push it thus would serve only to demonstrate either the banality of the category itself or the desperation of theologians to find connections with modern culture" (Pope, 2005, p. 174) (figure 1).

It may well be the case that, as Léonie Caldecott recently observed in her contribution to the appropriately named volume *Flickering Images*, "The cinema bears more than a passing resemblance to the cave in [Plato's] *Republic*, where we sit watching the flickering images and shadows of the *Matrix* trilogy on the wall" (Caldecott, 2005, p. 50), but it is the *uncritical* use of theology in film that should prompt us to exercise caution. It is tempting to suggest, in light of the proliferation in recent years both in university modules and in textbooks in the field of theology/ religion and film, that any interaction between theology and film is an innovative and exciting way forward for the discipline of theology, but this is to overlook the inadequacy of much of the work that has been produced in this area. Before we even begin to look at the interface between theology and film, we have to acknowledge that there is no one normative or objective theological framework through which one may attempt to enter into a conversation. It is one thing to suggest that there is scope for "doing theology through film," but "theology" is not an objective or monolithic term. There is a multiplicity of ways of "doing theology" – dependent on whether you are an Anglican, Roman Catholic, Methodist, Quaker, or Russian Orthodox Christian, or, for that matter, whether you are non-practicing or non-believing. These tensions are in evidence within even the same volume of a recent textbook in this area, *Cinéma Divinité: Religion, Theology and the Bible in Film*. Whereas William Telford, one of the book's editors, explains that he approaches theology as an academic or intellectual discipline capable of being practiced irrespective of one's faith (Telford, 2005, p. 26), Gerard Loughlin writes in the book's introduction that "theology can only really be undertaken in faith, the communities and cultures of those who understand themselves to stand in relation to a

Figure 1 The crucifixion pose of Phil Connors (Bill Murray) in *Groundhog Day* (Harold Ramis, 1993) is a prime illustration of the attempt to read Christ-figures into films on the basis of their purported visual correlation with the New Testament Jesus.
Photograph: Columbia/Tri-Star/The Kobal Collection

transcendent source, and recognize and seek to understand such a relationship" (Loughlin, 2005, p. 3). He even goes so far as to argue that any theology that is undertaken outside of such a relationship "has no real object of learning, and is a kind of vacuity" (ibid.). It may, further, be the case that you are a Reconstructionist Jew, a Zen Buddhist, or a Sufi Muslim. Are all theological explorations going to be the same? Without attending to what Marsh refers to as "the specifics of what religions (in all their internal diversity, as well as difference from each other) actually claim and promote" (Marsh, 1998, ¶11), it is misleading and condescending to even begin to attempt a theological conversation in this way.

Developing a Methodology

There is also the consideration that theologians will necessarily disagree among themselves as to the appropriate *method* by which to engage with film. One of the most vitriolic contributions in recent years has come from Steve Nolan, an English Baptist minister, who has argued that the methodology that most theologians favor – a literary approach to film – is inherently flawed. Castigating the work of John May, Robert Johnston, and others (including my own writing in this area), who tend to see film as a "visual story," Nolan argues that "film is not literature – and a literary approach is not sympathetic to film" (Nolan, 2005, p. 26), since it fails "to treat film in its own terms" (ibid.). In its place, Nolan uses the methodology of Lacanian film theory with a view to seeing that "the event of making and watching a film becomes a set of signs pointing us to a range of meanings which will always exceed the signs themselves" (ibid., pp. 26–7). His main argument is that "to earn critical respect theologians must answer the question: what have theology or religious studies brought to the study of film other than subjective opinion?," and he concludes that theological film critics have "succeeded only in leaving their readers with the question: 'So what?'" (ibid., p. 27). Melanie Wright has made a similar claim in her 2007 publication *Religion and Film: An Introduction.* For Wright, literary and filmic texts necessarily make different demands of their respective audiences, in that "A written text draws on verbal sign systems," whereas "in film a multiplicity of different signifiers (aural, visual, verbal) are contained within the space of a single frame or series of frames" (Wright, 2007, p. 21). While acknowledging that such tendencies are not surprising in that most theology and religious studies practitioners have historically privileged literary texts over other media, Wright is concerned that too little of the work published to date in the area of theology/religion and film has picked up on the fundamental incongruity between literature and film. In her words, "film's basic building blocks are the shot (the photographic record made when film is exposed to light, or its digital equivalent) and the editorial cut (the transition between shots, made in the pre-digital age by splicing the end of one shot to the beginning of another) but little

8

religion (or theology) and film work explores these fundamentals" (ibid., p. 22). In a nutshell, to quote Jolyon Mitchell, "The danger is that the attempt to 'read' a film turns it into something that it is not: a written text. Films cannot be reduced to mere words to be analyzed. Other skills, such as visual sensitivity, are required to analyze a film" (Mitchell, 2005, p. 744). In relying upon literary models of film criticism, the rich resources of film criticism and theory – such as sound, editing, cinematography, and *mise-en-scène*, as well as theoretical approaches including psychoanalytic, semiotic, formalist, impressionistic, poststructuralist, Marxist, feminist, and gay and lesbian[1] – are thereby being ignored. As Wright sees it, key questions are thus raised "about what is really going on in the discussions that purport to bring the worlds of film and religion into dialogue" (2007, p. 22), and she asks whether, despite the plethora of books and courses in this area, *film* is really being studied at all.

Yet, although it is demonstrably the case that most of the work undertaken by theological film critics is to "read" films as texts, with parallels made to literary criticism – the writings of Robert Jewett and Larry Kreitzer spring most obviously to mind – this is nevertheless a useful starting-point for our understanding of theology and film. Wright is no doubt correct that "A decent course on film within a theology and/or religious-studies program should regard familiarizing students with key areas of film-studies practice as one of its aims" (Wright, 2007, p. 23), but too much can be made of the "literature" vs. "film" dichotomy. The fact that much of film criticism over the years has also gone down the path of "reading" films as "texts" (Hollows & Jancovich's 1995 *Approaches to Popular Film* is one such example) suggests that, as Anthony Clarke puts it, "film still holds significant connections with literature" (Clarke, 2005, p. 61). Alister McGrath's anthology of *Christian Literature*, published in 2001, presents clear grounds for interchange with the study of film, as denoted by the discussion that appears in his preface concerning what is precisely meant by the term "Christian literature." He writes that no definition "has yet been offered which is immune from criticism or modification" (McGrath, 2001, p. xiv), but the four questions he then proceeds to ask are particularly germane to the theology–film field:

- Is the essentially "Christian" element in literature [for which we could substitute film] related to its content, its form, or the interpretation offered?
- Must a piece of writing [or a film] be *exclusively* Christian to count as "Christian literature" [or film]?

- Can a minimalist definition be offered, by which "Christian" means "not offending Christian sensibilities," or "not contradicting Christian beliefs"?
- Is fiction disqualified from being a Christian literary [or filmic] form on account of its non-factuality? (ibid.)

McGrath then follows these questions with the identification of three broad categories within which "works which would generally be agreed to be regarded as 'Christian literature'" (ibid.) could be said to fall. The first of these comprises those works "which are specifically written to serve the needs of Christians – such as prayers, devotional works, and sermons" (ibid.). The filmic equivalent would be movies whose explicit aim is to bolster the faith of Christian audience members. A film such as *The Omega Code* (Robert Marcarelli, 1999), whose producers are affiliated with the Christian cable channel Trinity Broadcasting Network, is a particularly good case in point. The film, which draws on the Torah, the Book of Revelation, and Michael Drosnin's novel *The Bible Code* for its inspiration, delineates an apocalyptic war between the forces of darkness and light, and is cited on the evangelical website Christian Spotlight on the Movies – a site whose explicit aim is, in an age of what it identifies as lying, greed, pornography, adultery, fornication, rape, and murder, to present the Gospel of Jesus Christ in ways that traditional missionaries cannot (Taylor, 1996) – as "THE film for Christians to recommend. It is THE film to take the 'lost' to see. We should support this film with the 'best' word-of-mouth advertising we can give it. *The Omega Code* deserves all the enthusiasm of *Star Wars*" (Downs, 1999). Although McGrath does not specifically refer to a missiological dimension, his assertion that works that belong in this first category "are a response to the nature of the Christian faith, and can be seen as both responding to the needs of that faith and expressing its nature" (ibid.) would certainly accommodate those cultural products that seek to do more than simply preach to the converted. Accordingly, the critical reaction to Mel Gibson's chronicle of the last 12 hours in the life of Jesus, *The Passion of the Christ* (2004), would also legitimate inclusion in this category. Although it is not a self-contained piece of work that can be judged simply on the basis of what happens on screen, inasmuch as if one is already a committed Christian then one will be much more likely to understand and better placed to accept the graphic depiction of violence on offer than if one is approaching from an outsider's perspective, these words from another Christian Spotlight contributor suggests that there is a strong missiological dimension to this picture: "I am closer to Jesus now after witnessing his sacrifice for me in its full horror and brutality. My hope is that somehow this film will be taken as a witnessing tool around the world... because I believe in this film there is the power to bring millions to Christ" (qtd in Willis, 2004). A more detailed exposition of films that belong in this category will appear later in this chapter in a discussion of the fifth of H. Richard Niebuhr's models of "Christ" and "culture" (Niebuhr, 1952, ch. 6).

McGrath's second category encompasses general literature that is not specific to the Christian faith, but that has been "shaped or influenced by Christian ideas, values, images, and narratives" (McGrath, 2001, p. xiv), irrespective of whether the writers would identify themselves as Christian. The lyrical ballads of Wordsworth and Coleridge would thus qualify in this section. This links with how, for Robert Johnston, "Some movies are simply inexplicable except from a Christian theological perspective" (R. Johnston, 2000, p. 51). A film such as *The Da Vinci Code* (Ron Howard, 2006) would be an obvious candidate for inclusion here. For what is relevant is not whether a movie can propagate or sustain the Christian faith (though anecdotal evidence suggests that, after reading the Dan Brown novel or watching the film adaptation, *The Da Vinci Code* caused an upsurge in the number of people keen to join Opus Dei), but the extent to which Christian beliefs, doctrines, teachings, and history have strongly influenced – even inspired – its subject matter. In the case of *The Da Vinci Code*, the plot hinges on the quest to find the Holy Grail of Christian legend, the identity of Mary Magdalene, and the disclosure that one of the lead characters, Sophie Neveu (Audrey Tautou), is the last living descendant of Jesus Christ. However, the fact that one can spot Christian themes in a film is not the same thing as saying that the filmmaker is "covertly affirming a Christian perspective" (R. Johnston, 2000, p. 70). As with the discussion above concerning the uncritical appropriation of cinematic Christ-figures, where there is often a tendency to falsely baptize a film character as a functional equivalent of Jesus Christ (see Kozlovic, 2004), movies do not need to be explicitly Christian in their content or form to be theologically significant. It is much more appropriate to see film as an expression of broader cultural[2] influences that may or may not encompass distinctively Christian elements. The intentions of film directors will sometimes "cohere with theological interests and purposes, even if those intentions are very diverse and not overtly religious or theological" (Marsh, 2004, p. 107) – and this should be sufficient. It may be the case that an audience watching *The Da Vinci*

Code or *Edward Scissorhands* (Tim Burton, 1990) will find theological motifs in these films, and read them as theological – even faith-inspiring – texts, but it does not ultimately matter if we can penetrate the mind(s) of the filmmaker(s) and glean whether or not they had a theological agenda in creating them. Sometimes, albeit unintentionally, it may well be the case that a non-explicitly Christian film will be more faith-inspiring for viewers than the likes of *The Omega Code* and Gibson's *Passion*. Writing in the context of theological aesthetics, and the religiosity of sacred works of art, Pie-Raymond Régamey argued some fifty years ago that a pious and faith-oriented perspective (along the lines of McGrath's first category, perhaps) is not always the most helpful anyway:–

> It is not surprising if the works that the pious artist produces for pious people manifest clearly the dull, dispirited devotion that belongs to the common faith of many today... We have to conclude that in certain cases a non-Christian will have a deeper, more genuine, and more effective feeling for the theme or function of a work than will a Christian.
>
> (Régamey, 2004, p. 224)

Régamey's argument is that if the artist begins from the starting-point of faith, the work of art concerned may be "artificially manipulated for the good of the cause" (ibid.), and that there may be among non-believers a "far more intense and demanding" process at work "than is to be found among many Christians!" (ibid., p. 225).

Of course, this is very different from the first of McGrath's categories, where confessional works, made by Christians and for Christians, were discussed. However, it is in McGrath's third, and final, category that we find a further development of the relationship between theology and literature (and, by implication, film). This is where the influence of Christianity is apparent, as in categories one and two, but there is evidence of an "appropriation, development, or modification of Christian assumptions" (McGrath, 2001, p. xv). Rather than merely illustrate and reflect Christian ideas, along the lines of films that bear witness to purported Christ-figure motifs such as *E.T. The Extra-Terrestrial* (Steven Spielberg, 1982) and *One Flew Over the Cuckoo's Nest* (Milos Forman, 1975), this third category comprises those works that challenge and even subvert dominant theological paradigms, for example by setting up a dichotomy between what Christianity traditionally espouses on matters of doctrine or ethics and what happens in experience. The aforementioned *The End of the Affair*, which questions and even subverts fundamental tenets of Catholic teaching concerning the rationality of the cosmos, the existence of miracles, and the beneficence of the Creator, is a good case in point. There is, further, the case of films such as *Pleasantville* (Gary Ross, 1998) and *The Truman Show* (Peter Weir, 1998) that not only draw on Christian ideas pertaining to the Creation and Fall of the Book of Genesis but subvert them, inasmuch as it is suggested in these movies that it is theologically beneficial to accept change and disorder rather than live in a sterile, prelapsarian, Edenic paradise, in order for human beings to realize their potential and growth and to exercise their free will. Two of Clint Eastwood's recent films could also be said to correspond to this third category as, in both *Mystic River* (2003) and *Million Dollar Baby* (2004), the efficacy of the Church is challenged. Although the former was cited earlier as a less helpful example of what Steve Nolan would call "superficial equivalences of realist representation" (Nolan, 2005, p. 43), once we move beyond the Christ-figure analogy, *Mystic River* could also be seen as a searing indictment of those who, like the Marcum family in the film, see the Roman Catholic Church as "nothing more than a social institution," whose "teachings have no impact in their lives" (Burns, 2004, ¶18). Charlene Burns even goes so far as to suggest that the parable of *Mystic River* teaches us that, though "the symbols of Christianity have been adopted by our culture ... its substance has not" (ibid.), and that, in a fallen world, the institutional Church is actually complicit in that fallenness. This will be discussed further in the chapter on justice. In *True Crime* (1998), further, Eastwood can be seen to critique the representatives of the Church as suitable messengers of salvation, as epitomized in the depiction of an unctuous prison chaplain working on Death Row. The secularization of the struggle for redemption, from the Church to the "mean streets" of New York's Little Italy, that characterizes much of Martin Scorsese's early work – not least in *Mean Streets* (1973) itself – would also be a good example of this third category, since there can be seen to be a theology actually going on in these films. For all the condemnation that has been meted out by some Church groups to *The Da Vinci Code* for its supposed non-piety – in particular, its suggestion that Christ may have been married to Mary Magdalene and had a child – *The Da Vinci Code* is more akin to an Indiana Jones-style treasure hunt, along the lines of *National Treasure* (Jon Turteltaub, 2004), than a challenging or critical theological exploration of the Graham Greene (in literature) or Martin Scorsese (in film) kind, and this is where the line of demarcation between McGrath's second and third categories could be said to lie.

Christ against Culture

In light of the discussion so far, it is thus easy to concur with Anthony Clarke's claim that "Whereas some films clearly set out to portray Christian or religious events, such as the various 'Jesus' films, or explore particular religious themes, it would be theology's loss to confine our reflection to this category alone" (Clarke, 2005, p. 64). Significantly, however, for too long this has been the predominant way in which a theological engagement with culture has been practiced. Peter Horsfield encapsulates the situation well when he writes from his own experience in Australia that "A persistent issue I have found in working with church leaders around the subject of electronic media is their fear that engaging with electronic media seriously will compromise Christian faith" (Horsfield, 2003, p. 276). Horsfield continues that for most Church leaders:

> Christianity is a distinct body of ideas and practices, defined and defended most effectively in theological books and journals. In this common view, electronic media are seen as more than just another form of mediation: their very structure as well as common content are seen as a significant threat to Christianity as a thoughtful, ordered and authoritative faith structure.
>
> (ibid.)

There is thus a sense in which only a limited and partial engagement with culture can be permitted, since cultural activity is to a very real extent an anathema to Christian beliefs and values. The underlying consideration here would seem to be that Christianity and culture are divergent – and irreconcilable – entities, in a manner that corresponds to what H. Richard Niebuhr had to say on the subject. Niebuhr, an American Christian theologian based at Harvard Divinity School, proposed, in his seminal 1952 publication *Christ and Culture*, five ways in which Christ and culture can be said to relate, the first of which directly concerns us at this juncture. This first model is that of *Christ against Culture*. In Niebuhr's words, "Whatever may be the customs of the society in which the Christian lives, and whatever the human achievements it conserves, Christ is seen as opposed to them, so that he confronts men with the challenge of an 'either-or' decision" (Niebuhr, 1952, p. 54). There is a clear biblical antecedent for this model. In the First Letter of John, the world is pictured as a realm that is under the power of evil and "into which the citizens of the kingdom of light must not enter" (ibid., p. 61). As Niebuhr puts it, this worldly realm constitutes "a culture that is concerned with temporal and passing values, whereas Christ has words of eternal life" (ibid.). In the early Church, also, Tertullian can be seen to bear witness to this model, as betokened by his rejection of Christian participation in the Roman state, including military service, trade, philosophy, and the arts (ibid., p. 66). In the twentieth century, such an exclusivist picture would find a ready sympathy in the theology of Karl Barth, for whom, as discussed at the beginning of this chapter, God is Wholly Other and theology should thus be self-validating (Barth, 1967, p. 39). Barth was mindful of the fact that, if we are not careful, theology could all too easily become a mere tool for the promotion of a wholly human agenda, as was the case, Barth thought, with Rudolf Bultmann's program of demythologization and appropriation of Heideggerean existentialism. In short, for Barth, nothing that is created by humans can enable revelation to happen, since there is no point of consciousness between God and man – only God can reveal God, and as human beings we are utterly lost before God. Regarding the concept of "beauty," for example, Barth believed that it was dangerous to apply such a human and secular adjective to the transcendent God:

> If we say now that God is beautiful, and make this statement the final explanation of the assertion that God is glorious, do we not jeopardize or even deny the majesty and holiness and righteousness of God's love? Do we not bring God in a sinister because in a sense intimate way into the sphere of man's oversight and control, into proximity to the ideal of all human striving?
>
> (Barth, 2004, p. 315)

The downside of this approach, however, is that it is not particularly dialogical – indeed, there is extremely limited scope for entering into a conversation between "theology" and "culture." The ultimate authority and point of reference of what is and is not acceptable emanates from pre-established theological norms. In his influential publication *Knowing God*, James Packer epitomizes the problem from a Calvinist position. Stressing the Protestant preference for the written word over images, Packer, writing in 1973, believes that even reverential pictures and statues of Jesus contravene this position, since "those who make images and use them in worship, and thus inevitably take their theology from them, will in fact tend to neglect God's revealed will at every point. The mind that takes up with images is a mind that has not yet learned to love and attend to God's Word" (Packer, qtd in R. Johnston, 2000, p. 75). As we shall see later, this goes against the grain of how for Paul Tillich – who was brought up a Lutheran – neither the religious nor the secular realm "should be in separation from the other," since both "are rooted in religion in the larger sense of the word" (Tillich, 1964, p. 9), but during the course of the twentieth century, since the inception of film, the *Christ against Culture* position has been particularly influential. It is explored, for instance, in Mark Joseph's book *The Rock & Roll Rebellion* (1999), where the point is made that "From the moment Elvis first swayed his hips and Bill Haley rocked around the clock, rock and roll has been on a collision course with millions of Americans . . . It was seen as the Devil's music and to be avoided at all costs" (Joseph, 1999, pp. 1–2). In this light it is worth noting the following quotation from David Noebel with respect to the Beatles, cited in the same volume:

> They wanted to subvert Western culture. They were pro-drugs, pro-evolution, and pro-promiscuous sex; anti-Christ and more . . . Rock music is a negation of soul, spirit and mind, and is destructive to the body . . . The muscles are weakened, the heartbeat is affected, and the adrenal glands and sex hormones are upset by continued listening . . . It's also been shown that rock music destroys house plants. If it destroys God's plants, what's it doing to young people?
>
> (in ibid., p. 3)

This position also coincides with the "Condemnation" model identified by William Romanowski in *Eyes Wide Open: Looking for God in Popular Culture* (2001, p. 12). While such an approach is manifest in such consumer tactics as boycotts, Romanowski suggests that "it is perhaps more pervasive as an attitude that aligns Hollywood or popular culture with the realm of evil as opposed to the Kingdom of God" (Romanowski, 2001, p. 12). Accordingly, "If the popular arts are 'of the devil,' the only recourse for Christians is complete abstinence," to the point, indeed, that, for some churchgoers, only the complete renunciation of secular culture "is the mark of a true believer" (ibid.). Further evidence of this position can be seen in Robert Johnston's "Avoidance" model (R. Johnston, 2000, pp. 43–5). In *Reel Spirituality*, Johnston refers to the large numbers of Christians who have grown up in homes where it is believed that, even if movies are not actually sinful, "the cinema was at least not morally uplifting or a good use of leisure time" (ibid., p. 24) and should thus be avoided. As Johnston puts it, "The father of one of my friends worried, for example, about what would happen if he were in a theater when Jesus returned. Surely Jesus would not approve!" (ibid.) Writing in the introduction to Herbert Miles's 1947 publication *Movies and Morals*,

Hyman Appleman went so far as to castigate movies as "next to liquor, the outstanding menace to America and to the world," while for Miles himself movies were believed to constitute "the organ of the devil, the idol of sinners, the sink of infamy, the stumbling block to human progress, the moral cancer of civilization, the Number One Enemy of Jesus Christ" (qtd in R. Johnston, 2000, p. 43; see also Clarke & Fiddes, 2005, p. ix). John Lyden refers to similar ideas in his 2003 publication *Film as Religion*, where the point is made that sexual themes in films initially gave rise, in America at the beginning of the twentieth century, to prohibition and censorship. The police in Chicago, for instance, were authorized to confiscate any films that they deemed to be "immoral" or "obscene" (Lyden, 2003, p. 127).

Especially in its early days, the Church as a body also played a prominent role in attempts to control the movie industry. In 1929, the Catholic Movie Code in America called for censorship of nudity and explicit sexuality and for the positive reinforcement of religious, family, and societal values over against what it perceived as the decadence of the film industry. This code became the basis for the Hays Office Code, which was named after Will Hays, an elder in the Presbyterian Church as well as chairman of the Republican Party, who became the first president of the Motion Picture Producers and Distributors Association in 1922. Hays believed that, at a time of social uncertainty (specifically in relation to the Depression), film should be employed to bolster national morale, and that the mission of the film industry should be one of prescribing what audiences ought to feel rather than reflecting what they were actually experiencing and suffering. This is demonstrated by the recommendation of Joseph Breen, head of the Studio Relations Department at the Hays Office, in a letter to Samuel Goldwyn in 1937 concerning the screenplay for the film *Dead End* (William Wyler, 1937). For Breen counseled that the picture should not emphasize "the presence of filth, or smelly garbage cans, or garbage floating in the river" (qtd in Tuska, 1984, p. 137), but conform to more conservative and inoffensive standards. Breen was a devoted Roman Catholic, and his involvement with Hollywood was recently dramatized in Martin Scorsese's biopic of the life of Howard Hughes, *The Aviator* (2004), in which Breen is depicted as remonstrating with Hughes over the inappropriateness of portraying nudity on screen, specifically in the context of the disclosure of Jane Russell's breasts in Hughes's film *The Outlaw* (1934). Similar tensions can be seen to exist in the objectives of the Catholic Legion of Decency, founded in 1933, the present-day incarnation of which is the United States Conference of Catholic

Bishops' Office for Film and Broadcasting. The Legion asked its members to "remain away from all motion pictures except those which do not offend decency and Catholic morality" (qtd in Johnston, 2000, p. 36), and Johnston notes that within just a few months of this pronouncement seven million to nine million Catholics had observed it to the letter. Indeed, in 1934, Cardinal Dougherty of Philadelphia referred to this edict as "binding all in conscience under pain of sin" (ibid.), and cinema attendance in Philadelphia subsequently dropped by 40 percent. In more recent years, the film *Priest* (Antonia Bird, 1994), which depicts a Roman Catholic cleric in a Liverpool parish indulging in a homosexual relationship, was denounced by the American cardinal John O'Connor for being "as viciously anti-Catholic as anything that has ever rotted on the silver screen" (in Ortiz, 2003, p. 186).

It is worth stating at this juncture that it would be wrong to conclude that all Roman Catholics see film as the epitome of all that is unholy and as a barrier to the promulgation of Christian values. As will be discussed in relation to the third of Niebuhr's five categories, there are many within Catholicism – including, not least, Martin Scorsese – for whom film can expand the theologian's understanding and enable a greater insight to be achieved. This sacramental and incarnational approach may be at odds with the Catholic Movie Code and the Catholic Legion of Decency, but Catholic film juries over the years (under the auspices of SIGNIS) at such festivals as Venice, Locarno, and Cannes have increasingly been able to see film as an important arbiter of cultural meaning, where it is the responsibility of the Church to read "the signs of the times." When *Priest* was shown at the Berlin Film Festival in 1994, it is significant that the Catholic members of the Ecumenical Jury issued a press release acknowledging that issues of "clerical celibacy and homosexual relationships of priests are a real problem of the Catholic Church," but signaling that the Church should not be avoiding or denying sexually related issues but should "confront, reflect on and clarify them" (qtd in Ortiz, 2003, p. 187). Provocative and controversial though the film's issues may be, the jury's statement sought to draw attention to the many "positive Christian themes and values" that they found to be "strongly present" in Antonia Bird's film, such as "the search for God, the involvement of the faith community, prayer, the Eucharist, solidarity, forgiveness," and "reconciliation" (ibid.). Notwithstanding the very real threat that many Catholics genuinely feel is created by film, the opportunity afforded by the silver screen to enter into dialogue with culture should not be underestimated. That the press release was endorsed by the bishop of Berlin, with the film then scheduled for screenings to Catholic communities across Germany (ibid.), does suggest that the goalposts have the capacity to be moved. At the very least, as Johnston notes, many people who previously urged Christians to abstain from cultural engagement now argue for *caution* instead. In his words, "Given the advent of the television age, abstinence is less and less a practical (or practiced) option" (R. Johnston, 2000, p. 59).

That said, however, whereas in Catholicism there are clear signs that a position of complete abstinence is not widely endorsed, new forms of conservatism, especially in Protestant America, have returned to the top of the agenda. In the *Explorations in Theology and Film* volume, published in 1997, mention was made of the assertiveness of the so-called "New Right" (see Marsh & Ortiz, 1997c, p. 246), which "bemoans the decline of 'Christendom'" and mourns "the loss of the impact of Christianity upon Western, cultural values," with a view to reasserting "traditional values" and "reclaiming Christianity's proclamatory voice in Western society" (ibid.). Accordingly, unless film is suitable for family viewing and promotes family values, the old tensions between the sacred and the profane, the religious and the secular, "theology" and "culture," will persist. In the words of the conservative critic Michael Medved, "In our private lives, most of us deplore violence and feel little sympathy for the criminals who perpetuate it; but movies, TV, and popular music all revel in graphic brutality, glorifying vicious and sadistic characters who treat killing as a joke" (qtd in Lynch, 2005, pp. 84–5). More will be said on this particular point in the chapter on violence. For the moment, though, it is significant that even films that espouse traditional values of "good" versus "evil" are not immune from attack from conservative Christians, as the criticism of the *Harry Potter* books and movies has shown. J. K. Rowling's 2000 entry in the series, *Harry Potter and the Goblet of Fire*, was attacked by some Christian groups for its ostensibly sympathetic portrayal of witchcraft, yet, as Lyden observes, the *Harry Potter* stories "deal largely with a conflict between those who would use magic for good and those who would use it for evil, so that its morality is quite traditional" (Lyden, 2003, p. 249). In his book *The Last Temptation of Hollywood*, Larry Poland goes even further: "If there is no 'chilling effect' for film and TV producers from the deeply religious majority in America, we will be seeing child molesting, cannibalism, sado-masochism, bestiality, and even 'snuff' films soon accepted as 'art' on the major movie screens of America" (qtd in R. Johnston, 2000, p. 44). Since Poland's book is a play on the title of Scorsese's 1988 Jesus film, *The Last Temptation of Christ*, brief reference to the controversy that this inspired among conservative groups would not be out of place, not least because it was, in Robin Riley's eyes, "one of the most prominent episodes in the recent history of popular culture to challenge fundamental beliefs about the sacred" (Riley, 2003, p. 1), engendering as it did a feverish debate between religious conservative protestors and liberal progressive defenders. Whereas, on the one hand, in his adaptation of Nikos Kazantzakis's novel, Scorsese may have seen himself "as an important instigator of social change, bringing about new ways of seeing Jesus Christ" (ibid., p. 38), it has been argued, conversely, that all that really happened is that liberal progressives and religious conservatives "became locked in a struggle for legitimacy, attacking the weakness of the opposition while reaffirming their own institutional legitimacy" (ibid., p. 3). Riley's detailed investigation into the way in which Scorsese's fictionalized biopic polarized America, *Film, Faith, and Cultural Conflict*, is a significant work, since his study of the various and competing ways in which the film was received and perceived – from a work of blasphemy and sacrilege that ought to be destroyed, to a challenge, which must be surmounted, to religious expression of which the freedom is protected by the American Constitution – says much about the state of relations in modern America. On the one hand, there are those who are critical of a theological engagement with culture (along the lines of Niebuhr's *Christ against Culture* model), and on the other, there are those, such as Universal Studios, which produced the film, for whom "no one sect or coalition has the power to set boundaries around each person's freedom to explore religious and philosophical questions whether through speech, books or films" (qtd in ibid., p. 69).

It is hard not to conclude from this that a fissure has thereby opened between conservative and liberal positions in America today. At one point, Riley even labels Scorsese a "heretic" (ibid., p. 11) and claims that "Critics that argue for the unfettered right of a film to blaspheme are in effect campaigning for the right to selectively offend the members of those they disagree with, namely religious conservatives, by abusing their religious beliefs" (ibid., p. 95). Since it is Riley's contention that as "a protected representation of free speech," *Last Temptation* "serves to sanction the persecution and victimization of religious conservatives" (ibid., p. 117), is the solution to ban outright anything that offends? It is our view that, whether we are speaking of religious fanaticism and fundamentalism (or, for that matter, the media's trivialization of cultural values and moral standards), there is much work to be done in continuing mutual conversation instead of resorting to authoritarian edict, censorship, or even hostilities as remedies for the cultural crisis of the new millennium. Otherwise, it is hard to see how, to cite Riley in the conclusion of *Film, Faith, and Cultural Conflict*, there can ever be a renewed commitment to the processes of dialogue and reconciliation, "opening the way for honest and constructive dialogue between competing segments" (ibid., p. 127). It cannot be denied that the removal of rancor and scapegoating (a prominent theme in Riley's book) is a genuinely good thing, but at the cost of freedom of religious expression it is difficult to see how the banning of films and other cultural products that offend is going to bring us any closer to what Riley identifies as the "ideal" of "a more tolerant society" (ibid., p. 123).

The prognosis is not altogether promising, as the release of Gibson's *Passion* in 2004 served to exacerbate the tensions even further. However, in a twist of irony, whereas the *Last Temptation* controversy in 1988 may have involved religious conservatives falling victim to an unsympathetic and intolerant media and legal system, which ultimately sanctioned the right of Scorsese's film to be released, Gibson's ultra-orthodox version of the Jesus story was sanctioned by conservative groups and scorned by liberals. Scorsese's biopic may have fueled similar antagonisms, but when conservative Christians such as Pat Buchanan saw the debate over Gibson's film as "a religious war going on in our country for the soul of America" (qtd in Berenbaum & Landres, 2004, p. 8), it is clear that, unlike in 1988, Gibson's film is seen to lie on the winning side! Despite claims that the film is anti-Semitic (see Deacy, 2005, pp. 117–26), some of the film's defenders – including Gibson himself – have turned such allegations on their head, claiming that to criticize the film is tantamount to attacking Christianity itself (Berenbaum & Landres, 2004, p. 8). In the words of Berenbaum and Landres in their book *After* The Passion *Is Gone*, Gibson's defenders "spun" these counter-claims "as evidence that there was a conspiracy to destroy the film and discredit Christianity" (ibid., p. 3), which in turn allowed Gibson, they allege, to portray himself as a martyr and a hero. As Jeffrey Siker sees it, "Gibson's film can be seen as a kind of embodiment of these more conservative voices, a reactionary counterpunch to current developments in historical research and in constructive Christian theology" (Siker, 2004, p. 144), not least in the way that the film has "touched a nerve with Christians who believe that scholars and church leaders alike are selling out some of the deepest doctrinal commitments of their faith" (ibid., p. 143).

This has enormous ramifications for our understanding of the relationship between theology and culture. As William Cork notes, having conducted a study of internet discussions of *The Passion* among evangelical Protestant groups, the "emotional defense of the film" has had the concomitant effect of "preventing objective discussion of the questions that it raised" (Cork, 2004, p. 38). Although Cork sees some positive benefit in the use of blogging and web-posting, in that participants' online interaction "is a bonding experience" (ibid., p. 42) that can bring "together people of different backgrounds or beliefs who might never meet in the brick-and-mortar world" (ibid.), it is significant that he qualifies his conclusion that internet communications can serve the positive function of passing "on to a younger generation what we have already learned and shared" with the following clause: "provided that they are used effectively for education and understanding" (ibid., p. 41). It is the very absence of an educational dimension that was responsible for initiating J. Shawn Landres and Michael Berenbaum's collection *After* The Passion *Is Gone* in the first place. As the editors explain in the introduction, "Mel Gibson has the right to make and distribute almost any kind of film he likes, but the rules of civil society and scholarship require that he and his defenders respect the rights of critics, scholars, and others to analyze and evaluate the film" (Berenbaum & Landres, 2004, p. 7). Crucially, the editors affirm their opposition to those defenders and critics alike who "use threatening or demonizing language to denigrate those who do not share their views" (ibid., p. 8), to the point that "This book attempts what too many of *The Passion*'s defenders, as well as some of its critics, refused to do: to engage in reasoned scholarly discussion" (ibid., p. 10). Whatever the views of the book's contributors, what lies at the heart of their endeavors is "a spirit of collaborative scholarly inquiry that acknowledges the possibility of other positions even as it respects each person's right to assert his or her own viewpoint" (ibid.). Since, as one of the contributors, David Elcott, attests, "*The Passion of the Christ* is not about Jews; it is about an increasingly polarized America" where "Religious assaults that divide us into the forces of absolute good and absolute evil are a sure recipe for increased hatred" (Elcott, 2004, p. 240), Gibson's film is clearly a barometer of the tensions that exist in contemporary America between conservative and liberal Christians over the use – and abuse – of cultural agencies.

Such is the state of play in America today that, in 2005, 12 Imax cinemas refused to show films that refer to the theory of evolution for fear of a backlash from conservative Christians. Such educational films as

Cosmic Voyage (Bayley Silleck, 1996), *Galapagos: The Enchanted Voyage* (David Clark & Al Giddings, 1999), and *Volcanoes of the Deep Sea* (Stephen Low, 2003), many of which are shown in Imax cinemas located in science museums, were withdrawn, following written comments from audience members such as, "I really hate it when the theory of evolution is presented as fact" and "I don't agree with [the filmmakers'] presentation of human existence" (qtd in BBC News, 2005). According to Lisa Buzzelli, director of the Charleston Imax Cinema in South Carolina, "We have definitely a lot more 'creation' public than 'evolution' public" (ibid.). Despite the constraints identified by David Jasper in his contribution to *Explorations in Theology and Film*, namely that, when "used in the wrong hands," both theology and film can be "dangerous and powerful instruments" (Jasper, 1997, p. 236), it is our contention, a decade later, that we can do nothing else but bring culture and theology into serious dialogue in an effort to understand the post-9/11 world in which we live, where we have indeed seen "wrong hands" wreak havoc. Although the specific context within which Jasper was writing is that – not least in the discussion of films that bear witness to Christ-figure motifs – "the shadow of theology is ever present in stories which would never be conceived of in themselves as theological or even religious" (ibid.), a comparable warning could be raised here in relation to the way in which films such as Gibson's *Passion* have been employed to sanction an exclusivist and reactionary theology. Referring to its intense display of violence, Susannah Heschel goes so far as to argue that *The Passion* "sanctifies a nationalistic memory of the horrific events of September 11: a Passion of America during which innocent, defenceless Americans were attacked over and over in a most brutal fashion in an unthinkable, unprecedented, unwarranted brutal assault that killed thousands of innocent people and left thousands of families bereft" (Heschel, 2004, p. 177). Similar dangers are in evidence in the links that Mark Juergensmeyer makes between the film's phenomenal success and "the current preoccupation with religious terrorism" (Juergensmeyer, 2004, p. 279). Although, as Juergensmeyer notes, those who perpetrate terrorism in the film are Jewish rather than Muslim – as evinced by "the shadowy, bearded and robed figures" (ibid., p. 281) of the Jewish Sanhedrin – he proceeds to ask whether it is

> such a stretch to imagine that in Middle America, any bearded, robed enemy
> of Christendom might be viewed as a part of a generic "Other" capable of
> the most hideous anti-American terrorist acts? ... [T]hey could be any of the
> shadowy, bearded and robed figures in America's image of terrorist

activists – the Ayatollah Khomeini of the Iranian Revolution, Sheik Omar Abdul-Rahman of the 1993 bombing of the World Trade Center, Sheik Abdul Yassin of Hamas, or Osama bin Laden of al-Qaeda.

(ibid., pp. 281–2)

Another danger presented when films are "used in the wrong hands" arises from the tendency among more conservative groups to expound a critique of a film that is what Lynch calls "very high on criticism and very low on thoughtful analysis" (Lynch, 2005, p. ix). As Johnston suggests in *Useless Beauty*, "Some Christian movie critics offer a content analysis of movies as to their moral suitability," such as "the presence, or lack thereof, of sex, violence, coarse language, or a pagan worldview" (R. Johnston, 2004, p. 183). Some Christian websites such as Christian Spotlight tend to go down this path, which leads to a tendency to pit Christian "judgment" against what critics and secular audiences may be inclined to glean from the film. In the case of the Robin Williams family comedy *R.V.* (Barry Sonnenfeld, 2006), for example, in which a dysfunctional family embark on a road trip in a hired recreational vehicle to the Colorado Rockies, Christian Spotlight acknowledges that the picture "delivers several very funny moments" but also warns that "viewers must endure a seemingly endless line of crudeness (occasionally to the point of disgusting), rudeness, and immodesty along the way" (Soencksen, 2006). When it transpires that the rationale for the trip is that Bob Munro (Robin Williams) has to attend a crucial business meeting in Colorado during a planned holiday to Hawaii or else he will lose his job, and this is his way of attempting to balance his work–family priorities (inevitably to the satisfaction of neither his wife nor his children, none of whom know about the conflict), Christian Spotlight denounces what it sees as "a gigantic lie," and invokes passages from Luke 12 and Proverbs 23 as a retort to its perception of the film's tendency to promote "greed, covetousness, and materialism" (ibid.). The site also advises that "Though nudity and strong sexuality are absent, immodesty is rampant," with one character in particular showing "cleavage in every shot," which they fear will cause "male viewers" to be "distracted" (ibid.). Setting up a dichotomy between Christianity and culture – as made explicit in the stipulation that "impressionable teens may be influenced by the worldly character of this film" (ibid.) – Christian Spotlight cites Jesus's warning in Matthew 5:28 that "every one who looks at a woman lustfully has already committed adultery with her in his heart," and counsels that "It's a very high standard, but one we must not yield on" (ibid.). A similar criticism can be found in Michael Medved's review of *Superman Returns* (Bryan Singer,

2006), in which the conservative critic opines that children who see the movie will not fail to notice that "Lois Lane has followed politically correct trends to become an unwed mother, raising a kid of somewhat mysterious parentage" (Medved, 2006a). Medved is also quick to disparage *The Fast and the Furious: Tokyo Drift* (Justin Lin, 2006) for, among other things, its "vague drug references and leering views of loads of scantily clad hotties" (Medved, 2006b).

Not only does this sort of criticism inhibit the cultivation of a theological conversation, but, to cite Niebuhr regarding the first of his five theological models, it is inadequate to affirm the "sole dependence of Jesus Christ to the exclusion of culture," since "Christ claims no man purely as a natural being, but always as one who has become human in a culture...He cannot dismiss the philosophy and science of his society as though they were external to him; they are in him" (Niebuhr, 1952, p. 80). It may be possible to "withdraw from its more obvious institutions and expressions" (ibid., p. 81), but, as was suggested at the beginning concerning Barth, Bonhoeffer, and Moltmann, nothing we do is ever produced in a cultural vacuum. Even among Christians whose goal, or *telos*, is the future Kingdom of Heaven, it is impossible to completely separate oneself from one's worldly environment, as evinced in the New Testament when St. Paul wrote to the Christian community at Corinth concerning marriage (1 Cor. 7), the role of women in worship (1 Cor. 11: 2–16), and the tenability of eating meat sacrificed to pagan gods (1 Cor. 8: 4–13). Niebuhr, similarly, wrote that "Though the whole world lies in darkness, yet distinctions must be made between relative rights and wrongs in the world, and in Christian relations to it" (Niebuhr, 1952, p. 84), and that

> Christians are just like other men, needing to rely wholly on the gracious forgiveness of their sins by God-in-Christ, that Christ is by no means the founder of a new closed society with a new law but the expiator of the sins of the whole world, that the only difference between Christians and non-Christians lies in the spirit with which Christians do the same things as non-Christians.
>
> (ibid., p. 90)

The *Christ against Culture* position thus has serious drawbacks. However, it is worth noting that this model can also work in reverse, with a "Culture against Christ" approach the hallmark of many recent works in film studies. It is not so much that an explicit anti-Christian or anti-theological position is taken, more that contributions from theologians and religious studies specialists tend to be either neglected outright in work carried out by film theorists or given decidedly short shrift. A particular case in point is Peter Matthews's review of *Explorations in Theology and Film* in February 1998 for *Sight and Sound*, where it is said that "It's hard not to be touched by the book's naïve desire to be now and with it, even if the total effect is as acutely embarrassing as those church services that try out rock music to fetch back the dwindling flock" (Matthews, 1998, p. 30). Is this not simply an inversion of Barth's call for a separation between culture and theology?

Christ of Culture

Niebuhr's second model of the interrelationship between Christ and culture is qualitatively distinct from the *Christ against Culture* position, as it sees theology as firmly embedded in, rather than in opposition to, culture. In this second approach, which Niebuhr refers to as *Christ of Culture*, we see an agreement between these two entities to the extent that those who subscribe to this position will feel equally at home in the Christian community and in what Niebuhr terms the "community of culture," and will "feel no great tension between church and world, the social laws and the Gospel, the workings of divine grace and human effort, the ethics of salvation and the ethics of social conservation or progress" (Niebuhr, 1952, p. 93). In this model, which Johnston sees as a liberal Protestant perspective (R. Johnston, 2000, p. 59) and which according to Niebuhr himself could be labeled "Culture-Protestantism" (Niebuhr, 1952, p. 94), there is deemed to be no threat or antagonism on the part of its defenders between Christianity and society. Rather, a two-way process is involved of interpreting culture through Christ and Christ through culture. The seeds of this approach stretch back to the very origins of the Christian Church, where, for Justin Martyr in the second century, Platonism was employed to communicate the Gospel. Justin argued that as divine wisdom had been spread throughout the world, it was not surprising if aspects of the Gospel were reflected outside of the Church. Accordingly, Christianity might be said to build upon and fulfill those anticipations of God's revelation that can be found in pagan philosophy (and for that matter the Old Testament). By the fifth century, St. Augustine had become one of the greatest champions of using secular culture, arguing that if ancient culture and philosophy could be appropriated by Christians then this could only serve the cause of Christianity. Niebuhr also gives the example of the Gnostics of the second century who sought to "reconcile the gospel with the science and philosophy of their time" (Niebuhr, 1952, p. 96), namely, a belief system that saw salvation to be possible not through faith but through knowledge. Niebuhr argues that the Gnostics may have been scorned in their day, but that their position was not fundamentally different from "those folk in our day who find in psychiatry the key to the understanding of Christ, or in nuclear fission the answer to the problems of eschatology" (ibid.). Niebuhr may also have had in mind here the theology of Rudolf Bultmann in the twentieth century, for whom the appropriation of Heideggerean existentialism was a vital way of communicating the *kerygma* or proclamation, and the significance of the Christ of faith, in a scientific and technological age. In all such instances, Christ will always be the dominant motif (for all his reduction of the Christian proclamation to existentialist philosophy, no one could accuse Bultmann of being less than Christo-centric), but secular thought-forms and agencies have the capacity to resonate with, and even amplify, the extent to which the Christian message can be discerned.

In the case of the medium of film, this two-way interaction and exchange between Christ and culture have reached their apotheosis in the work of those such as Anton Karl Kozlovic for whom Christ's life and ministry have provided the benchmark for so many popular films (Kozlovic, 2004). Seeing Christ as a role model or exemplar, and the prototype of such movie characters as Edward Scissorhands, E.T. and *The Green Mile*'s (Frank Darabont, 1999) John Coffey, the recent proliferation of work on cinematic Christ-figures is a particularly good illustration of Niebuhr's second model. According to Niebuhr, "Jesus often appears as a great hero of human culture history; his life and teachings are regarded as the greatest human achievement; in him, it is believed, the aspirations of men toward their values are brought to a point of culmination" (Niebuhr, 1952, p. 54). This is not wholly distinct from Matthew McEver's claim, in a 1998 article published in the *Journal of Religion and Film*, that, in films whose protagonists may be designated Christ-figures, "humanity is indebted to those who dare to confront, challenge our thinking patterns, and willingly suffer for it" (McEver, 1998, ¶29). Forging a correlation between cinematic Christ-figures and the New Testament Jesus, McEver argues that Jesus is very much present "on the silver screen" (ibid.), albeit "not as a prophet and teacher from Nazareth" but as "an unlikely redeemer in a prison" (Lucas Jackson in *Cool Hand*

Luke [Stuart Rosenberg, 1967]), "a mental hospital" (Randle P. McMurphy in *One Flew Over the Cuckoo's Nest*), "a class room" (John Keating in *Dead Poets Society* [Peter Weir, 1989]), or "inside the home of an abused child" (Karl Childress in *Sling Blade* [Billy Bob Thornton, 1996]). Underlying McEver's claim is the implicit suggestion that these functional equivalents of Jesus Christ are performing a role that is analogous to that of the New Testament Jesus but that, crucially, cannot be understood in isolation from the Jesus of history and/or the Christ of faith. There is no talk of these Christ-figures replacing Christ whether as role models or as agents of salvation and redemption. Quite simply, McEver's position appears to be that filmic Christ-figures are doing the job that Jesus himself once did but that, in an age when film audiences have lost the appetite for biblical epics (though in light of the furore surrounding Gibson's *Passion* this is questionable), audiences tend to get more out of going to see a Christ-*like* figure on the cinema screen than a representation of Jesus himself.

In marked contrast, then, to Niebuhr's *Christ against Culture* model, the *Christ of Culture* is a reductionistic approach that sacrifices Jesus to the interests of the prevailing culture. Rather than Christ being seen as superior to culture, the two entities are inextricably connected so that, when we watch a film, for instance, it is impossible to isolate the beliefs and values communicated in that picture from prevailing suppositions and ideas concerning Christ. Neither would it be possible to see film-watching as merely a leisure-time or recreational activity that can be set apart from the religious sphere. On the positive side, this model would appear to demonstrate that, in an ostensibly secular age, religion has not been eviscerated or destroyed and that secular agencies need not be construed as being antithetical, or in opposition, to the affairs of religion. In an age in which many Western intellectuals in such fields as anthropology, sociology, and psychology "have anticipated the death of religion as eagerly as ancient Israel anticipated the Messiah," and have thus looked forward to "the dawn of a new era in which, to paraphrase Freud, the infantile illusions of religion will be outgrown" (Stark & Bainbridge, 1985, p. 1), the abundance of literature on cinematic Christ-figures would certainly suggest that the so-called secularization thesis is outmoded and that religion is evolving and mutating to meet new circumstances, rather than in an inexorable decline. On the negative side, however, Pope is right to counsel that there is something lacking in this model. As he sees it, there is a qualitative difference between any "transcendence" that we may experience in film and "transcendence" as traditionally conceived in religion:

> If it is the case that the cinematic experience is one of transcendence, this transcendence is more the recognition of human need than a response to contact with the divine. It may be a transcendence of the self, of personal limitations...But is this really an encounter with the "wholly other" as some would claim? More importantly, is it only the *appearance* of the real or the noumenal that religious encounter and experience have usually been held to be?
>
> (Pope, 2005, p. 170)

In other words, the same language may be invoked in both a theological and a secular context, but the referent is not the same. When a term such as "redemption" is utilized in Protestantism, it is likely to refer to the restoration of the torn fabric of personal relationships between God and his "fallen" Creation, and exclusively denotes the activity of Jesus Christ coming into the world by God's grace to bring about the salvation of sinful humanity by means of his substitutionary and atoning death on the Cross, thereby freeing humans from slavery to sin. When it is used in the context of a film, however, does it refer to the same thing? *The Shawshank Redemption* (Frank Darabont, 1994) is a film that contains the word "redemption" in the title, and its tagline reads "Fear can hold you prisoner. Hope can set you free," suggesting that something vaguely theological may be taking place, but any "redemption" that there might be going on in the film is a far cry from article 15 of the Church of England's 39 articles of faith, where it is affirmed that Christ "came to be the Lamb without spot, Who, by sacrifice of himself once made, should take away the sins of the world" (qtd in Gibson, 1902, p. 439). This is not to belittle the medium of film, but merely to suggest that, while acknowledging that words such as "theology" and "redemption" are heterogeneous, and that there are many approaches by which a theologian may wish to conduct a theological conversation, any attempt to link theology and film by means of extrapolating words and ideas from one context and appropriating them into another is fraught with difficulties. As Niebuhr counsels, it can often end up being the case that Christ is treated as "little more than the personification of an abstraction" (Niebuhr, 1952, p. 117), and that "sometimes it seems as if God, the forgiveness of sins, even prayers of thanksgiving, are all means to an end, and a human end at that" (ibid., p. 121).

Similar problems are expounded by William Romanowski in *Eyes Wide Open* in relation to his "Consumption" model (see 2001, p. 13). In contrast to his aforementioned "Condemnation" approach, Romanowski notes that "most Christians watch pretty much what everyone watches, with little thought about how faith might affect viewing habits and criticism" (ibid., pp. 12–13), and it is here that he identifies the problem that arises when one immerses oneself too deeply into the world of popular culture. For, although such an approach can be interpreted as "an affirmation of cultural involvement" (ibid., p. 13), the downside is that Christians may naïvely consume popular culture "without critical Christian appraisal" (ibid.). In other words, there may be a tendency to indulge in what film and other cultural products have to offer without acknowledging that some films will more readily lend themselves to theological exploration than others. Just as there are various different "theologies" available (Roman Catholic, Anglican, Methodist, and so on), "film" is not a monolithic or homogeneous medium, and cannot function in an analogous manner to theology (and nor should it be expected to). David Jasper's chapter in *Explorations in Theology and Film*, entitled "On Systematizing the Unsystematic: A Response," was particularly critical of the function of film vis-à-vis that of theology, and is one of the most cited pieces of work in the theology–film field in subsequent years. As Jasper sees it, "Theology, within the Judeo-Christian tradition or otherwise, emerges from more problematic and disturbing material than Hollywood dare show" (Jasper, 1997, p. 244), and, quite simply, theology and film belong to two different orders of things. Indeed, as he sees it, the cinema is "effective in as much as, demanding nothing of the viewer, it seems to offer the viewer the power to understand without the need seriously to think or change" (Jasper, 1997, pp. 242–3; see also Loughlin, 2005, pp. 1–2; Deacy, 2001, p. 9). He has his eyes set in particular on the escapist and illusory dimension of Hollywood cinema, the sole function of which, according to Jasper, is to "help us through the tedium of inactivity" (ibid., p. 235). Johnston similarly claims that "All too frequently, movies are controlled by crass commercial interests" that "merely provide escape or indulge our prejudices and fantasies, oversimplifying life in the process" (R. Johnston, 2000, p. 87). As a result, movies are inclined "to create spectacular special effects in order to generate a crowd rather than to portray the nuances of everyday life" (ibid.), and it is here that Jasper's concerns about the discordance between what Hollywood does and what theology does come to the fore.

As I have argued elsewhere, serious religious reflection does not consist of an identification with a merely transitory, ephemeral wish-fulfillment realm, but, rather, makes the contradictions and discontinuities of reality much clearer, and any transformation that exists is necessarily of a radical and more rudimentary kind (Deacy, 2005, p. 26). When the Christian tradition talks about human beings being able to enter into a new covenant with God by means of the Incarnation, this is necessarily far removed from the manner in which popular cinema continues to foster a suspension of disbelief or submission in the darkness of the movie theater to the sights and sounds of the big screen. As more and more people continue to partake in the ritual of attending the cinema, then, coupled with the hegemony of Hollywood, Marsh is right to counsel that this could be "identified as no more than a form of controlled escape, and a trite one at that, from postmodern fragmentation" (Marsh, 2004, p. 133). The fact that what he calls the "disjointedness" of life is handled through "avoidance" (ibid.) raises, by its very nature, theological questions and concerns. It links, for example, with how for Paul Tillich, while in principle "everything that has being is an expression, however preliminary and transitory it may be, of being-itself, of ultimate reality" (Tillich, 2004, p. 210), not every manifestation or interpretation of popular culture comprises or bears witness to this dimension of depth. Specifically, where the object of worship is not God but may, for instance, be a film text or the movie stars and celebrities it features, Tillich believed that one is thereby being idolatrous because the object concerned is transitory and temporal, causing the worshiper (or idolater) existential disappointment. As when we accord ultimate worth to relationships, power, and wealth, we will, argued Tillich, ultimately be let down because they will not satisfy our deepest spiritual needs. By contrast, people who think that life makes sense and transcends minor things have come to know God whether they know it or not. On this basis, therefore, it would be dangerous to attempt to conflate Christianity and culture along the lines of Niebuhr's second model since there is a danger that one will end up ascribing ultimacy and depth to that which is not ultimate or even especially deep.

Considering that Tillich is often cited as a theologian whose work most enables a fruitful dialogue between theology and film to arise, in light of his claim that neither the religious nor the sacred realm "should be in separation from the other," since both "are rooted in religion in the larger sense of the word, in the experience of ultimate concern" (Tillich, 1964, p. 9), his skepticism regarding cultural forms *per se* taking on a religious dimension is not without significance. It also links with how, for Bultmann, the influence upon us of technology and the media can alienate us in a manner that is equivalent to what the New Testament writers had in mind when they spoke of demonic powers ruling our world and of our being "fallen" creatures (see Bultmann, 1953, pp. 24–5). Bultmann's disdain for the way in which the mass media can control us and lead us away from appropriating God's grace is another illustration of how the *Christ of Culture* model is deficient, and suggests that film and popular culture might be impediments, rather than open invitations, to theological engagement. Films that ostensibly bear witness to theological motifs – in the form, for instance, of Christ-figure analogies – can never, therefore, be a substitute for the real Jesus Christ, on this interpretation. As Jasper sees it, in relation to Hollywood cinema, many films simply "mimic theology without theology's claims for methodological order and reflection" (Jasper, 1997, pp. 237–8) and do not require the same form of intellectual assent that theology demands. In his 1997 contribution to *Explorations*, Jasper is particularly critical of the first two *Terminator* movies (James Cameron, 1984, 1991), which he sees as "capacious and largely empty containers" (ibid., p. 238), where once the stage has been set the viewer is not required to think any further, but is sent on a rollercoaster ride. In marked contrast, Jasper refers to the "fire of religious passion" that underscores the writings of the Hebrew prophets, which could never be categorized in the same way as providing entertainment value within a viewing environment "that is ultimately reassuring and safe" (ibid.). The tendency for films to delineate happy endings is a particular moot point, here, as, in Jörg Herrmann's words, this is "a concession to the needs and desires of the consumer" (Herrmann, 2003, p. 198), whereas in marked contrast Christian culture perceives social realities in which the contradictions and discontinuities of life are apparent. In a social and material sense, also, rather than simply in terms of the psychological or transformative effects that a film may have upon a viewer, there are clear functional differences between what Christian communities and film communities tend to do. As Herrmann points out, "[b]irths, deaths and weddings cannot be celebrated well in the cinema" (ibid., p. 199), just as, in mainstream movies at any rate, "existential crises" cannot adequately "be coped with" (ibid.) in the same way as by theologians or clerics.

The appropriation of films for films' sake is thus a major problem for theologians. No matter how persuasive a Christ-figure motif may appear to be, Clive Marsh makes the judicious point that "We would be unwise to try and conduct a theological conversation, however useful its subject matter may be, with a 'bad film,' " which he defines as "a film which people simply would not want to watch" (Marsh, 1997, p. 32). Without disputing that not all of what Hollywood produces is banal, in an age of movie sequels and remakes – does the world really require the likes of *Miss Congeniality 2: Armed and Fabulous* (John Pasquin, 2005) or the virtual scene-by-scene re-creation of *The Omen* (John Moore, 2006)? – it is hard not to concur with Benjamin Svetkey's observation, published in an *Entertainment Weekly* article, that "pretty much *all* of the big commercial films being released by major studios these days have a certain written-by-chimps-locked-in-a-room-with-a-laptop quality," wherein "[s]tory lines veer in nonsensical directions, dialogue is dim or dopey," and "characters have the heft of balsa wood" (qtd in R. Johnston, 2000, p. 101). Whereas theology may use the language of *kerygma*, films tend to veer in the direction of kitsch, and for every film with a Christ-figure motif, can we really say that Christology is more important to the film's producers than commercialism? This is not to say that religion or theology does not have a stake in commercial matters. Indeed, the grounds of Canterbury Cathedral, the birthplace of the Christian Church in the United Kingdom, rely heavily on National Lottery funding – the completion in 2000 of the International Study Centre in the cathedral precincts is a case in point – and there is a very fine line between its status as a sacred site and as a tourist haven. Similarly, when Michelangelo painted the Sistine Chapel it was a job undertaken on commission (see R. Johnston, 2000, p. 87). However, in an age where "spectacle seems to be supplanting drama based in storytelling," and every "script must have a script doctor, and stars often demand the privilege of rewriting their lines," the net result of which is that "cohesive stories become little more than a collection of choppy scenes" (R. Johnston, 2000, p. 101), is it altogether surprising if any theological engagement that has the capacity to take place is too threadbare to warrant serious scrutiny? A case in point is Wolfgang Petersen's 2006 film *Poseidon*, a remake of the seminal 1970s disaster movie *The Poseidon Adventure* (Ronald Neame, 1972), about which Paul Arendt, writing for the BBC Films website, remarks:

> Chucking the characters from Paul Gallico's novel overboard and paring backstory to a bare minimum, Petersen fills the space with setpiece after setpiece, hardly giving the audience room to draw breath. It's a refreshing approach, but since the new characters are pretty dull, the experience is more of a jolly rollercoaster than a scary movie.
>
> (Arendt, 2006)

Ironically, given the discussion above about the tenuous utilization of messianic-figure motifs, *Poseidon* has actually jettisoned the original film's overt theological referent, in the form of Gene Hackman's Bible-spouting preacher, who leads a select band – the chosen people, no less – of the ship's passengers and crew through the waters to freedom, Moses-style. As the *Observer*'s Philip French puts it: "The special effects are stunning and there are more corpses around than you'd find on a Napoleonic battlefield, but the characters are a dull lot, and the original's allegorical element with 'the Reverend' Gene Hackman as a muscular Moses figure has been dropped" (French, 2006). Perhaps we have now reached a point in our culture not only where "The world presented by films tends to be neater, more orderly, and has satisfactory endings...in which vice is punished and virtue rewarded, families are reunited, and lovers mate for life" (Lyden, 2003, p. 45), but in which the presence of a biblical analog (whether a Christ-figure or a Moses-figure) is deemed to add an undue layer of complexity to the proceedings, and so is better off being omitted altogether. If any conflicts that take place within the length of the film are resolved by the denouement, and however "bad the situation of the characters may be at various points in the story, by the end all will be tidy and we will be reassured that all is well with the world" (ibid.), is there any scope for serious theological engagement? Moltmann and Pannenberg may have believed in the importance of hope and in the need to revolutionize and transform the present – a motif that is central to so many contemporary films – along the lines of Stephen Brown's claim that "If the cross identifies itself with our present human condition then the resurrection is God's promise of a future transformation" (Brown, 1997, p. 232), but this is a far cry from the tendency in films to "offer an entry to an ideally constructed world" (Lyden, 2003, p. 4). As Lyden puts it, "We often hope and wish for a world like the one we see in the movies even though we must return to a very different world at the end of the show" (ibid.).

Although it would be wrong to suppose that this *Christ of Culture* model was one that Niebuhr himself espoused, one advantage of this approach is that it demonstrates the extent to which the realms of theology and culture overlap to a much greater extent than is commonly perceived. This fits in with John Lyden's own model for looking at the interface between religion and culture, as delineated in *Film as Religion*, where he suggests that "theology cannot stand outside culture any more than any other aspect of human religion or culture can do" (Lyden, 2003, p. 17), and that "there is no absolute distinction between religion and other aspects of culture" (ibid., p. 2). Lyden's premise is that we tend to designate certain activities as "religious" because they conform to a pre-set pattern or model that we recognize from religious traditions with which we are acquainted, and, as a corollary, we overlook the religious provenance of anything that does not conform to such a typology. Accordingly, "Once we give up narrower definitions of 'religion' that only identify it with formal institutions that go by that label, we can recognize that multiple religious influences affect each one of us" (ibid., p. 135). In lieu of the classic distinctions between "theology," or "religion," and "culture," Lyden advocates a more nuanced position, in keeping with Niebuhr's *Christ of Culture* model, that sees all aspects of culture as having a religious angle or propensity, and that, crucially, does not require us to have to choose one side over another (as in Niebuhr's first model). Just as a Christian who studies Islam is not thereby abandoning their Christian heritage by being open to the beliefs and values of another religious tradition, so Lyden emphasizes that neither is a Christian "worshipping false gods each time they go to the cinema" (ibid., p. 135). As has already been suggested, with reference to Justin Martyr, St. Augustine, the Gnostics, and Bultmann, no religion can exist unless it adapts to, and borrows from (and even incorporates), prevailing religious and cultural influences, and Lyden develops this position by suggesting that film and other cultural products are performing a functionally equivalent role to that of religious traditions. In his words, "It may be that the insistence on a distinction between religion and culture mainly signifies a battle between one kind of religion and another," so that just as in biblical times monotheism was defined in relation to polytheism (cf. Cohn-Sherbok & Cohn-Sherbok, 1994, p. 4), so today traditional religions define themselves in relation to secular culture instead. Instead of secularization, and the eclipse of traditional religion, we thus have the evolution of new forms of religious expression.

While Lyden has a point, it is questionable, in an age when conservatism is back on the agenda – in the form, for instance, of the "Christian Right" in the United States – whether this is the whole picture. This model is more likely to hold sway in liberal circles than among more evangelical and conservative Christians for whom culture presents a demonstrable threat to traditional beliefs and values. It may well be the case for Lyden that the interaction between religion and film may be deemed comparable to the dialogue that exists between religions (so that to enter into a theological conversation with a film comprises a form of inter-religious dialogue), but it is hard to find eager support for a position that takes it as a given that no one "religion" is right or that there is no one legitimate or normative world-view, thereby allowing for "genuine differences in approach and perspective so that our judgments do not condemn others simply for disagreeing with us" (ibid., p. 126). He is, however, far from wide of the mark in stressing that traditional religious groups have tended to respond to the threat produced by secular films (as shown in relation to the Catholic Legion of Decency) *as though they constituted alternative religious sites.* In Lyden's words, "By relating to it either as a demonic threat to their own religion, or a mirror image of it, religious film critics were essentially already viewing film through the categories of religion" (ibid., p. 132). Indeed, similar questions were being addressed, albeit in a radically divergent way, as shown by the controversies over *Dead End* and *Priest,* in which both films were deemed by Catholic church groups in particular to be raising the same sort of questions (relating to street culture and celibacy, respectively) but in ways that were antithetical to one another. While Lyden's claim may initially seem overstretched, not least because church groups have never accorded films the status of an alternative religious tradition, along the lines of Islam, Buddhism, or Judaism, this may, paradoxically, corroborate Lyden's argument, since anyone espousing an anti-film polemic would naturally be inclined to discredit, rather than dignify with a higher status, the alternative that it presented. To give an example, Lyden refers to the manner in which "early Christian explorers of the Americas were reluctant to call the practices of the 'Indians' by the name of religion" (ibid.), and we could similarly cite the more recent tendency post-9/11 among moderate Muslim groups to denounce the purported Islamic predilections of suicide bombers, thereby not exalting their terrorist acts to the status of a "holy war" being conducted in the name of Allah.

On this basis, therefore, the medium of film may be performing an analogous function to that of traditional religious groups, not least through addressing comparable if not equivalent issues to those found in Christianity, Hinduism, and Sikhism. As will be seen in the second part of this volume, when specific themes are examined, films can raise theologically fecund questions pertaining to a whole range of ostensibly "religious" questions, including abortion (for which we might cite *Citizen Ruth* [Alexander Payne, 1996], which examines questions of free choice and the sanctity of human life against the backdrop of an increasingly polarized conservative Christian America), euthanasia (as sensitively handled in *The Sea Inside* [Alejandro Amenábar, 2004]), and a just war (as delineated in an animated film such as *Antz* [Eric Darnell & Tim Johnson, 1998] and such documentaries as *The Fog of War: Eleven Lessons from the Life of Robert S. McNamara* [Errol Morris, 2003] and *Fahrenheit 9/11* [Michael Moore, 2004]). Since such films are not, however, purporting to grapple with religious or theological issues as a means of illustrating or bearing witness to religious traditions – in other words, they are not missiological works – then Lyden's claim that films have the capacity to function religiously in their own right (Lyden, 2003, p. 34) should not be dismissed out of hand. M. Darroll Bryant wrote in 1982 that "as a popular form of the religious life, movies do what we have always asked of popular religion, namely, that they provide us with archetypal forms of humanity – heroic figures – and instruct us in the basic values and myths of our society" (Bryant, 1982, p. 106). Although Bryant qualifies this claim by making a distinction between a religious and a secular culture, in that, since the Enlightenment, the former, which "seeks to mediate a transcendent order," has been associated in secular circles with superstition,[3] whereas the latter "has no referent beyond itself and consequently worships itself" (ibid., p. 105) – to the point that "modern cultures have outgrown religion" (ibid.) – Lyden's approach shares much common ground with Bryant. Indeed, for Bryant, the act of going to the movies is a participation "in a central ritual of our technological civilization" (ibid., p. 102) and where "the 'stuff' of everyday life can be taken up and magically transformed; base metals are turned into gold" (ibid., p. 103). It is significant that Bryant lays emphasis upon the origin of the term "culture," which, derived from the Latin *cultus*, means "worship," and signifies that "a culture grows out of intimate life with the gods" (ibid., p. 105). In the words of Garrison Keillor,

> If you can't go to church and, for at least a moment, be given transcendence; if you can't go to church and pass briefly from this life to the next; then I can't see why anyone should go. Just a brief moment of transcendence causes you to come out of church a changed person.
>
> (qtd in R. Johnston, 2000, p. 100)

This quotation, which is also cited by Ken Gire in his book *Windows of the Soul: Experiencing God in New Ways*, is then followed by this response from Gire:

> I have experienced what Garrison Keillor described more in movie theatres than I have in churches. Why? . . . movies don't always tell the truth, don't always enlighten, don't always inspire. What they do on a fairly consistent basis is give you an experience of transcendence. They let you lose yourself in somebody else's story.
>
> (R. Johnston 2000, p. 100)

In other words, film is not just analogous to, or a functional equivalent of, traditional religious agencies, but may actually be even more adept at functioning religiously than its traditional counterparts. As John Updike, author of *The Witches of Eastwick* (1984) and the more recent *Terrorist* (2006), once wrote:

> the cinema has done more for my spiritual life than the church. My ideas of fame, success and beauty all originate from the big screen. Whereas Christian religion is retreating everywhere and losing more and more influence; film has filled this vacuum and supports us with myths and action-controlling images. During a certain phase in my life film was a substitute for religion.
>
> (qtd in Herrmann, 2003, p. 190)

Similar testimony is provided by British journalist and author John Walsh, whose *Are You Talking to Me? A Life Through the Movies* (2003) comprises an autobiographical account of the power that film can have. Writing about the interconnectedness of movie images and the vagaries and vicissitudes of real life – "[t]hey offer you images of a counterlife that you might, but probably won't ever, live" (Walsh, 2003, p. 311) – Walsh reflects upon the way in which films had the ability to leave such an indelible impression while he was growing up that, when he lost, at the age of 19, "the last vestiges of religious faith" (ibid., p. 310), it fell to the movies to provide the values and aspirations through which life-decisions are made. Recollecting that "My parents didn't disapprove of the cinema as a temple of sin, they simply ignored it as an irrelevance in their children's education" (ibid., p. 22), Walsh describes at length his first ever visit to the cinema, to see *Mutiny on the Bounty* (Lewis Milestone, 1962). He recalls that "The Odeon loomed above us like an enormous temple. It took up as much space as our local church and seemed to bulge with light, eclipsing all the other buildings on one side of the square" (ibid., p. 24). He continues that "We sat, all fourteen of us plus two teachers, line-abreast across a whole row, chattering and gazing at the Odeon's mile-high ceiling, the complicated sculptures on the facing walls, the great proscenium arch" (ibid., p. 27), and refers also to the "massive stage in front of the film" as "a sort of epic altar" (ibid.). Both at the time and in subsequent years, Walsh attests to the life-changing capacity of the silver screen, whereby "when we've seen everything we were supposed to see, have been strung out by the drama, dinned into submission by the galloping soundtrack, carpet-bombed by the special effects, made to laugh aloud or weep real tears, we make a connection with the screen that's life-changingly powerful" (ibid., p. 13). Similarly, Walsh affirms that "all my life I had been storing up images and dialogue and epiphanies from the movies that had come to mean more to me than my own true-life experiences" (ibid., p. 12). Contending that "the cinema screen works an insidious magic on the emergent consciousness, and leaves us *charged with feeling* in ways that we only dimly understand" (ibid., pp. 16–17), Walsh's testimony is a prime example of how, in a Durkheimian sense, film can provide communities of cinema-goers with the means to affirm shared values in the way that traditional churches may once have done. As he says in relation to his penchant for watching horror movies:

> So many movies featured crucifixes, Satanic faces and sacrificial victims that it was easy to confuse the church-stuff and the cinema-stuff. They were both alarmingly keen on death and darkness...It seemed an odd form of enjoyment, to sit in a dark cinema watching mad people with staring eyes making each other bleed in dark rooms and spooky exteriors, but no odder than to kneel for half an hour in a crepuscular church, listening to tales of crucifixion with a moaning organ accompaniment.
>
> (ibid., pp. 44–5)

Such testimony also goes some way toward rebutting Christine Hoff Kraemer's dismissal of the premise of Lyden's *Film as Religion*, whose "interreligious approach," she argues, "threatens to put contemporary films and rich religious traditions thousands of years old on equal terms" (Kraemer, 2004, p. 249). While Kraemer argues that it is necessary to honor the autonomy and integrity of both religion *and* film, she feels that "to compare them as if they were equal risks disadvantaging film, which by its nature cannot be as complex as a world religion" (ibid.). Despite the similar force of Jasper's claim, adduced earlier in this chapter, that film is too illusory and undemanding a medium to enable a systematic theology to take place, the testimony of the likes of Walsh and Updike would suggest not simply that films *can* perform a religious function, but that they can do so in a way that is no less enchanting, nourishing, emotionally intense, and transcendental.

Having looked in detail at the extreme positions presented by Niebuhr's first two models of the interrelationship between Christ and culture, the rest of this chapter will consist of a synopsis of the last three of Niebuhr's positions, which is where he believed the majority of Christians tend to reside. Arguing that most Christians embrace neither of the two extreme positions delineated above, Niebuhr argued that "the fundamental issue does not lie between Christ and the world...but between God and man" (Niebuhr, 1952, p. 124). In other words, rather than see

the Christian response to culture as being a position of outright condemnation or outright accommodation and interpenetration, he felt that
most Christians – whom he referred to as belonging in "the church of
the centre" (ibid.) – are inclined not to see the distinction as one between
"Christ" and "culture," since it is not possible to separate the works of
human culture from the grace of God, *who makes all works of culture
possible in the first place.* At the same time, neither can Christians separate
this grace from cultural activity – "for how can men love the unseen God
in response to His love without serving the visible brother in human
society?" (ibid., p. 126). In *Explorations in Theology and Film*, the last
three of Niebuhr's positions were consolidated into one section on how
Christ and culture can be in critical dialogue with each other (see Marsh,
1997, p. 28), but here more detailed consideration will be given to each
of these three models, which are *Christ above Culture, Christ and Culture
in Paradox,* and *Christ the Transformer of Culture.*

Christ above Culture

In this model, which Niebuhr identified as a *synthetic* approach, and
which tends to hold particular sway among Roman Catholics, Christ is
seen to complete and fulfill culture. Without going so far as to reconcile
Christ and culture in the manner of Niebuhr's second model, both Christ
and culture will be affirmed by this third model, but, crucially, the distinctions between them are maintained. This is why the model is referred
to as *synthetic*, since there is a synthesis at work between Christ and
culture, and those who espouse this position do not dilute or compromise
the *dual* nature of Christian interaction – that is, between looking after
the affairs of this world and building toward the goals of the next. Seeing
Christ as both *continuous* and *discontinuous* with the affairs of this world,
Niebuhr cites two passages from Matthew that best encapsulate this
position: Matthew 5:17 and 22:21. In the former, Jesus proclaims, in
the Sermon on the Mount: "Think not that I have come to abolish
the law and the prophets; I have come not to abolish them but to fulfil
them." In the latter passage, Jesus enjoins the Pharisees to render
"to Caesar the things that are Caesar's, and to God the things that are
God's." In both instances, Jesus does not decry human culture *per se*,
and indeed does not see it as inherently without goodness or value.
However, human culture is *incomplete*, and in need of fulfillment, which
can only be achieved by complementing reason with revelation, nature

with grace, and secular society with the Christian Church. This was very much the position of Thomas Aquinas in the thirteenth century, for whom there was a huge gulf between Christ and culture, but there is scope for a natural theology to emerge, to the point, indeed, that, according to Niebuhr, Aquinas "combined without confusing philosophy and theology, state and church, civic and Christian virtues, natural and divine laws, Christ and culture" (Niebuhr, 1952, p. 136). Culture, on this model, is God-given, and, while the model does not reject the importance of human activity, culture nevertheless entails the exercise of divine power with which it has been sacramentally endowed from above. As the French Neo-Thomist philosopher Jacques Maritain saw it, "Artistic creation does not copy God's creation, it continues it. And just as the trace and the image of God appear in His creatures, so the human stamp is imprinted on the work of art – the full stamp, sensitive and spiritual, not only that of the hands, but of the whole soul" (Maritain, 2004, p. 327). There is, therefore, a sense in which nature is believed to comprise a spark of the divine, and whereby "The artist, whether he knows it or not, consults God in looking at things" (ibid.).

In this Roman Catholic-based approach, a number of film authors and critics have argued, similarly, that the values conveyed in film are preparatory to Christian revelation. In his 1970 work *Theology Through Film*, Neil Hurley asked whether movies will "serve that reason which, after all, is the universal spark of the divine which the Stoic philosophers believed to bind all men together in some mysterious cosmic fraternity" (Hurley, 1970, p. 3). For Hurley, film has the ability to expand the theologian's understanding and enable filmgoers to cultivate their sense of what it is to be fully human. This is a marked difference from the way Catholic film criticism was employed in the *Christ against Culture* model, in which the tendency was to disparage films for their tendency to lead audiences astray. In this *Christ above Culture* approach, the objective is not to render moral judgments, but to attain greater insight about human experience and destiny. John May is a prominent Roman Catholic writer who fits into this mold. In books such as *Image and Likeness: Religious Visions in American Film Classics* (1992) and *New Image of Religious Film* (1997), May inquires into the possibility that films represent a visual analog of religious or sectarian questions, including whether the universe is friendly, hostile, or indifferent, and whether human beings are independent from or interdependent with the cosmos (and "higher things"). Michael Bird's contribution to his co-edited (with John May) collection *Religion in Film* (1982) is also a particularly good illustration of this process, as, in his chapter "Film as Hierophany," Bird argues that art can point toward the "holy" (without being able to go so far as to capture it), and that "art can disclose those spaces and those moments in culture where the experience of finitude and the encounter with the transcendent dimension are felt and expressed within culture itself" (Bird, 1982, p. 4). It is not a film's "religious" subject matter, but the medium itself, that determines the religiosity of a film, caught as it is between the incarnational (which Bird construes as a rootedness in reality itself) and the transcendent element, that is, a glimpse of something beyond the material world. Impossible though it is to portray the Infinite on screen, Bird believes that the finite can be represented, and that film's simple, realistic style – which enables the real emotions of film characters, in all their anxieties, to be communicated – is capable of pointing to, and anticipating, our true longing and need for the Infinite.

The French film theorist and critic, and father of the French New Wave, André Bazin similarly held that the aesthetic core of cinema was comprised of an innately sacramental dimension, wherein the movie camera, through photographing the world, bears witness to the miracle of God's creation. According to Bazin, it is through film that the surface of the world can be faithfully copied in art, thereby fulfilling an innate human need to stop the constant flow of time by preserving it in an image. Whereas a painting, no matter how lifelike, is never anything other than a work of human art and contrivance, a photograph or film shot "holds an irrational power to persuade us of its truth because it results from a process of mechanical reproduction in which human agency plays no part," and amounts to "just what happens automatically when the light reflected from objects strikes a layer of sensitive chemical emulsion" (Matthews, 1999, p. 23). In Bazin's words, "Photography affects like a phenomenon in nature, like a flower or a snowflake whose vegetable or earthly origins are an inseparable part of their beauty" (qtd in ibid.). In line with the synthetic model, Bazin believed that film is "preordained to bear endless witness to the beauty of the cosmos" (Matthews, 1999, p. 23), and is able to do this more and more effectively as technology improves, since technical advances insure that an ever more perfect approximation of the real (for which we might substitute Bird's understanding of the "holy") becomes possible. The filmmaker who preferred montage and editing to the realist style was thus, from Bazin's perspective, committing "a minor heresy – since it arrogated the power of God, who alone is entitled to confer meaning on the universe" (ibid., p. 24). Language such as this may be an anathema to many film theorists, for whom religious language and thought-forms have no rightful place in the secular and rational discipline of film studies – as Matthews puts it, "the merest rumour of the transcendental is enough to scandalise most film theorists" (Matthews, 1999, p. 23) – but this must be judged alongside the fact that "Bazin is the single thinker most responsible for bestowing on cinema the prestige both of an artform and of an object of knowledge" (ibid., p. 22) and of establishing film studies as an intellectual discipline. Even John Hill and Pamela Church Gibson's benchmark volume on the critical theories, debates, and approaches to the study of film, *The Oxford Guide to Film Studies*, which conspicuously excludes any mention of approaches from within religious studies, biblical studies, or theology, nonetheless acknowledges (in the volume's sole reference to religion) that Bazin's aesthetic "was religious and founded in the faith that the cinematic image could reveal the world in fact and spirit and confirm the temporal and spatial thereness of the world with the camera's meditative eye" (Kolker, 1998, p. 16). Before we get too carried away, however, the qualification must be added that, despite Matthews's warning that talk of religion is an anathema to purist film theorists, Matthews himself is very far from amenable to seeing all interactions between theology and film as productive. Matthews wrote the aforementioned negative review of the *Explorations in Theology and Film* for *Sight and Sound* (Matthews, 1998, p. 30), in which he is highly selective about what amounts to good and bad instances of theological engagement. Approaches that conform to the stature of Bazin's synthetic approach can be countenanced (and Matthews refers in this regard in his review to "The transcendental trio of Bresson, Dreyer and Ozu"), but any engagement "with worldlier texts, including *Field of Dreams* and *Awakenings*" (ibid.) is disparaged. Matthews's general acceptance, though, that, at least in principle, theology and film need not be treated as discrete subject areas is to be welcomed.

A similar approach can be found in the work of the filmmaker and film theorist Paul Schrader, whose *Transcendental Style in Film* (1972) is a groundbreaking publication in this area. Though a Dutch Calvinist, rather than a Roman Catholic, Schrader's approach is particularly amenable to the *Christ above Culture* model in that his premise is that the realistic style evokes a sense of transcendence by pointing beyond the austerity and barrenness of the everyday world toward a higher, transcendent reality. Going a stage further than Bird, in that he believes the "holy" *can* be captured on film, Schrader's premise is that even among filmmakers from different religious and cultural backgrounds (and to this end his book examines the work of Japan's Yasujiro Ozu, France's Robert Bresson, and Denmark's Carl Theodor Dreyer), the seemingly simple and bare – even ascetic – style of filmmaking that is employed can show forth the presence of the transcendent. It may, for instance, be that there is scope for seeing, in the face of a film character, something of God's grace, and the more that films convey the finite in this manner, the greater their capacity for pointing beyond themselves and disclosing the Infinite, or Transcendent. Accordingly, in Schrader's words, "Transcendental style, like the [Catholic] mass, transforms experience into a repeatable ritual which can be repeatedly transcended" (Schrader, 1972, p. 11). Another Calvinist theologian who deals with Roman Catholic themes in film is Roy Anker, whose *Catching Light: Looking for God in the Movies* was published in 2004. Focusing on film stories, Anker suggests that "when it does show up, grace befalls unlikely and unsuspecting people in surprising and unforeseeable ways that are quite beyond human prediction, conception, or charting" (Anker, 2004, p. 17). Quoting from John 3:16 – "For God so loved the world that he gave his only Son, that whoever believes in him should not perish but have eternal life" – Anker contends that "God bathes this world in love and that love goes everywhere, even into the damnedest places" (ibid.). He also cites the aforementioned John Updike, whose 1963 novel *The Centaur*, which concerns the relationship between a father and son as they are forced to spend three days together in a snowstorm, contains the following quotation:

> *All joy belongs to the Lord.* Wherever in the filth and confusion and misery, a soul felt joy, there the Lord came and claimed it as his own; into bar-rooms and brothels and classrooms and alleys slippery with spittle, no matter how dark and scabbed and remote, in China or Africa or Brazil, wherever a moment of joy was felt, there the Lord stole and added to His enduring domain.
>
> (Updike, 1963, p. 267)

Even if a religious vision is not intended by a filmmaker, the important criterion here is that a film is believed to inspire a religious vision. Accordingly, it is that religious themes are being read not so much *into* films, as in the plethora of literature on Christ-figures, as *onto* films, in which, to cite Lyden, "the religious interpretation fulfils and completes the secular cry of pain and suffering" (Lyden, 2003, p. 27).

There is, therefore, a strong sacramental dimension to this model, in which the physical can be an important, and even necessary, gateway to the spiritual (although there will be variations here, as shown by the inclusion in this section of Paul Schrader, a Dutch Calvinist). In this model, on the premise that the created order (and human condition) must be acceptable to God or else He would not have sent His son into the world in the form of the Incarnation, and in a manner not wholly distinct from panentheism – which sees everything as being in God and God as being in everything – the physical is often venerated, to the point that success is seen as only coming about when one confronts the world through action, thereby making the world better through having acted in it rather than suffering in silence and doing nothing (see Blake, 2000, p. 16). Like the bread and wine at the Eucharist, which, rather than merely being symbols, are believed to comprise the actual body and blood of Christ, it may be flowers, costumes, paintings, taxi drivers, boxers, prostitutes, contraband weapons, a baby's smile, water, fire, a nightclub, a parking garage, or sexual love that mediate a transcendent reality. As the American Catholic priest and sociologist Andrew Greeley affirms, filmmakers can sometimes disclose God's presence even more intensively than God has chosen to do through creation itself, with the medium of film being especially amenable to the making of sacraments and the creation of epiphanies because of its "inherent power to affect the imagination" (Greeley, 1988, p. 250). Richard Blake, a professor of fine arts at Boston College and a Catholic priest, also explores this terrain in his 2000 publication *AfterImage: The Indelible Catholic Imagination of Six American Filmmakers*, in which attention is given to six film directors, each of whom had an early exposure to Catholicism, which, like a flash-bulb, has left "an afterimage on the artistic imagination long after it has been removed, or in many cases, after the artists have removed them-selves from the stimulus" (Blake, 2000, p. xv). Blake also affirms that even though these filmmakers – Martin Scorsese, Alfred Hitchcock, Frank Capra, John Ford, Francis Ford Coppola, and Brian De Palma – may be inclined to "shut their eyes and turn away to other, non-Catholic stimuli" in later years, "the afterimage intrudes and adds a halo of meaning to the object of their conscious attention" (ibid.). Observing that Catholi-cism may not always appear explicitly in their films, such as in the form of churches, crucifixes, and statues, is a far cry from presuming that God is neither present nor active in the world. As Blake says in relation to Scorsese's films, "His characters act out their lives in interaction with the persons and things of this material universe, and through these objects of everyday experience they may eventually find some form of redemption" (Blake, 2000, p. 38). The challenge for the theologian is thus to undertake a critical reading of religious influences in film that may lurk so far beneath the surface that they are not even detected on a conscious level by the filmmakers themselves. As Gerard Loughlin, another prominent Catholic theologian who works in the area of theology and film, recently pointed out, there are many directors, not least Ingmar Bergman and Luis Bunuel, who "disavow religious intent but remain haunted by theological themes," and for whom "the disparities of life still call for spiritual consolations, even if those proffered by religion are found wanting" (Loughlin, 2005, p. 9). Indeed, Bunuel was, in Loughlin's words, "an atheist, but a devout one, who cleaved to the God he denied" (ibid.).

It will often, therefore, be a secular reality that mediates, and discloses, a spiritual or transcendental reality. In the case of Scorsese's films, Blake argues that when, in *Taxi Driver* (1976), the alienated and dysfunctional protagonist, Travis Bickle (Robert De Niro), expresses his distaste for the filth and decay that suffuse the New York City streets where he plies his trade, and anticipates that "Someday, a real rain will come and wash all the scum off the streets," he is echoing the Catholic belief that baptismal waters do not merely symbolize purification *but actually accomplish this action*. While acknowledging that Travis is not overtly or consciously foreseeing that God will use rain as the instrument of his cleansing of the squalid and sin-suffused sidewalks, Blake attests that "he does give the rain an active role in purifying the city streets in a way that is remarkably consistent with a Catholic understanding of the effects of the sacrament of baptism" (Blake, 2000, p. 37). A not dissimilar motif can be found in Umberto Eco's medieval detective novel, *The Name of the Rose*, a film version of which was directed by Jean-Jacques Annaud in 1986. In a narrative set in an Italian monastery in 1327, a young monk, Adso of Melk, is at one point torn between the demands of the celibate life he has chosen and the enchantment of a young peasant girl with whom he enjoys a furtive, but incandescent, sexual relationship, which, paradoxically, only serves to reaffirm his sense of the sublime ordering of the cosmos. To quote from the novel:

> It was ... as if – just as the whole universe is surely like a book written by the finger of God, in which everything speaks to us of the immense goodness of its Creator, in which every creature is description and mirror of life and death ... – everything, in other words, spoke to me only of the face I had hardly glimpsed in the aromatic shadows of the kitchen.
>
> (Eco, 2004, p. 279)

Adso also speaks of "the whole world" being "destined to speak to me of the power, goodness, and wisdom of the Creator," with the young girl – "sinner though she may have been" – fulfilling the role not of a temptress, or an obstacle to divine grace, but "a chapter in the great book of creation, a verse of the great psalm chanted by the cosmos" (ibid.). Rather than as a mortal sin, Adso sees his physical relationship as "a part of the great theophanic design that sustains the universe" and as a "miracle of consonance and harmony," to the point, indeed, that as "if intoxicated, I then enjoyed her presence in the things I saw, and desiring her in them, with the sight of them I was sated" (ibid.).

While there is a serious downside to this model, in that, as Niebuhr himself noted, "The effort to bring Christ and culture, God's work and man's, the temporal and the eternal, law and grace, into one system of thought and practice tends, perhaps inevitably, to the absolutizing of what is relative, the reduction of the infinite to a finite form, and the materialization of the dynamic" (Niebuhr, 1952, p. 150), it is clear that this synthetic approach holds much sway, particularly in Roman Catholic circles. Christ may be *above* culture, but a radical and transformative reverence for the (God-given) material order is instrumental to this model, and lends itself to a reciprocity between the sacred and the profane, the material and the spiritual, "theology" and "culture." It is also notable that this approach does not fall into the trap of Niebuhr's second *Christ of Culture* position, which tends to conflate Christianity and culture to such an extent that critical and theological rigor is lost, such that there is little scope for differentiating between the plethora of different types of theology and different types of film that may be susceptible to a theological interpretation. It would be wrong to suggest, however, that there is a homogeneity or uniformity to the synthetic model. For example, in spite of Bazin's belief that only long, uninterrupted, and continuous shots are able to "divine the real," it is notable that one of the best illustrations of the synthetic model can be found in the cinema of Martin Scorsese, which employs a heavy use of montage and editing. In situating his characters in a busy and violent universe as they search for redemption, the jolting and disorientating effect that editing creates arguably makes it easier, rather than more difficult, for the audience to bear witness to the spiritual struggles that Scorsese's protagonists are experiencing. Indeed, Scorsese has spoken in the past of his desire that the viewers might be part of the tapestry of his films and have their noses bloodied by being bombarded with a multiplicity of sights, sounds, and sensations. As he says of *Raging Bull* (1980), "I wanted to do the fight scenes as if the *viewers* were the fighter, and their impressions were the fighter's" (qtd in Dougan, 1997, p. 65), thereby identifying with the need of Jake La Motta (Robert De Niro) for purification and vindication. Or, to give a more recent example, the arguably futile quest of Billy Costigan (Leonardo DiCaprio) for retribution, purgation, and vindication amid the seedy milieu of a mob syndicate in *The Departed* (2006) owes much to the violence, carnage, and assault that are inflicted not only on the other characters in the film but, viscerally, on the film audience at home or in the cinema. Had Scorsese opted to make his films in the realist tradition, using *mise-en-scène* and deep-focus cinematography (in which both the foreground and the background are equally in focus) in order to objectively lay bare the realities of the world, it is unlikely that the films would have achieved the same effect of bringing the audience into an intense confrontation with the bloodshed and carnage that La Motta and Costigan experience in the boxing ring and the "mean streets" of South Boston, respectively. Though an anathema to Bazin, films that use close-ups, fast cuts, jagged dissolves, and swirling camera pans, as well as those that employ such stylistic flourishes as elaborate set decoration and colorful, even garish, costumes (as in *The Age of Innocence* [1993] and *Casino* [1995]), are prime examples of how a spiritual reality may be embodied in, and mediated by, the physical universe, and where, to quote Richard Blake, the viewer "will discover spiritual meaning" (Blake, 2000, p. 32). Ultimately, therefore, the synthesis between Christ and culture transcends the matter of which style of filmmaking – realist or montage – is being employed by the director.

Christ and Culture in Paradox

In this model, which is a more Protestant-based position, there is an emphasis less on the synthesis that has the capacity to arise between theology and culture, and more on the *dualism* between Christ and culture, with all of the attendant opposition and bifurcation that this entails. Rather than looking at the way in which, through sacramentality, there is a synchronicity between Christianity and culture that Christianity tends to complete and fulfill, this dualist model is inclined to juxtapose the combination of Christ and culture (which for the synthesists is maintained by divine grace) with a recognition of the disunity and distinction that ultimately lie between them. Although, as Niebuhr recognized, there are similarities here with the *Christ against Culture* model, in that dualists will refuse to accommodate the claims of Christ to the norms of secular society, the difference is that, for those who subscribe to this fourth model, humankind is believed to exist in a tension between two conflicting demands – that of Christ and that of secular authorities and institutions. In Niebuhr's words, "man is seen as subject to two moralities, and as a citizen of two worlds that are not only discontinuous with each other but largely opposed" (Niebuhr, 1952, p. 56). This is not the end of the matter, however. As the "paradox" of the heading suggests, Christians who subscribe to this model tend if not to overcome this dualism then at least to live with this tension – with all of the attendant sin, suffering, and injustice that this conflict necessarily brings – with a view to securing a justification that lies beyond history. This is not to diminish the pervasiveness of the sin and depravity that dualists believe is an inextricable part of inhabiting a fallen world, but it is hoped that this fallenness, from which we cannot escape, will eventually lead, by God's grace, to a restoration of our prelapsarian condition. Whereas the *Christ against Culture* position holds that we can abstain from worldly impurity, this dualist model is rather more nuanced, holding that we belong to our culture, and that we cannot remove ourselves from it, but that God sustains humankind in it (and by it). As a result, for the dualist, attempting to evade or renounce culture, as in the first model, is simply an untenable position, and it is therefore nonsensical to claim that only by withdrawing from culture will salvation be assured. As Niebuhr says in relation to St. Paul, "His experience with Galatian and Corinthian, with Judaizing and spiritualizing Christians had taught him...that the anti-Christian spirit could not be evaded by any measures of isolation from pagan culture" (Niebuhr, 1952, p. 167), such as by abstaining from meat sacrificed to pagan gods or abandoning family life in favor of a celibate lifestyle.

Accordingly, although, on this dualist rendering, there is something inescapably negative about secular culture, it can nevertheless serve the function of a necessary evil. It may be the case that, in Niebuhr's words, "All human action, all culture, is infected with godlessness, which is the essence of sin" and that "reason in human affairs is never separable from its egoistic, godless, perversion" (ibid., p. 159), but it is believed that secular laws can act as a not insignificant corrective, preventing sin from becoming even more pervasive than is presently the case. Without going so far as the synthetic position, according to which culture is directed toward the attainment of positive values, the dualist will begrudgingly accept the norms of secular culture since they may be the only remedy for and restraint against even greater sinfulness. No matter how independent culture may be from Christ or Church law, there is no alternative, for those who subscribe to this model, to being caught up in the – albeit temporal and transitory – affairs of this world. Provided that Christians derive their knowledge and freedom about what to do in the secular sphere from their Christian ethics, beliefs, and values – so that they live out, as best as possible, a Christian life – then the fundamental tensions between Christ and culture, though by no means overcome, can at least be held together, with a view to gaining new insight from that dialogue or interchange. This has important ramifications for the study of theology and film, since there is no need to attempt, on this interpretation, to foster artificial or contrived connections between theology on the one hand and film, or culture, on the other. Rather than claim, as so much of the Christ-figure literature does, that a film is more Christian or theological than it actually is, the dualist would be inclined, rather, to focus on dissimilarities rather than elementary narrative or thematic convergences. The autonomy of both theology and film needs to be respected, and there can be no scope for simply "reading" theology into film in light of the radical discordance between what Christianity and culture comprise. A film that disturbs or challenges, rather than simply enlightens, would be a prime example of this theological model. Rather than go down the path of, say, reading *Fight Club* (David Fincher, 1999) as a religious or theological film because it contains discernible Christian vocabulary – such as the enigmatic inclusion of seven "I am" sayings that correspond to the language of the Fourth Gospel, along the lines of "I am Jack's smirking revenge" and "I am Jack's enflamed sense of rejection," as well as the constant references in Fincher's audacious exploration of the redemptive power of physical violence to spiritual rebirth, including "Every evening I died and every morning I rose again...Resurrected" – a dualist response would be more inclined to highlight how and to what extent the film's exploration of nihilism and self-mutilation differs at key stages from a traditional Christian reading.

A recent publication that might be said to correspond to this model of *Christ and Culture in Paradox* is *Flickering Images: Theology and Film in Dialogue*, edited by Anthony Clarke and Paul Fiddes of Regent's Park College, Oxford. In his chapter "When Text Becomes Voice: *You've Got Mail*," Fiddes undertakes a critical reading of the romantic comedy *You've Got Mail* (Nora Ephron, 1998), in which Meg Ryan and Tom Hanks play rival bookshop owners who develop an anonymous email correspondence with each other, by placing alongside the film's pairing of "text" and "voice" the New Testament pairing of "letter" and "spirit," as delineated in 2 Corinthians 3:6. While noting that there is "nothing overtly 'religious' about this film" (Fiddes, 2005, p. 108), Fiddes finds that, despite exposing "patterns of text, voice and presence in human life where a Christian thinker can see the presence of God" (ibid.), the film fundamentally differs, in its life-affirming and over-optimistic ending, from Christian eschatological ideas about the End. Attesting that all "endings in human art offer us an echo and an image of the final End" (ibid., p. 109), Fiddes is concerned that the fantasy denouement, in which the protagonists are finally reconciled despite their incompatible attitudes to business – Hanks's character, Joe Fox, is a corporate shark while Ryan's Kathleen Kelly runs a small, family corner shop that puts the well-being of its customers above economic greed and financial acumen – offers no more than "an escape from life, a happy-ever-after world which fails to connect with the world in which we are living" (ibid., p. 110). Whereas in Shakespeare's comedies "some dark strain remains in the final harmony, some note of discord or incompleteness" in which "one of the characters remains unreconciled, or we are made aware of the passing of time and the threat of death pressing in, or there is something about the relation between the lovers that makes us suspect that troubled times lie ahead in the midst of the happiness" (ibid.), in filmic romantic comedies it is characteristically the case that all conflict and dissension are miraculously and implausibly resolved. Fiddes argues that the Christian understanding of the final End brings both closure and openness and comprises "a new beginning in which there will be room for the development of persons, in which there will be journeys to make, adventures to be had and purposes to be fulfilled" (ibid.). Despite being charmed by the cozy and life-affirming ethos of *You've Got Mail*, Fiddes is nonetheless aware of the radical discontinuity between how the film and Christianity interpret questions of resolution and finality.

Similar ideas are developed by Robert Jewett, a Pauline scholar for whom Pauline theology should take account of the movies. His premise, as delineated in *Saint Paul at the Movies: The Apostle's Dialogue with American Culture* (1993) and *Saint Paul Returns to the Movies: Triumph over Shame* (1999), is that St. Paul's teaching, as chronicled in his New Testament epistles, was shaped more by the popular culture of his day than by any formal religious or educational training, as denoted by the time that he used to spend evangelizing in such secular locations as the workshop, lecture hall, and street corner. Jewett hypothesizes that Paul, placing himself "where other people were, to communicate the gospel on their turf" (Jewett, 1993, p. 5), "would have been a discerning partner in discussing secular movies had they been available in his time," with the issues that they raise and stories they tell "reminiscent of conversations in the workshops where he spent most of his life" (ibid., p. 6). Jewett's approach is to relate the films discussed, which include *Star Wars* (George Lucas, 1977), *Tootsie* (Sydney Pollack, 1982), and *Grand Canyon* (Lawrence Kasdan, 1991) in the first volume, and *Unforgiven* (Clint Eastwood, 1992), *Babe* (Chris Noonan, 1995), and *Mr. Holland's Opus* (Stephen Herek, 1995) in the sequel, to a specific passage from St. Paul's epistles – such as the theme of comfort in 2 Corinthians 1 in the case of *Tootsie*, and Romans 12, which discusses honoring the lowly, in the case of *Babe* – with a view to treating both with equal respect and bringing their common themes into relationship "so that a contemporary interpretation for the American cultural situation may emerge" (ibid., p. 7). Laudable though this is, however, there is a vital and not insignificant disclaimer that links with the dualist reading as expounded by Niebuhr. For, rather than simply seeking analogies between ancient and modern texts and situations, in the form of "an interpretive arch," one end of which is anchored in St. Paul's day while the other is rooted in contemporary (American) culture, Jewett believes that this is not a relationship of equals. Although he stresses the need to treat each film under discussion with respect, his non-negotiable position is that "the Pauline word is allowed to stand as primus inter pares," that is, the "first among equals," since, unlike film, the Bible has "stood the test of time by revealing ultimate truth that has gripped past and current generations with compelling power" (ibid., p. 11). Acknowledging that motion pictures can also be "inspired," and conceding that the Bible should not be an overbearing partner in the hermeneutical dialogue, Jewett contends that, unlike films, "biblical texts have sustained the life and morals of faith communities in circumstances both adverse and happy over several thousand years" (ibid., p. 12).

Since Jewett's rationale is to read the films under discussion against the standard of Paul's epistles, the net result is that the films are consistently treated as lightweight or incomplete conversational partners. After making a number of effective claims about *Mr. Holland's Opus* and its relationship to the discussion of fame and self-commendation that Paul expounds upon in 2 Corinthians 3, Jewett concludes that, ultimately, "Paul's viewpoint seems healthier than the anticipation evoked by the conclusion" (Jewett, 1999, p. 85) of the film. Jewett is referring here to the scene in which an inspirational high-school music teacher, Glenn Holland (Richard Dreyfuss) – who has hitherto considered himself a failure because, due to his pedagogical duties, he never managed to find the time to accomplish the dream of completing his own musical symphony (the "opus" of the title) – is finally accorded, upon his retirement, the recognition and acclamation that his 30-year career has warranted, when his former pupils perform a surprise rendition of his unfinished magnum opus in the school hall. Despite finding this "a moving scene, especially for those of us who have been influenced by a great and devoted teacher or pastor" (ibid., p. 72), Jewett attests that "We do not need the endorsement of those we serve resounding through the auditorium, because in Christ we already have divine endorsement that is not dependent on our achievements" (ibid., p. 87). Likewise, in relation to the end of the John Grisham-based legal thriller *The Firm* (Sydney Pollack, 1993), Jewett argues that although he admires the protagonist, Mitch McDeere (Tom Cruise), for developing, by the picture's denouement, "a newfound commitment to the law because it treats all persons equally," he is concerned that this film "does not develop the radical implications of freedom as Paul does" (ibid., p. 144).

Furthermore, just as Fiddes found the ending of *You've Got Mail* to be theologically problematic because of its failure to delineate a sufficiently ambiguous sense of closure (in a manner that conforms to that which has come before in the movie), so Jewett is critical of the ending of *Groundhog Day* (Harold Ramis, 1993), in which an egocentric television weatherman, Phil Connors (Bill Murray), who is punished by spending the worst day of his life over and over again in a small American town, finally finds peace and restitution (and an end to the cycle of repetition) upon finding true love with his producer, Rita (Andie MacDowell). Despite finding rich parallels between the film and what Paul has to say in Galatians 6 concerning the dangers of reaping the rewards of the flesh as opposed to those of the spirit, Jewett feels that the important motif running throughout both Galatians and the film, namely, that we should avoid "seizing the day in an opportunistic manner" and instead overcome "the prideful illusions that the times and seasons can be brought under human control," as well as the concomitant tendency to think that other people "can be mastered and seduced to suit our own rhythm and ego needs" (ibid., p. 102), is squandered by *Groundhog Day*'s "fairy-tale" ending. In Jewett's words:

> The lovers come down the steps of the bed and breakfast at the end of the film, and Phil, gazing at the fresh snow, says, "It's so beautiful. Let's live here." A false note is struck as their station wagon is seen making tracks through the freshly fallen snow, indicating the promise of a new life in

Punxsutawney for a couple who will live here happily ever after. Especially for Phil and Rita, whose matured vocations require the broadcasting facilities of Pittsburgh, this ending is wide of the mark. Given the cultural appeal of an idyllic life in an isolated town or safe suburb, this is one more illusion of the flesh.

(ibid.)

In marked contrast, Jewett suggests that when St. Paul writes in Galatians 6 about "reaping a harvest," "doing what is right," and "working for the good of all" (ibid.; cf. Galatians 6:7–10), a more serious treatise of living responsibly by "the fruit of the Spirit" (cf. Galatians 5:22), with the attendant focus on "love, joy, peace, patience, kindness, goodness, faithfulness, gentleness, self-control" (Galatians 5:22), is set forth. Whereas St. Paul was calling upon the early Christian community in Galatia (in southern Asia Minor) to seek the welfare of their neighbors in both good times and bad, and to be freed by Christ "from our culturally shaped compulsions to embrace selfish love" and our penchant for escaping "the complexities of vocation and mutual responsibilities" (Jewett, 1999, p. 102), it is questionable whether *Groundhog Day* is able in quite the same way to counter "the despair of a cyclical life that goes nowhere" (ibid., p. 99) and to enable audiences of the film to sow to the Spirit and thereby be in a position to "reap eternal life" (Galatians 6:8). Films are simply unable, for Jewett, to impart the same depth of insight and to have the same transformative effect as the apostle Paul was able to convey in his epistles concerning the way we should be responding to such pivotal Pauline themes as justification, shame, honor, grace, love, and righteousness. Although the "language and metaphors of the Bible still retain their power in some of our most secular artifacts" (ibid., p. 183), not least in a film such as *The Shawshank Redemption* where the Bible is used as an instrument of oppression by a sadistic prison warden and as a means of escape, by literally housing the key to salvation, by an innocent inmate, Jewett is under no delusion that only a cautious and tentative critical appropriation of film by the Pauline scholar will facilitate a theological (and more specifically Pauline) conversation.

Instructive though Jewett's approach is, however, there are a number of limitations to his position. He may be clearly acquainted with the narrative of the films under discussion, and there is little doubt that he judiciously enters into dialogue with his chosen texts, but, as he admits in the prologue to *Saint Paul at the Movies*, he is not a film critic – "I have neither the talent nor the training" (Jewett, 1993, p. 8). This is not a problem *per se*, since he is a Pauline scholar whose primary audience is students and fellow biblical scholars interested in hermeneutics, but his work is littered with references to the need for a film to carry a "prophetic power" and to offer the "potentially vivid counterweight of biblical stories and ideas" (ibid.) to culture's more secular and even religion-less values and norms. Jewett may hope to engender "a respectful dialogue that is sensitive to the contemporary relevance of both the film and the biblical text" (ibid.), but any dialogue that has the potential to take place is hampered by the fact that this is a one-sided conversation, in which the parameters of the debate have already been framed by the New Testament writings alone. Even when, as happens at one point in a discussion of the theme of vengeance in relation to Romans 12:19–21 and *Pale Rider* (Clint Eastwood, 1985), Jewett concedes that St. Paul is being inconsistent, in that on the one hand he is calling on the Christian community to pray for its enemies but on the other he urges obedience to the government that is responsible for punishing and killing its criminals (as outlined in Romans 13:2, the person who "resists the authorities resists what God has appointed, and ... will incur judgment"), Jewett resolves the problem by proposing that this is a "holy inconsistency" (Jewett, 1993, p. 131). In other words, where we encounter a flaw in St. Paul's judgment and logic, the fault is more likely to be ours rather than the apostle's – "Is there perhaps a deeper, more divine logic at work here? ... Is there not perhaps a deeper understanding of the human psyche in Paul's apparent inconsistency than in our cultural simplicities?" (ibid.).

On no occasion does Jewett concede that St. Paul may be in the wrong, and nor does he countenance that a film may offer a more erudite or judicious reading of theological themes than St. Paul's epistles. In unapologetically dualist terms, Jewett believes that, as he says in his chapter on *Unforgiven*, in marked contrast to the "distinctively Christian story of regeneration through sacrificial love," our culture is predisposed to preach the gospel of "regeneration through violence" (Jewett, 1999, p. 161). Since these two contradictory options cannot be brought together – "When the two models of redemption are held up before us, side by side ... it should become clear that either choice will eliminate the other" (ibid.) – we must therefore choose one over the other, and Jewett leaves his readers in no doubt as to where his allegiance lies. Ultimately, Jewett is dedicated to seeing his work as missiological in nature, with "a commitment to pursue the saving power of the gospel" (Jewett, 1993, p. 9), so that, to paraphrase Paul in 1 Corinthians 9:22, it might bring at least some of his readers, and those who view these films, to salvation. Is Jewett not, though, judging his selection of films against a standard by which they were never meant to compete? It is one thing to argue that film can be part of a hermeneutical conversation, but when he argues, for instance, that violent retaliation, along the lines of that meted out in *The Shawshank Redemption* by one of the subsidiary characters, a prison inmate called Elmo Blatch (Bill Bolender), to the wife and lover of Andy Dufresne (Tim Robbins) – who was in turn framed for their murders – "is an all too typical reaction" without the presence of "the love of Christ that can heal the shame of being treated with contempt" (Jewett, 1999, p. 174), Jewett goes too far, criticizing a film for its failure to perform an evangelistic function that it had never set out to fulfill.

For this reason, a more useful, and fully dialogical, approach can be found in George Aichele and Richard Walsh's recent collection, *Screening Scripture: Intertextual Connections Between Scripture and Film* (2002), which explicitly sets out in a manner that is qualitatively distinct from "most books that bring together Scripture and film" (Aichele & Walsh, 2002, p. ix) not to privilege the scriptural side of the exchange. Rather than presume, in the manner of Jewett, that a scriptural text (or a biblical scholar's reading of it) is paramount and that if a film should deviate from that interpretation "on some particular issue, theme, character, plot, or story" (ibid.) then the film in question is simply flawed, Aichele and Walsh's volume does not presuppose that there is only one, monolithic interpretation of a text. Instead, their aim is to "bring the selected movies and biblical texts into a genuine exchange that will open up illuminating connections between them" (ibid.). For example, in the case of the media satire *Pleasantville* (Gary Ross, 1998), in which two teenagers from the 1990s are transported to the prelapsarian world of a hermetically sealed 1950s television sitcom, and struggle to create some semblance of humanity and authenticity in what they discover is no Edenic fantasy but an artificial, reactionary, and oppressive milieu, Aichele argues in his chapter "Sitcom Mythology" that "The cinematic rewriting of the biblical stories of Eden and the Flood in *Pleasantville* not only juxtaposes them, but it also recycles them in a way that challenges the Christian reading of those stories" (Aichele, 2002, p. 116). He suggests that the supposedly paradisiacal world that the two teenagers enter "was never especially innocent," but, rather, "bland and pasty" (ibid., p. 119), in accordance with the claim I have adduced elsewhere that although this is an environment where everyone is always wholesome and in high spirits, the fact that there are no dangers, uncertainties, risks, or surprises prompts the question: "would we want to live in such a world?" (Deacy,

2005, p. 127). Indeed, would it not do us a disservice as human beings to live a life where we are not required to think or be challenged, and where we operate within a set of carefully prescribed boundaries and limitations – both mentally and geographically (ibid.)? Rather than see this film, as a number of Christian internet contributors have done, as an attack on traditional biblical morality and Christian values (see Deacy, 2005, p. 128) – where, as one Christian Spotlight respondent puts it, "good is completely slandered," with the film constituting "a twisted allegory of Genesis" (Rettig, 1998) – Aichele approaches the film from a different angle, proposing that it should challenge our reading of Scripture, instead of (along the lines of Jewett) simply using Scripture to challenge our reading of the film. The film may therefore raise questions about the intrinsic goodness of Eden, but this is an inescapably good thing, on this reading, since few would disagree, at least within a postmodern context, that the meaning of all texts must be continually negotiated and renegotiated between that text (including Scripture) and the interpreter, for there is no objective or absolute reading of any text.

Accordingly, since meaning is never intractably fixed, but lies between texts and in "intertextual configurations of texts that intersect one another in a wide variety of ways" (Aichele, 2002, p. 9), it would clearly be absurd to argue that the biblical text should be treated with a degree of reverence and seriousness that no other text (or, indeed, film) could possibly aspire to. In contradistinction to Jewett's approach of according the Bible the upper hand over modern secular cultural products, it is much more appropriate if and when two (or even more) texts can challenge or even subvert readings of each other. A fruitful example of this approach is given by Jeffrey L. Staley in his contribution to Aichele and Walsh's volume, entitled "Meeting Patch Again for the First Time: Purity and Compassion in Marcus Borg, the Gospel of Mark, and *Patch Adams*," in which an attempt is made to read, intertextually, the Gospel of Mark, Marcus Borg's novel *Meeting Jesus Again for the First Time* (1994), and the Robin Williams film comedy *Patch Adams* (Tom Shadyac, 1998). Noting that both Mark and the film explicitly address the dangers involved when purity boundaries are crossed in the name of compassion, Staley argues that viewers are given "a new way to understand the political challenge" (Staley, 2002, p. 228) presented by the Jesus of Mark's Gospel. In juxtaposing four contemporary American institutions of purity – a mental institution, a university, the food industry, and a hospital – with the purity codes that appear in Mark's Gospel – in the challenges to authority raised by Jesus' exorcisms (3:20–30), his teaching (1:21–2), his eating with sinners (2:15–17), and his healing of the sick (1:40–5, 2:1–12) – Staley finds that one is enabled to "move beyond surface-level critiques of the film that merely focus on its storytelling devices and its emotional tone" (ibid., p. 226) and can see how both the film and the biblical text present viewers "with an alternative vision of life that challenges traditional cultural values" in the form of subversive wisdom and a politics of compassion. This is very far removed from the world of Jewett!

Christ the Transformer of Culture

Whereas the dualist approach, as epitomized by Jewett, tends to encourage cultural conservatism, with cultural laws and standards assumed to belong to what Niebuhr referred to as "the temporal and dying world," thereby comprising no more than "restraining forces, dykes against sin" and "preventers of anarchy" (Niebuhr, 1952, p. 190), the fifth of Niebuhr's five models takes a much more positive attitude toward culture. In lieu of the tendency in dualism to lay particular emphasis on the fallenness of creation, those who subscribe to this conversionist model will agree with the dualists (and for that matter those who subscribe to the *Christ against Culture* position) that human culture is far from perfect, but with the crucial difference that they will not simply hold to the negative position of mere endurance in anticipation of a future, eschatological (and trans-historical) deliverance from this world. Rather, Christ is believed to be capable of converting and transforming the existing fallen culture, so that a much more affirmative and hopeful position is adopted. Instead of using the dualist's language of justification and redemption from sin, the conversionist will be much more inclined to stress, like the synthesist, the incarnational and sacramental dimension of culture – albeit without the more extreme veneration of culture that pervaded Niebuhr's third model. The present dimension of existence will thus be accorded a more central role than it will for the dualist, for whom, as Niebuhr pointed out, "spiritual transformation cannot be expected this side of death" (ibid., p. 191). As a result, in this eschatological present, the emphasis will be on renewal, with culture able to point to the glory of God. Niebuhr cites St. Augustine as one of the most obvious exponents of this position, in that, according to Augustine, Christ is the transformer of culture by his redirection, reinvigoration, and regeneration of "that life of man, expressed in all human works, which in present actuality is the perverted and corrupted exercise of a fundamentally good nature" (ibid., pp. 209–10). In response to this corruption, Jesus was believed to have come to earth to heal and renew that which had been perverted – to restore and reorient that which had been led astray by sin. There is nothing in culture that cannot be transformed and converted, on this interpretation.

This fifth model – which Lyden claims was Niebuhr's preferred approach, although this may simply be because Niebuhr does not offer a critique of this model in the same way as he does for the other four – can also be seen to underscore the theology of John Calvin, for whom the secular order was not simply a corrective to evil but also served the positive function of promoting human welfare. In Niebuhr's words, "what the gospel promises and makes possible, as divine (not human) possibility, is the transformation of mankind in all its nature and culture into the kingdom of God" (Niebuhr, 1952, p. 217). As with F. D. Maurice, leader of the Christian Socialist Movement in the nineteenth century, for whom the conversion of humankind from self-centeredness to Christ-centeredness was a fundamental theological axiom, the thinking here is that there is no aspect of human culture that Christ does not have the capacity to transform. Ironically, however, whereas Maurice thereby advocated universal salvation, and the promise of redemption for all, Calvin's theology highlighted the deep fissure between those who were predestined, or elected, to eternal salvation and those who would be consigned for an eternity to eternal damnation. It may not be entirely accurate, therefore, to associate Calvin with this fifth model in the way that Niebuhr suggests. However, more modern forms of Calvinism would seem to fit much more effectively, not least in light of Karl Barth's twentieth-century revisiting of Calvin's thoroughgoing form of predestination, in which it is believed that we have all been made acceptable to God, and God has extended unlimited love to us, because of Christ's atoning death for humankind's sins. For Calvin, in marked contrast, the death of Christ merely takes away the penalty of sins of those on whom God has already chosen (indeed, predestined) to have mercy – that is, the sins of the elect – and so does not apply to the whole human race. Although Barth himself stopped short of advocating universal salvation, it is notable in terms of Niebuhr's fifth model that Barth's updating of Calvinist teaching has positioned creation in a much more positive relationship to God than that which was hitherto the case, since, as Christ is the ground and goal of all creation, humans are thereby unable to undo what Christ has done. As the author of creation and salvation, Christ has restored the covenant with God, the net result of which is that all of creation lies in an essentially positive relation to God. Despite Barth's association with the *Christ against Culture* model cited earlier in this chapter, it may be no less apposite to see him as an albeit partial proponent of Niebuhr's conversionist position.

One possible application of this model to the theology–film conversation can be seen in the way in which Christians may be inclined to create a Christian version of "secular" culture by appropriating it with a spiritual dimension. As with the aforementioned *The Omega Code*, which infused the action genre with an overtly eschatological sensibility in order to be palatable to Christian audiences, the hallmark here is explicit Christian belief. Although more spiritual than explicitly Christian, a more recent example of the conversionist model is the documentary film *What the Bleep Do We Know!?* (Mark Vicente, Betsy Chasse, & William Arntz, 2004), a part metaphysical treatise, part educational tract, and part New Age self-help manual that attempts, with interviews from both the scientific and decidedly unscientific communities, to offer lay audiences new insight into the phenomenon of quantum mechanics. The film's premise is that, just as quantum physics shows us how phenomena are always transformed by observation, so our perception of reality can be changed if we are willing to give up traditionally held suppositions about the whys and wherefores of the universe and our place within it. As well as the allegation that mass meditation is scientifically proven to have reduced crime rates in Washington DC, one of the claims advanced in this film is that humans have the capability of changing the molecular structure of water simply by looking at it. Accordingly, since human beings are comprised of 90 percent water, then, by observing ourselves, we too have the capacity to change at a fundamental level thanks to the laws of quantum physics. Not surprisingly, the film has received a critical mauling from a number of professional scientists, among them Simon Singh, a particle physicist from Cambridge University, who accuses the film-makers of distorting science to fit their own agenda and suffusing the film with "half-truths and misleading analogies," if not "downright lies," as well as duping "millions into mistaking pure claptrap for something of cosmic importance" (qtd in "Inside Story," 2005, p. 4). In like manner, Richard Dawkins, professor of the public understanding of science at Oxford University, directs his invective not simply at "the dishonesty of the charlatans who peddle such tosh, but the dopey gullibility of the thousands of well meaning people who believe it" (qtd in ibid.). However, in seeking to suffuse "secular" scientific culture with an albeit quasi-religious sensibility, in terms of the film's ostensible claim that the distinction between science and religion becomes increasingly blurred once we realize that, ultimately, both are describing the same phenomena, there is a danger that the confessional or evangelical dimension will override all other considerations – aesthetic, scientific, intellectual.

The danger with this fifth model, therefore, is that the religious imagination will become impoverished as the need to transform and suffuse culture with a spiritual dimension becomes the overriding object-ive. If confessional intent overrides artistic or aesthetic quality, then it is not surprising if, as has happened in the case of *What the Bleep Do We Know!?*, it proves difficult to find an interested or appreciative audience beyond the strict confines of the community, or sub-community, that has engendered it. As Steve Rose, writing in the *Guardian*, notes, while the film ostensibly endeavors to present itself as "populist scientific enquiry," it eventually reveals itself to comprise no more than a "mushy self-help manual for a new religion" – or, worse, "a manifesto for a new religion" (Rose, 2005). Rather than transform or convert secular culture, therefore, all that it succeeds in doing is "muddying the waters" (ibid.), and drawing attention to its ghettoized origins. Stella Papamichael simi-larly draws attention to the filmmakers' "cultist" orientations, in which they appear to be encouraging viewers "to come out of the metaphysical closet" (Papamichael, 2005). Rose also argues that *What the Bleep* is "one to file alongside other pseudo-mystical phenomena like the kabbala and *The Da Vinci Code*," and denounces the film as "a product that's happy to rake in the cash by exploiting our lack of knowledge, or even contributing to it" (Rose, 2005). Despite the attempt by one of the film's three directors to dispel reservations by assuring audiences that no funding was received from any religious or spiritual organization in the making of this film, a number of commentators have drawn attention to the fact that one of the "experts" cited in *What the Bleep* is the 35,000-year-old spirit of an ancient warrior from the lost city of Atlantis known as Ramtha the Enlightened One, who is presently being channeled through the body of a woman living in Washington. Furthermore, all three of the film's directors are known to have studied at the Ramtha School of Enlightenment. As Ruthe Stein, writing in the *San Francisco Chronicle*, thus concludes, the "biggest puzzlement" surrounding *What the Bleep* is "what it's doing in major movie theaters around the country when it so clearly belongs on one of those small cable channels given to peculiar programming," leading her to conclude that this "independently pro-duced feature must have some hefty moneybags behind it to afford this level of distribution" (R. Stein, 2004). Although Niebuhr himself does not advance any criticisms of this fifth model, it is clear that, in practice, there are intellectual and artistic problems concomitant with the application of this approach.

Such a dynamic of converting or transforming secular culture with an explicitly religious or spiritual sensibility can also be identified in the Contemporary Christian Music (CCM) industry that was set up in the early 1970s by American evangelical groups as a religious alternative to the mainstream "secular" entertainment industry. A hybrid of rock music ("the devil's music," no less) and Bible-based song lyrics, this approach entails, in Romanowski's words, "co-opting existing musical styles and adding 'Christian' lyrics in the current vernacular," thereby attempting to evangelize and reach out to the "spiritually lost" (Romanowski, 2000, p. 105). Although CCM was created solely on the basis of lyrical content rather than musical style (see Joseph, 1999, p. 5), there is also a sense in which, on this reading, rock concerts might be seen to take on an experiential (and even worship-oriented) role that is functionally equivalent to attending and participating in a church service. Similarly, the creation and distribution of records and CDs might be deemed synonymous with the evangelical task of "saving souls" – where "souls" are consumers, and the more a "Christian" product sells or receives radio airplay the more "souls" are thereby saved. The proliferation in recent years of satellite television channels is also a case in point. In Britain, for example, GOD TV has been running for over a decade – "freely providing life-changing programming to 390 million people" with a view to winning "one billion souls" as it "feeds from Jerusalem to the ends of the earth 24 hours a day" (http://www.god.tv). As with Christian bookshops and youth festivals, there is only room for popular art that evangelizes, praises, or exhorts. The strategy has thus changed in conservative evangelical circles from rejecting popular culture, in the manner of Niebuhr's first model, to rebranding it in their own image, so that, to give an example adduced by Lyden, "rock 'n' roll is no longer 'the devil's music' if it can be given lyrics focused on God rather than sex and drugs" (Lyden, 2003, p. 18).

Arguably, one of the greatest examples in Britain of an artist who conforms to this model is Cliff Richard, who announced his conversion to Christianity during a Billy Graham rally in London in 1966. There is a difference, though, in that whereas, as Mark Joseph points out, in America "successful artists who experienced life-changing conversions were encouraged to give up their loyal audiences, who may have been interested in hearing what their favourite artists had to say, and were relegated to the [CCM] ghetto and urged to make music for fellow believers" (Joseph, 1999, p. 6), Richard has always worked, successfully, in the mainstream. While acknowledging that a career in the music industry involves "working alongside acts which you may feel are in bad taste or offensive" and which "puts you in a place where your beliefs are under pretty constant attack from people who entirely reject Christian standards" (qtd in Joseph, 1999, p. 99), Richard concluded that "Running away from the world is no answer to its challenge ... so I decided to stay put. Paul told the Corinthians at Corinth to stay in the position in life they were in when they were converted" (ibid.). In tandem with Niebuhr's fifth model, therefore, since, as Richard earnestly believes, "I can only say to people who are not Christians that, until you have taken the step of asking Christ into your life, your life is not really worthwhile" (ibid.), the objective is to attempt to transform culture from within. On the downside, however, as with *What the Bleep*, the danger is that a reductionist agenda is in place, whereby confessional intent becomes the sole objective and "religion" is, at it were, introduced through the back door. In Richard's own words, "I am a Christian, so nothing I ever do now is secular. Even when I sing a pop song that doesn't mention Jesus, it's still a Christian song, because I am presenting it. If my record is played on a mainstream radio station, they are playing a Christian record whether they know it or not" (qtd in Joseph, 1999, p. 100). Such is the strength of personality that, he continues, "You can sing about lost love and found love, and about love that's going to last forever. Then once people love you, you can slip them something that really explains what love is about" (ibid.). Rather than be taken on its own terms, the suggestion, here, is that music is only efficacious when it is harnessed – even manipulated – for missiological purposes, and cannot be judged on its own terms.

Richard's 1999 hit record *Millennium Prayer*, which saw the words of the Lord's Prayer set to the music of *Auld Lang Syne*, perhaps best epitomizes this process. The fact that it so deeply polarized audiences – with fellow music artists George Michael and Mel C castigating the song as a "heinous piece of music" (qtd in BBC News, 1999b) and as "ripping off fans" (qtd in BBC News, 1999c), respectively – suggests that not everyone is persuaded by the attempt to Christianize popular culture in this way. Indeed, George Michael went so far as to call the enterprise "vile," arguing that "Just knowing there has been a Christian campaign for it – I think it is so exploitative of people's religion ... I think there are people out there who feel it is their duty to buy this record on the eve of the millennium. That is a really horrible reason for a number one record" (qtd in BBC News 1999b). Controversy also erupted at the time when BBC Radio 2 omitted Cliff Richard's *Millennium Prayer* from its playlist, with a spokesperson for the station explaining that "We are very supportive of him as an artist but his new single was considered not to be of broad enough appeal to be included" (qtd in BBC News 1999a).

Another problem with this transformative model is that there is often a confluence between confessional and commercial interests to such an extent that, with its emphasis on such commercial considerations as "industrial growth, increased market share and greater profits," there has been a systematic dilution and reduction of the evangelical message, whether in satellite television or the Contemporary Christian Music scene, to "the goals and strategies of the commercial marketplace" (Romanowski, 2000, p. 108). On the GOD TV website, for example, viewers are urged to "Become a Business Angel" (www.god.tv/partner/UK/businessangel.aspx). Four dictionary definitions of "angel" are then offered, namely, "A benevolent celestial being that acts as an intermediary between heaven and earth," "A representation of such a being in the image of a human figure with a halo and wings," "A kind and lovable person" who "manifests goodness, purity and selflessness," and "A financial backer of an enterprise" (ibid.). With emphasis on this fourth definition, the channel's website then explains its rationale: "With a God-given passion to reach the lost and equip the Church, the vision of GOD TV is so vast that it is going to take a multitude of Kingdom-minded financiers to accomplish this mission" (ibid.). In a somewhat dubious translation of Deuteronomy 8:18 – which, in the RSV translation, sees Moses calling upon Israel to "remember the LORD your God, for it is he who gives you power to get wealth" – GOD TV uses this passage from the Mosaic law to incite business leaders, which it then identifies as those "who lead corporations, companies or have their own businesses," to "earnestly remember the Lord our God, for it is He who gives power to gain wealth" (ibid.). One thousand "business angels" are then asked to support the channel with a gift of "£3000 or more per year or £250 per month" (ibid.). Similar issues arise in the Contemporary Christian Music scene, where, in 1982, Amy Grant's album *Age to Age* sold over a million copies, paving the way for Grant's evangelical record company WORD to sign a co-production and distribution deal with A&M Records. Yet, as Romanowski reports, this led to tensions among evangelical Christians, as Grant's music was deemed to have become less Christianized (Romanowski, 2000, p. 117). Whereas she had, in the past, performed songs called "My Father's Eyes,"

"El Shaddai," and "Praise to the Lord," her subsequent music, such as her 1991 album *Heart in Motion* and, in 1997, *Behind the Eyes*, was deemed by more conservative Christians to be "religiously shallow" (ibid.), with her 1985 album *Unguarded* lambasted by one reader of *CCM Magazine* as "moral and ethical humanism with a very slight religious perspective ... From Amy's ungodly album cover to her mediocre message, I see no attempt at true evangelism" (qtd in ibid.). In sum, therefore, whatever the merits of Niebuhr's fifth model, it is clear that, to judge by the examples cited from film, music, and televangelism, Christians have a long way to go before Christ will succeed in infiltrating, converting, and transforming secular culture. If anything, this position is the weakest (practically if not intellectually) of Niebuhr's five models, and arguably the most difficult to apply to the interface between theology and film.

Concluding Reflections: "High" and "Low" Culture

While the purpose of this chapter has been to highlight the range of perspectives that exists on the interrelationship between theology and culture, using the five models adduced by H. Richard Niebuhr as a frame of reference, it is apparent that the differences between the five positions cited by Niebuhr are often subtle in form. For example, the fifth model, though clearly distinct from the dualist approach, nevertheless shares that position's tendency to be deeply suspicious about the efficacy of secular products *per se*, at least insofar as they remain in a pre-transformed and unconverted state. And, although it has much in common with the synthetic approach, the difference is that the fifth model does not view culture as *already* in relation to Christ, but only as having the *potential* to become so. It is also different from the second model, *Christ of Culture*, because although both share the propensity to seek a dynamic interaction between Christ and culture, Niebuhr's fifth model is governed and propelled by the Christian faith, and specifically Christ's redemptive power to transform and convert the secular order, and does not see Christ and culture as coterminous and interchangeable. George Marsden may thus be correct in his claim that "Virtually every Christian and every Christian group expresses in one way or another all five of the motifs" (qtd in Glanzer, 2003, ¶7), and it is worth noting that even Niebuhr himself acknowledged that "a construction has been set up that is partly artificial" and "no person or group ever conforms completely to a type" (Niebuhr, 1952, p. 56). The idea that there is such a clear-cut distinction between "Christ" on the one hand and "culture" on the other can, indeed, be misleading. No theological activity can ever be conducted in a cultural vacuum, yet there is something conspicuously abstract and even ahistorical in Niebuhr's distinction between the two. Underlying his typology is the inaccurate suggestion that a line of demarcation exists between the two constructs of "Christianity" and "culture," and that Christianity, or at least the Church, ultimately comprises a monolithic category which can be set apart from the equally monolithic and static realm of "culture." Maybe, in order to adequately highlight the extent to which all theological reflection is ultimately, and inescapably, culturally bound, the typology should be reframed as "the culture of Christianity ... and other cultures" (qtd in Glanzer, 2003, ¶7), along the lines of what Marsden has suggested. Such an approach would at least have the advantage of drawing attention to the existence of *sub*-cultures. As John Howard Yoder puts it, "There is no reason that what we should do about war, and about farming, and about epic poetry, and about elementary education, and about pornography ... and about heavy metal, would gain by our trying to treat each of those segments of 'culture' in the same way" (qtd in ibid.).

Furthermore, as Johnston notes, there are occasions when a theologian "might adopt several different approaches to the conversation between movies and theology depending on the film in view or the audience addressed" (R. Johnston, 2000, p. 59). Even Johnston himself, a Protestant theologian whom Lyden associates with the *Christ and Culture in Paradox* model, because of the dialogical nature of Johnston's program (Lyden, 2003, p. 22), defies easy categorization, since his own leanings tend to be toward the Catholic-oriented synthetic model. Indeed, in *Reel Spirituality*, Johnston claims at one point that film "can usher us into the presence of the holy" (R. Johnston, 2000, p. 87), and that film stories that "portray the truly human bind their viewers with the religious expressions of humankind" and "awaken a holistic sense in their viewers, providing windows of meaning" (ibid., p. 158). He goes even further than this when talking about the films of Peter Weir, in the case study that appears at the end of his book. There, Johnston bemoans the fact that "we seldom notice God's sacramental presence in the ordinary experiences of life, including our moviegoing. We fail to hear God speak" (ibid., p. 173). Together with his attestations that "The movies of Peter Weir can help the church recover something of life's mystery and grace" and that "The intimations of Spirit/spirit found in his movies are real expressions of grace and have strong biblical warrant, if we would but listen" (ibid., p. 189), this clearly suggests that we should exercise caution before pigeonholing theologians and critics as belonging to particular typologies. This is no less true of James Wall, whose article "Biblical Spectaculars and Secular Man," published in Cooper and Skrade's 1970 volume *Celluloid and Symbols*, would indicate that he subscribes to the dualist model in light of his assertion that a film's vision "can be said to be 'religious' in the Christian sense if it celebrates humanity or if it exercises with conviction a strong agony over moments where humanity is actually distorted" (Wall, 1970, p. 56). On the other hand, in his later writings in the 1990s for the *Christian Century*, Wall has argued for a more sacramental view of things, as betokened by his claim that "God is active but often in disguise, and where signs of the spirit are waiting to erupt from novels, movie screens and bully pulpits" (qtd in R. Johnston, 2000, p. 60).

Despite such ambivalence, however, a general picture may be seen to emerge. While there are many Christians who would subscribe to the two more extreme positions of *Christ against Culture* and *Christ of Culture*, the majority of Christian contributions to the dialogue between Christ and culture tend to relate to the last three of Niebuhr's five positions. Whereas in the first model, where film cannot contribute to Christian theology at all, and in the second, where there is an over-zealous attempt to converge Christ and culture, in the dualist, synthetic, and conversionist models film can clearly contribute to Christian theology *although Christian theology brings its own agenda to the conversation*. Since, for there to be a proper dialogue, theology must expect to be challenged in the process, this is more likely to be achieved in models three to five than in the first approach, where theology resolutely refuses to engage with culture through fear of contamination, and the second, where "anything goes" and, as David Jasper's critique has evinced, there is an absence of critical rigor. Of the three latter positions, which in *Explorations in Theology and Film* were synthesized into one generic model entitled *Theology in critical dialog with culture* (Marsh, 1997, p. 28), it is the dualist model of *Christ and Culture in Paradox* that is most resistant to simply welcoming uncritically all that culture has to offer (cf. ibid., p. 27), in view of the model's tendency to judge popular culture on the basis of pre-formed theological assumptions. It is our view that an important way forward for the theology–film field is to insure that a much more dialogical and two-way conversation can emerge that allows both theology and film an equal voice in the exchange, rather than (as in the dualist model as conceived by Jewett) a position that seeks a dialogue but only on the proviso that Christianity calls the shots. An approach more in keeping with the positions adopted by the contributors to Aichele and Walsh's *Screening Scripture*, rather than Jewett's *Saint Paul at the Movies*, is thus pivotal in this regard, not least because the contributors to the former volume stress the need to undertake a hermeneutical conversation with Scripture, but one in which biblical texts are just one of many voices struggling to be heard among the swirling, fermenting currents of contemporary culture, and none has primacy over any of the others.

Such an approach finds a ready parallel not so much in the work of Niebuhr as in Gordon Lynch's revised correlational approach to the theology–culture exchange, as delineated in a recent Blackwell publication, *Understanding Theology and Popular Culture* (Lynch, 2005, p. 103f.). According to Lynch, such a position "values a complex conversation between the questions and insights of both religious tradition and popular culture, and allows for the possibility that both religious tradition and popular culture can be usefully challenged and transformed through this process" (ibid., p. 105). Rather than, in the form of what Lynch refers to as the correlational method, simply looking for theological answers to cultural questions in the manner of Jewett, there is a much greater emphasis in the revised correlational approach on the extent to which theology can itself learn from (and be changed or challenged by) secular culture – even to the point that one may wish to reject aspects of one's theological tradition that are deemed to be deficient or harmful. Although Lynch associates my own work with the correlational model (ibid.), the *revised* correlational approach would be more in keeping with the claim adduced in *Faith in Film* that so complex is the relationship between theology and film that film may even have "taken on many of the functions that we would historically associate with traditional religious institutions" (Deacy, 2005, p. 137). Provided that the relationship is a critical and dialectical one, then film and other agencies of secular culture can be seen to comprise a far cry from the way in which adherents to the *Christ against Culture* model have tended over the years to deride motion pictures (and in particular Hollywood) as a form of distraction from – and, indeed, a counterpoint to – more demanding and erudite pursuits. Whereas, to cite one example, in the words of Richard Harries, kitsch "is the enemy of all that is true, good and beautiful" and "an enemy of the Christian faith and must be exposed as such" (Harries, 2004, p. 354), the theology–film debate today has moved on a long way, to the extent that film is often deemed an equal dialogue-partner rather than a merely commercial enterprise that, as the British literary critic

F. R. Leavis, writing in the early-to-mid-twentieth century, believed, is unable to replicate the ability of other art forms such as poems and novels to educate, inform, and confront (cf. Lynch, 2005, p. 6).

There is no room, however, for complacency. Although films can often perform an important cultural and societal role, American art critic Clement Greenberg's diagnosis in the 1930s and 1940s of forms of entertainment (not least kitsch) that offered their audiences easy pleasures without requiring from them any intellectual assent or aesthetic response (cf. Lynch, 2005, pp. 6–7) is not without its more recent advocates. Though a committed movie buff, Mark Kermode, who regularly reviews films for BBC radio and television and for *Sight and Sound* magazine, and has written two entries in the British Film Institute Modern Classics Series on *The Exorcist* (William Friedkin, 1973) and *The Shawshank Redemption*, lambasted *Pirates of the Caribbean: Dead Man's Chest* (Gore Verbinski, 2006) – the sequel to a film inspired by a Disney theme park ride – on the BBC2 arts program *Newsnight Review* on July 7, 2006, for representing "the death of Western civilization." It is not that Kermode is adverse to popular film, as his infatuation with (often low-budget) horror films attests. However, film is demonstrably not capable of facilitating a theological discussion *per se*, and Kermode's disenchantment with artistically impoverished summer blockbuster fare is a salutary reminder of the dangers involved in going down the path of the second of Niebuhr's five models. Although he was writing in the context of television, Neil Postman's comprehensive critique of electronic media, *Amusing Ourselves to Death* (1986), has serious ramifications for the way we look upon film in the late twentieth and early twenty-first centuries. A media theorist and cultural critic, Postman argued that whereas print culture (the dominant form of communication in the nineteenth century) encouraged coherent, orderly, serious, and rational discourse with propositional content, television epitomizes an image-based culture where fragmented, rather than coherent, multi-sensory images, which emphasize feeling and sensation over rationality, predominate. Even when television programs deal explicitly with religion, Postman draws attention to the qualitative distinction between worship that is conducted in a consecrated space, such as a church, synagogue, or temple, and how, when it comes to television, audiences will experience religious programs in the same semi-attentive manner that they will soak up game shows or soap operas – that is, while they are eating, talking, going to the toilet, or doing "push-ups" (Postman, 1986, p. 119). Since, according to Postman, audiences of religious programs cannot, by definition, be "immersed in an aura of mystery and symbolic otherworldliness" when in the "presence of an animated television screen," it is highly "unlikely" that television "can call forth the state of mind required for a nontrivial religious experience" (ibid.). In a nutshell, "[e]verything that makes religion an historic, profound and sacred human activity is stripped away" when it is presented on television – "there is no ritual, no dogma, no tradition, no theology, and above all, no sense of spiritual transcendence" (ibid., pp. 116–17). The danger for Postman "is not that religion has become the content of television shows but that television shows may become the content of religion" (ibid., p. 124). As John P. Ferré points out, in his paraphrase of Postman:

> The producers of religious programs know the viewing habits of the audience, including the fact that with a quick press of a button the religion could be gone and a soap opera could appear, so they compete for viewers with upbeat programs that exude health, wealth and beauty. They promote values that have everything to do with audience share, but nothing to do with the rigorous demands of true religious devotion ... [where even] God is subordinate to the evangelist.
>
> (Ferré, 2003, p. 87)

With the lines between worship and entertainment blurred, in which the minister plays the role of entertainer, electronic media thus perform an insidious role in our society, one which is inimical to genuine religious engagement – to the point, indeed, that Postman even refers to this as "blasphemy" (Postman, 1986, p. 123). His British counterpart, Malcolm Muggeridge, was also of the view that television was a medium of fantasy in contradistinction to the reality of the Christian message, such that, had Christ returned to earth in the twentieth century and been invited to appear on television then, according to Muggeridge, he would have declined the opportunity, since his province was one of truth whereas television is bound up with illusion. In Muggeridge's words, "We have created a Frankenstein-like monster, an enormous apparatus of persuasion such as has never before been known on earth," which says to those whom it influences: "satisfy your greed, satisfy your sensuality, that is the purpose of life" (qtd in Grant, 2003, p. 121).

The dangers of being subsumed into an electronic, visual culture are also illustrated well in a number of motion pictures. In François Truffaut's *Fahrenheit 451* (1966), for instance, we see a chillingly prophetic vision of a future age where books are ritually burned ("Books disturb people; they make them anti-social") and the citizens are controlled and manipulated by television. As Bernard Brandon Scott sees it, the film "paints a picture in which one of the driving ideologies of the Western liberal tradition, the equality of all humans, becomes in the hands of the new media a tool for leveling and controlling society," and that instead of "inducing freedom" fosters only "anarchy" (Scott, 1994, p. 273).[4] In *Being There* (Hal Ashby, 1979), reading and writing are peripheral concerns since the protagonist is illiterate. Indeed, Chance Gardiner (Peter Sellers) is a blank slate, whose entire understanding of the world has been derived from television. He has learned all his values – how to behave, how to smile, and how to be pleasant and calm – from TV. When he enters the "outside world," he becomes an instant celebrity, and is a natural performer on television, because this is the tool that has literally formed him. At the end, he is even touted as a possible future president of the United States. Another case in point is *Network* (Sidney Lumet, 1976), a satire on the commercialization of American news broadcasting, in which a TV news anchorman, Howard Beale (Peter Finch), suffers a nervous breakdown live on air and launches a series of rants against the network that had recently decided to fire him because of a fall in ratings. He lambasts the very industry that has molded him, turning into an on-air prophet. However, when ratings begin to soar, especially when Beale threatens to "blow my brains out" live on peak-time television, his employers react by turning the nightly news into a type of game show in order to foster the unprecedented audience share, and the entertainment division of the network takes over the news division. In an apocalyptic tone that is reminiscent of Postman, Beale – the "mad prophet of the airwaves," as he comes to be known – denounces television as

> the gospel, the ultimate revelation. This tube can make or break presidents, popes, prime ministers. This tube is the most awesome goddamn force in the whole godless world. And woe is us if it ever falls into the hands of the wrong people ... Television is not the truth. Television is a goddamn amusement park. Television is a circus, a carnival, a traveling troop of acrobats, storytellers, dancers, singers, jugglers, side show freaks, lion tamers, and football players. We're in the boredom killing business.

This thus connects well with Postman's premise that we are "amusing ourselves to death" and that when "a population is distracted by trivia, when cultural life is redefined as a perpetual round of entertainments ... - when, in short, a people become an audience and their public business a vaudeville act, then a nation finds itself at risk; culture death is a clear possibility" (Postman, 1986, pp. 155–6).

In light of such considerations, it is not surprising if church leaders are often predisposed to disdain what the media has to offer as unworthy of theological attention. As Peter Horsfield, writing from an Australian perspective, notes:

> Many church leaders tell me – sometimes proudly, sometimes dismissively – that they are too busy to watch television or go to the movies. Their major media activities are reading books and journals, activities that put them out of touch with the most common media practices of the people to whom they are supposed to be communicating.
>
> (Horsfield, 2003, p. 274)

Such concerns, though sincere and considered, are inclined to judge the value of a cultural product on the basis of where it sits on the high–low culture axis. A distinction will be made between high and popular culture, so that films (and TV) will tend to be seen to comprise throwaway entertainment, whereas the printed form contains an intellectual (and theological) rigor. Paul Tillich is a case in point. Despite his contention in *Theology of Culture* that neither the religious nor the secular realm "should be in separation from the other," since both "are rooted in religion in the larger sense of the word, in the experience of ultimate concern" (Tillich, 1964, p. 9), Tillich's theology also underscores the dangers inherent in presupposing that *popular* culture can be amenable to a theological conversation. For the mere fact that for Tillich "Ultimate concern is manifest in the aesthetic function of the human spirit as the infinite desire to express ultimate meaning" (Tillich, 1964, p. 8) and "refers to every moment of our life, to every space and every realm" (ibid., p. 41) does not mean that all works of art express God in the way that he describes. Indeed, so highbrow was Tillich in his approach to the arts that it is conspicuous that – even taking on board the consideration that much of his work was written in the first half of the twentieth century, when film was more of a fledgling medium – he chose not to refer to the medium of film at all in his *Theology of Culture*. Even when he referred specifically to the "visual arts" (Tillich, 1964, p. 71), the remit of the discussion was restricted to "the Byzantine, the Romanesque, the early and late Gothic styles," as well as Mannerism, Baroque, Rococo, Classicism, Romanticism, Naturalism, Impressionism, Expressionism, Cubism, and Surrealism. The cinema is not accommodated at all in his schema, prompting me to revisit the juxtaposition made in *Screen Christologies* of the way for Tillich everything that the human thinks, feels, and performs achieves its greatness and depth because of the active presence of a religious dimension to life, and the subsequent suggestion that film is taking on many of the functions of religion in contemporary society (Deacy, 2001, pp. 2–3).

A better conversation-partner than Tillich is Harvey Cox, who, writing in the 1960s, believed that a balance must be struck by theologians between an uncritical reception of popular culture and remaining in their ivory towers. Cox explicitly advocated moving "beyond a culture dominated by print," with what he called "its inherently elitist characteristics," to the point where electronic media has the potential to "facilitate a more democratic and more participatory society than we now have" (Cox, 2004, p. 254). While acknowledging that books play a vital role, Cox argued that as modes of communication they are "awkward" and "cumbersome," they "take too long to write, cost too much to publish, encourage a certain snobbish reliance on a pretty style and vocabulary, and clutter up houses and libraries to a degree that is already becoming nearly impossible to handle" (ibid.). Although this is to overstretch the point somewhat, inasmuch as books, like films, come in a variety of styles, forms, and genres, including those such as comic books, cartoons, dime novels, pulp fiction, and potboilers that do not fit into such a categorization, it is nevertheless germane to the present discussion that Cox claimed that "Print does not reproduce the full range of human communicative sonorities and gestures the way tapes and especially films do" (ibid.). Notwithstanding the fact that Cox's critique reads here as an over-simplistic dichotomy and is altogether too reminiscent of the world delineated in François Truffaut's aforementioned parody *Fahrenheit 451*, which was released in the same year as Cox's *The Secular City*, the "coming cultural revolution," as Cox put it, "from print to images" (ibid.) has undeniably given theologians the apparatus to engage more fully in a proper critical dialogue between theology and popular culture. Although Cox was of the view that the revolution had not yet arrived, in the sense that "Instead of a global village we have a global cluster of pyramids, a complex of vertical skyscrapers where signals come down from the tower tops but there is no way to answer back from the bottom" (ibid., p. 255), it is apparent in an age of reality TV, where audience testimony is regularly solicited (often by inviting the viewer at home to press the red button on their remote control to decide which Big Brother contestant to evict, a trend that extends even to news programs in which the audience is encouraged to text or telephone their views on the latest stories), that the contours have changed significantly in the last forty or so years.

As with the theology of Dietrich Bonhoeffer, of which Cox was an unqualified advocate in the 1960s, it is difficult not to agree with Cox that theologians (and the Church) should re-evaluate their relationship to the "secular" world, thereby rendering the distinction between different types of culture (high and low) an artificial and outmoded one. For Bonhoeffer, indeed, any attempt to separate theology from the affairs of the world actually entailed a denial of the unity of God and the world as achieved through the Incarnation. Since there is, on this model, no God apart from the world, no supernatural apart from the natural, and no sacred apart from the profane, then it would be theologically indefensible to argue that films, or any other agencies of popular culture, are anything other than a pivotal part of the way in which theology is practiced and understood. As Bonhoeffer's talk of "religionless Christianity" highlights, the goal of Christianity is not to be consumed by increasingly redundant rituals and metaphysical teachings that allow people to escape the challenge of the gospel, "but to be a man ... in the life of the world" (Bonhoeffer, 1963, p. 123; see also Deacy, 2007). It may well be the case, not least in an age where reality TV holds such sway, that there is much in popular culture that is mindless and trivial, but this should not inhibit (or prohibit) film and other media from provoking serious reflection on our lives and our society. Romanowski is thus right to call for "an engaged, critical, and productive involvement with the popular arts," one that is "grounded in a faith vision that encompasses all of life and culture" (Romanowski, 2001, p. 14).

Having surveyed Niebuhr's five models of the interaction between Christ and culture, and followed them up with some reflections upon where this leaves the theology–culture debate today in light of the variety of perspectives from both theologians and cultural commentators on the adequacy and suitability of entering into a conversation with "low" culture, the remainder of this book will consist of the discussion of a number of theological perspectives and filmic themes that will help facilitate a fertile two-way exchange between theology and film. The underlying assumption will be that, although Christians consume films like everyone else (thus concurring with Niebuhr's second model), Christian theology needs to harness appropriate critical tools in order to engage with such material, along the lines of the dialogical model advanced by Aichele and Walsh's *Screening Scripture* and by Lynch's revised correlational model. I would also concur with Clive Marsh's assessment that if dialogue between theology and film "is to locate itself appropriately within the study and critique of contemporary culture then it needs to be working with culturally significant material, including dominant examples of popular culture" (Marsh, 2004, p. 61). As a result, the rest of this book will comprise a detailed overview of the manner and extent to which a conversation between theology and film can enable us to gain some understanding of the role of women, the environment, violence, justice, war, and eschatology. A final, concluding chapter will survey the fruits of the exploration (with particular reference to the cinematic art of storytelling) and will consider just how helpful films are able to be in initiating a theological encounter with contemporary cultural concerns. It will be suggested that this can be achieved without the prophetic voices of either theology or culture dominating proceedings and diminishing the envisaged dialogical and reciprocal nature of the exchange.

Notes

1 This is not to say, of course, that theology does not embrace such theoretical approaches, also. We can, for instance, have psychoanalytical, Marxist, feminist, gay and lesbian, and poststructuralist forms of theology. Indeed, theology is never conducted in a vacuum and will draw upon all manner of ideological perspectives, whether these are consciously articulated or not. I am grateful to Jeremy Carrette for drawing my attention to this "conceptual overlap."

2 In this context, we are talking about broader *American* cultural interests. "Culture" should not be synonymous with "American culture" (this book could have been approached from the perspective of Bollywood and Indian culture, for instance), although in much (though certainly not all, as the chapter on feminism shows) of this book reference is made to American cultural interests.

3 It is worth noting in passing that the word "religion" derives from the Latin *religio*, meaning "to bind," and referred in the Roman Empire to those practices that were accepted by the state, in contradistinction to those that were in opposition to the status quo (*superstitio*). It is ironic, therefore, that, in terms of Bryant's argument, religion should have become synonymous in the modern world with superstition when they were originally polar opposites.

4 However, notwithstanding the merits of Truffaut's film in stimulating discussion regarding the critical capacities of visual culture, the film itself is a somewhat vacuous work when compared to Ray Bradbury's 1953 novel that inspired it. The film's literalistic tone and its failure to offer the same indictment of visual culture that is contained in the novel suggest that the dangers of being subsumed into a visual culture are not as well illustrated in some motion pictures as my initial claim would indicate.

Theological Perspectives and Filmic Themes

Part II

Theological Perspectives and
Filmic Themes

Introduction

In many respects, part II is a continuation of the debate that was precipitated in Marsh and Ortiz's *Explorations in Theology and Film*. Although that collection of essays did not specifically set out to address individual theological themes, with a view to engaging in intertextual dialogue between those theological themes and the themes of a number of filmic texts, Robert Johnston nevertheless identifies in *Explorations* "several theological themes" that in turn suggest "the intertextual methodology of the book" (R. Johnston, 2000, p. 141) – namely, mutuality, salvation, Christology, violence, liberation, Jesus, the human condition, spirituality, grace, and hope. Building upon the insights generated in *Explorations*, this part aims to present an ordered structuring of a number of topics and themes that are germane to theology. It may well be the case that, to cite from the concluding chapter of the first volume, "Film simply will not deliver a systematic theology" (Marsh & Ortiz, 1997c, p. 248), in that a theological discussion of film can do no more than "sift, sort and shape the results of the conversations" (ibid.) *that the systematic theologian has already placed on the agenda*. However, when looking at such themes as feminism, the environment, violence, justice, war, and eschatology, it is not inconceivable that a systematic theology – defined as "the ordered structuring of Christian theology's topics or themes" (ibid.) – can be constructively undertaken in conversation with film. It may necessarily be the case that the choice of topics has been selected and identified by the theologian first and foremost, since a film text in itself cannot impose such an ordering or structuring (it can only be brought in to the ensuing dialogue), but provided that the films themselves are treated with integrity and respect and allowed

 Chris Deacy

to speak in their own voice, the conversation has the capacity to be a fruitful and reciprocal one.

It is not our aim in this part to suggest that only those films that most easily harmonize with a particular topic or theme of theology should be discussed. Quite the opposite, in fact. As will be discussed in the chapter on violence, for example, films – not least revisionist Westerns along the lines of *Unforgiven* (Clint Eastwood, 1992) – can sometimes offer a more sophisticated and erudite slant on the efficacy of redeeming violence than a conversation that is limited to passages in the Bible that address issues of retribution, vengeance, and suffering might suggest. Fertile though the exchange may be, however, the point was made in *Explorations in Theology and Film* that theology and film *are*, ultimately, operating at different levels, with film working from the gut, first and foremost, in the form of the emotional impact movies have upon audiences, whereas theology "is necessarily abstract, and at one or two stages removed from concrete expression or encounter" (ibid., p. 249). To a point, this is undeniably true – films, like faith, often work on an experiential level, involving our emotions and causing us to laugh or cry, provoking anger or frustration one moment, and, perhaps, inducing melancholy or excitement the next. Yet it would be wrong to suppose that theology is incapable of operating in a comparable way. In the case of liberation theology, for instance, reflection and analysis give way to action. Rather than, like Marx, see theology as merely having described the world, and as an intellectual pursuit whose province is the spiritual, metaphysical, and transcendental, the objective for theologians of liberation, among them Leonardo Boff and Gustavo Gutierrez, is to *change* the world. Theology is therefore inextricably bound up with the social and political dimension, and sees human *action* as the point of departure for all reflection. In other words, to paraphrase the title of Spike Lee's drama of racial insecurities and tensions in 1980s New York, the theologian must *do* the right thing, rather than merely think it, with the empirical and experiential the primary, rather than secondary, motivation. The distinction advanced in *Explorations* between theology as an abstract intellectual discipline and film, whose raison d'être is the immediate and practical, is not, therefore, the full picture, even if in the West at any rate this is a distinction that has too often held sway.

It is not our intention in the pages that follow to simply draw up a checklist of films that can be seen to intersect with theology with respect to the chosen themes, so that we can say, for instance, that *The Verdict* (Sidney Lumet, 1982) deals with justice, *The Deer Hunter* (Michael Cimino,

1978) deals with war, *Vanilla Sky* (Cameron Crowe, 2001) deals with eschatology, and so on. To go down this path would be to fall into the trap of offering a merely illustrative form of theology, in a manner that is reminiscent of so much of the Christ-figure literature. What is important is not so much whether certain films shed light on important theological themes as the extent to which such a conversation can help us to view both film and theology in a new light. No two theologies will ever be the same – Bultmann and Boff might not, for example, see eye to eye on the issue of the necessity for *praxis* – just as no two filmgoers will interpret the same film in the same way. Accordingly, it would be absurd to suggest that what follows is an exhaustive account of how we may bring theological perspectives and filmic themes into a mutual and reciprocal conversation. Just as all theologians bring different insights to bear, in light of the specific, and diverse, faith communities from which their insights are derived (or, indeed, the absence of a faith community), so our selection of films is inevitably going to reflect, to some extent, the type of films we find stimulating – intellectually, aesthetically, and emotionally – and (in light of the previous discussion) the extent of our amenability to popular culture. As the aforementioned John Walsh (see chapter 1), growing up in England in the 1960s and 1970s, has found that his values and aspirations have been shaped by the movies that left such an imprint on him in his formative years – from *The Sound of Music* (Robert Wise, 1965) and *Bonnie and Clyde* (Arthur Penn, 1967) to *Cabaret* (Bob Fosse, 1972) and *Don't Look Now* (Nicolas Roeg, 1973) – so neither of us can claim that we have been dispassionate, agnostic, or detached in our selection of films. The filmmakers responsible for the films that are discussed in the pages that follow may not have been functioning as theologians, nor are these films discernibly theological texts. But audiences bring all kinds of perspectives and ideologies to a film – political, social, cultural, economic, as well as religious – and in turn these are brought into dialogue with the filmic text. Hopefully, signs of this dialogue will be on view in the ensuing explorations.

A range of genres will be looked at in the pages that follow, from romantic comedies to action movies, from Westerns to horror films, and from supernatural thrillers to documentaries. A brief word about categorization would, however, be helpful. Many of the films to be discussed cross thematic boundaries, so that, although they may appear in different chapters, links may be discernible between, say, war and violence, and eschatology and justice. To an extent, therefore, the boundaries between categories are always going to be artificial. Since, moreover, there is no limit to or restriction on the extent to which films, or genres of film, can challenge or provoke, it is clear that we need to treat each film with integrity, rather than merely see it as an example of a particular type or genre, especially given the tendency of films to depart from or subvert specific genre conventions. It can be extremely frustrating to find oneself in a video or DVD store and discover that, although films are listed alphabetically, they are located in different parts of the store depending on whether the manager has determined that a particular title belongs in the section on martial arts, horror, Westerns, comedies, action, or drama or whether it is a family or children's film. Where might *Raging Bull* (Martin Scorsese, 1980) appear? Is it a sports film, inasmuch as it ostensibly deals with the life of a middleweight boxing champion and considering that some of the movie's most powerful scenes are set in a boxing arena? Or would it be more fitting to find this film categorized in a section on biography or, simply, drama? Or, as the theme of redemption that permeates the film, culminating in a quotation on screen at the end of the credits from John 9, might indicate, would it be appropriate to designate it as a "religious" picture? What about *The Witches of Eastwick* (George Miller, 1987), which is a fantasy, comedy, romance, supernatural, feminist, and horror movie all rolled into one? Similar problems arise each year following the announcement of the Golden Globe nominations in Los Angeles, when members of the Hollywood Foreign Press Association are required to make a distinction between films that fall into the category of "drama" and those that are "comedies" or "musicals" (as if the latter category itself is homogeneous!). One of the reasons *Life is Beautiful* (Roberto Benigni, 1998), a "comedy" set in a Nazi prison camp during the Holocaust, was not nominated for a Golden Globe in 1998, despite going on to achieve Oscar nominations for Best Picture, Best Director, and Best Original Screenplay and to win an Academy Award for Best Actor, would appear to be related to the uncertainty among voters as to whether the film comprised a comedy/musical or, in light of its serious subject matter, a drama. Upon winning a Golden Globe four years later in the category of "Best Performance by an Actor in a Motion Picture – Drama" for *About Schmidt* (Alexander Payne, 2002), Jack Nicholson even expressed some ambivalence about the award in his acceptance speech, explaining to the assembled audience at the Beverly Hilton: "I don't know whether to be happy or ashamed, because I thought we'd made a comedy." When it comes to classifying "religious" films, the picture is even more complicated. Although some films overtly deal with religious or theological issues – biblical epics or Jesus-films, along the lines of *The Passion of the Christ* (Mel Gibson, 2004) spring obviously to mind – Robert Ellis makes the judicious point that

> [s]ome films, by contrast, would require a real struggle to extract any theological ore for further smelting. However, in the middle, and largely unexamined, a huge corpus of "popular" films awaits theological scrutiny and consideration. These films, often with "meaning" or significance embedded in the complexity of their production, tell stories about how human beings see themselves and their situations, their hopes and their fears.
>
> (Ellis, 2005, p. 11)

It is noteworthy that Ellis finishes his argument with the claim that, when it comes to genre, "almost every film is in some sense a 'religious film'" (ibid.).

With such considerations in mind, it is not our aim to approach genres in the pages that follow as monolithic entities, with clearly established lines of demarcation separating one from another. Despite Marsh's assertion that "Films within a particular genre work by satisfying a viewer's expectation," in that one may "go to a horror film in order to be scared," see "a period drama to become lost in the history and culture of the period in question," or view "a romantic comedy in order to laugh and weep" (Marsh, 2004, p. 77), there are many instances in which a film may challenge or surprise us by *playing with* and *subverting* genre conventions. It is undoubtedly true for many people that if their expectations in watching a film are not satisfied then, to cite Marsh, they are "likely to be disappointed by the film" (ibid.). However, one of the satisfactions that can be gleaned from a film comes when it takes the audience in a different direction than they might have expected. Despite a tepid review of Sam Raimi's first *Spider-Man* movie in 2002, Roger Ebert, writing in the *Chicago Sun-Times*, was blown away by the 2004 sequel, because the latter "demonstrates what's wrong with a lot of other superhero epics: They focus on the superpowers, and short-change the humans behind them" (Ebert, 2004b). Whereas in the original, Ebert laments the fact that Spider-Man (Tobey Maguire) "seemed to move with all the realism of a character in a cartoon," he enthuses about the way in which in the sequel Raimi "is able to seamlessly match the CGI and the human actors" and "gives weight" to all of the film's elements, including the story-line and special effects, which, in "a lesser movie from this genre," usually entail the audience perking up "for the action scenes" but having to "wade grimly through the dialogue" (ibid.). Here, in contradistinction, "both stay alive, and the dialogue is more about emotion, love and values" and "less about long-winded explanations of the inexplicable" (ibid.). Ebert thus labels *Spider-Man 2* "a superhero movie for people who don't go to superhero movies," while, "for those who do, it's the one they've been yearning for" (ibid.). It might be more apt, therefore, to say that, for many audience members, we go to, say, a horror movie or a romantic comedy – or, indeed, a film adaptation of a comic-book superhero – in the hope that the film concerned will *transcend*, rather than rigidly adhere to, its genre limitations and offer something refreshingly new, original, and authentic. In our search for dialogue between theology and film, we will be looking for films that confound, rather than merely subscribe to, the constraints of genre, and that take us into exciting and innovative directions – to the point, perhaps, that the searing indictment of revenge on display in Quentin Tarantino's *Kill Bill: Vol. 2* (2004) qualifies as no less theologically fecund than the more overtly "religious" film *The Passion of the Christ*, which was on release in the same period in Easter 2004.

Woman as Spectacle: Theological Perspectives on Women and Film

This chapter provides a new look at the often-stereotyped roles of women in film, which some claim is always built upon the model of sexual difference and dominated by male spectatorial desire (see Mayne, 2002, p. 28), and asks whether, in an age of wider than ever diversity in the cinematic marketplace, there has been any change in a culturally inscribed objectifying portrayal of women. Have contemporary female characters transcended or simply confirmed sexism in society in general and in the movie industry in particular? What are the ramifications of gender identity and objectification for the pursuit of theology?

We begin this chapter by first examining how the feminist critiques of theology and of the filmmaking industry and film theory evolved from the women's liberation movement of the 1960s, or what is known as the second wave of feminism.[1] We will then identify parallels between the feminist critiques of theology and film theory, with a view to asking whether women's increased "ownership" of theology and film, through scholarship and professional craft, has been enough to begin a reconstruction of the theological and filmmaking processes, or whether, to use the famous phrase of Audre Lord, "the master's tools will never dismantle the master's house"[2] – rather, are both theology and the film industry inherently/patriarchally/hopelessly flawed? And finally, we will take a closer look at two quite different cultures to discern some of the issues that appear to determine the cinematic representation of women and which invite theological reflection.

 Gaye Ortiz

The Feminist Movement

Although the two academic disciplines of theology and film theory are very different, they have been affected by the feminist movement of the past fifty or so years in many similar ways. In each, feminist scholars have challenged not only the traditional use of "tools" of academic methodology but also the focus of that methodological approach. In seeking to deconstruct, reconstruct, and re-vision these disciplines it has been necessary for feminists to identify their patriarchal underpinnings and to mount a challenge to them at many levels. As Ursula King says, "Patriarchy is not only about social, economic, religious and political power structures, but is rooted even deeper that that in attitudes, values, language and thought" (King, 1993, p. 24).

There are several theories about the establishment of patriarchy as the norm, some dramatically involving rampant hordes of nomadic warriors sweeping across the plains to invade and subjugate the goddess-loving, peaceful agricultural societies of the world. Whatever the origins, Rosalind Miles suggests that the patriarchal systems of religion were at first quite attractive to women, and the irony is that women "embraced and furthered the systems which would all too soon attack their autonomy, crush their individuality and undermine the very reason for their existence" (R. Miles, 1988, p. 91). In her book *Goddesses and the Divine Feminine*, Rosemary Radford Ruether has recently taken up the discussion about a much-disputed legacy of goddess worship and spirituality claimed by some feminists in the 1970s. From her exhaustive research there is no doubt that the desire to find a more egalitarian way of approaching the divine is widespread and comes as a result of the feminist critique of the status quo, in which patriarchy operates within a spectrum ranging from benign paternalism to androcentric cultural patterns to destructive and violent misogyny.

The rise in the perception of and reaction against patriarchy and sexism within social institutions in the last four decades has been defined as feminist consciousness at work. Feminist consciousness – which can be experienced by both women and men – can be described as a blinding flash of light: "it blinds in that it disorients and disturbs the viewers; it is light in the way it vividly illumines the whole landscape" (Lacugna, 1993, p. 9). The realization is that men have been the ones to formulate beliefs and write and transmit sacred writings, and have been the sole interpreters of them; they have created and controlled religious institutions, worship, and rituals. This insight is followed rapidly by another, which is, put simply, the principle of contemporary hermeneutics: that all inter-pretation is conditioned by the presuppositions and prejudgments of the interpreter. The revelation for budding feminist thinkers is: it's not all carved in stone after all! They (the male-dominated powers that be) only say that it is! This startling realization spurred on the women's movement, from Elizabeth Cady Stanton's remark that the sacred texts, creeds, and ecclesiastical laws of the leading religions "bear the impress of fallible man" (Stanton, 1993, p. 13) to Mary Daly's comment that "we are breaking the dam of sex stereotyping that stops the flow of being, that stops women and men from being integrated, androgynous personalities" (Daly, 1994, p. 354). Thus Phyllis Trible declares: "As a critique of culture and faith in light of misogyny, feminism is a prophetic movement, examining the status quo, pronouncing judgment, and calling for repentance" (Trible, 1992, p. 3).

Feminist Critique of Religion

Ursula King insists that feminist theology should not be characterized by what it is not but by what it aims to achieve. She points out that its task is both negative and positive: "Its negative task is the radical critique of all forms of sexism and androcentrism inherent in the language and thought forms of previous theologies...Its positive task is one of reform and reconstruction" (King, 1993, p. 159f.). And so begins a brief recap of the feminist critique of religion, in which we can identify three distinct stages. First, a critique of tradition. Denise Lardner Carmody states that "feminists are bound to be angry at the injustices found in the historical record. They are bound to think that women's second-rate status in most periods of history is a negative judgment against the human race" (Carmody, 1994, p. 9). Christianity has not done women proud in preserving their testimonies to faith. The awareness that there is an absence of women's voices in religious tradition has been written about by Ann Loades in *Searching for Lost Coins* (1987), in which she describes women's hunt for their religious and biblical history.

Another element of the feminist critique of religion is the portrayal of women in the Bible. The preponderance of stories in which women are property, tools, objects, or stereotypes is indignantly chronicled in Dowell and Hurcombe's *Dispossessed Daughters of Eve*: "As a history of religious consciousness the Bible traces in its narratives and its silences the secondary status of women" (Dowell and Hurcombe, 1981, p. 37). But almost a full century before Dowell and Hurcombe, Elizabeth Cady Stanton was compiling *The Woman's Bible* with a view to combating the Bible's negative image of woman, which both men and women accepted because of biblical authority. Stanton said that the nature of Christian belief, based upon a traditional interpretation of the story of Adam and Eve that assumed that women's subordination was God-given, made women into the "patient hopeless slaves" (Stanton, 1993, p. xix) they are. The critique of the traditional interpretation of the Bible – and of the theological acceptance that it implied for the male-dominated status quo – is ongoing and dynamic in feminist theology; the contributions of feminist biblical scholars whose research and writings have directly impacted upon film include Bach (1996), Exum (1996), and, more recently, Runions (2003). That the task of challenging millennia of social, cultural, and religious patterns that exclude women from full humanity (engaged in academically only in the past thirty or so years) is drawing its energy from an ever-growing number of feminist scholars is something that would gratify (but not mollify!) Elizabeth Cady Stanton and the early pioneers of feminist theology and biblical studies.

The second stage of a feminist critique of religion is the subsequent recovery of women in Judeo-Christian history. A fuller picture of the legacy of women can come about through reading texts to discover and uncover the contribution of women to the faith story; retrieval – if the right questions are asked and the right sources uncovered – is akin to good detective work. Also, reinterpreting stories can provide fuller contours of the biblical and historical legacy of women – anyone who has read Phyllis Trible's *Texts of Terror* knows how fascinating and moving that recovery process can be. Using literary criticism as her methodology and feminism as her perspective, Trible finds the theme of terror woven through the Bible: "If art imitates life, scripture likewise reflects it in both holiness and horror. Reflections themselves neither mandate nor manufacture change; yet by enabling insight, they may inspire repentance. In other words, sad stories may yield new beginnings" (Trible, 1992, p. 2).

That there were women in the Christian tradition throughout the centuries who wrote about the Bible and theology is still a well-kept secret; Patricia Demers exposes the wisdom and curiosity of these neglected thinkers in *Women as Interpreters of the Bible* (1992); Amy Oden's *In Her Words* (1994) encompasses early Gnostic writings, lives of martyrs, musings of mystics, religious, and laywomen in an anthology of Christian thought that makes us aware that so many more voices failed to be preserved as primary sources through the centuries. And *In Our Own Voices* (1995) features four centuries of religious writings from women in the American multicultural landscape. This text offers an affinity among the voices of "Christian, feminist, womanist, and mujerista theology, along with voices of Jewish, Muslim, and Buddhist feminist theology and those of Wiccan theology" (Ruether and Keller, 1995, p. 15). The skilled work of deconstructing and re-visioning the Scriptures is presented in Elizabeth Schüssler Fiorenza's *Searching the Scriptures* (1993) as a reclaiming of women's authority of interpretation.

The final stage of the feminist critique of religion is theological reconstruction, which incorporates newly understood historical material and contemporary feminist insights into theology. Whether it is the reshaping of doctrine – the service that Rosemary Radford Ruether has provided for systematic theology[3] – or the scholarship of Schüssler Fiorenza within biblical interpretation and feminist theology, the reconstruction is being done in a spirit of empowerment that is ecumenical, pluralistic, and global in approach. So much so that we can only speak of feminist *theologies*, which connect with other disciplines, make wide use of source materials, including writings from the margins (extracanonical or pre-biblical texts), and employ a wide range of interpretive strategies. Who or what determines the issues that appear on the feminist agenda? Categorization is not universally consistent, so that "women's rights" in the West might mean something completely different to women of Asia or the Pacific Rim. Kwok Pui-lan says that feminist theology must "develop an intercultural hermeneutics that heightens our cross-cultural sensitivity and underscores the relation between cultural-religious production and social and economic formation" (Kwok Pui-lan, 2002, p. 34).

There are feminists who have undertaken the critique of religion and have decided that a prophetic voice can only be heard from the outside; they have abandoned institutional religion and theology, seeing them as fatally flawed and reform as impossible. Mary Daly and Daphne Hampson continue to speak outside the margins as radical feminist theologians, promoting a post-Christian separation that envisions feminist sisterhood as the ideal community to challenge traditional patriarchal religion.

What seems to be most important in any feminist theory is that, for all the need to renew culture and religion in a visionary manner, the experience of women is the prime source from which theology draws its ideas and which it revisits in order to test its commitment to truthfulness. Susan Frank Parsons sees this experiential basis as problematic:

> for feminist theology to begin with experience means to enter into a rigorous process of discernment, in which one's experiences are tested for their authenticity. Experiences are not of equal worth. Because human lives are caught up in deceitfulness and pride, it is essential that one distinguish those experiences that are distorted, from those in which one is able to recognize, and thus become, one's own true self.
>
> (Parsons, 2002, p. 118)

Ruether takes this ideal a step further when she demands that the critical principle of feminist theology is to work for "the full humanity of all people, women and men" (King, 1993, p. 163). This is an ambitious task, to hold all of us to the standard of authentic humanity with all that entails for right relationship. It is a hopeful sign that theology has come a long way – and still has a long way to go – with the help and vision of feminism.

Feminist Film Theory

When feminism's second-wave consciousness-raising began in theology, a similar critique of film was growing out of the women's liberation movement, fueled particularly by the 1960s New Left in French politics and culture. Just as excited as feminist scholars unearthing theological writings by and about women, a delve into the vaults of filmmaking exposed early female pioneers who wrote and directed films. *Reel Women*, Ally Acker's amazing archaeological excavation of those women, tells us that in the silent era of film women dominated the industry. There, Marc Wanamaker is quoted as saying, "more women worked in decision-making positions in film before 1920 than at any other time in history" (Acker, 1993, p. xviii).

Feminist critique moved on rapidly from the early years of women's lib to engage with and shape many aspects of film theory. Reading the early writings of feminist film theorists like K. Ann Kaplan, Claire Johnston, Laura Mulvey, and Molly Haskell, one sees a concern with the roles and stereotypes imposed upon women in popular culture and, in particular, in the movies. These "cine-feminists" questioned the myth of film and its relation to a system of values that informs culture in our society. Claire Johnston observed that "myth transmits and transforms the ideology of sexisms and renders it invisible...and therefore natural" (C. Johnston, 1977, p. 409). But the most widely discussed theory arising from this time is the woman as spectacle. In the late 1970s there was debate surrounding the validity of psychoanalytically based film theory, and the language of that debate, with the centrality of castration and phallus, is evidence of this emphasis on objectified women in film. According to Laura Mulvey, her seminal work on the male gaze (Mulvey, 1977, pp. 412–28) was meant to apply to the popular mass entertainment culture, in which mainstream film "coded the erotic into the language of the dominant patriarchal order" (ibid., p. 414). Based on Freud's association of scopophilia (pleasure in looking) with objectifying people by subjecting them to a controlling gaze, the male gaze theory relies upon structuralism, semiotics, and psychoanalysis to examine the sub-texts of films. Mulvey highlighted Alfred Hitchcock's way of imposing on the viewer an uneasy identification with the voyeur in his films (e.g. *Psycho* [1960], *Rear Window* [1954]). The theory also concerned itself with the contrast between the *auteur* and the commercialization of the studio system, with Mulvey hoping for an alternative cinema that would subvert and discard traditional film convention, which would decline but not be mourned "with anything much more than sentimental regret" by women "whose image has continually been stolen and used" (ibid., p. 428) in a voyeuristic manner.

When we look at the development of feminist film theory, the nature of female pleasure is addressed in the question: "Is there a cinematic aesthetic specific to women?" This question opens the debate over the discourse of women and the issue of female spectatorship. Does a female spectator have an intuitive, unquestioning emotional response to what she sees on the screen? It might be possible to argue that, because films are said to wash emotionally over the audience, who "feel" a film long before they analyze it, it is not a gender-related issue: we are all held captive by the silver screen. But the implication that there can be a reaction in an essentialist manner, for example common to all women, assumes a uniformly passive experience through an implicit and patriarchal assigning of qualities. Anti-essentialists argue that "there is no single trait or characteristic (or no group of traits or characteristics) that is 'essentially' female, that by itself definitively captures the essence of womanhood" (Eller, 2003, p. 14). However, there were female filmmakers such as Barbara Hammer (*Menses* [1974], *Multiple Orgasm* [1976]) who championed women's experience of their bodies in the early days of feminist filmmaking and whose work in that sense promoted an essentialist view of women.

One effect of the women's liberation movement was that women began to make films "by, for and about women." They were influenced by the 1960s avant-garde trend in cinema, which appealed both to the personal and to women's creativity. Although Maya Deren had been a pioneer in the 1940s as an American independent director – herself influenced by the surrealist movement – it was much later that women began to form cooperative film communities in order to support the activities and projects arising from feminist concern for social change. However, the Audre Lord quotation that is found earlier in this chapter frames the primary paradox for feminist filmmakers of that time: how to use the "tools" of filmmaking while subverting both the convention of the representation of women in film and the very act of filmmaking itself. In a dialogue dating from 1967 between experimentalist filmmaker Storm De Hirsch and independent feature filmmaker Shirley Clarke, the impact of gender upon filmmaking is addressed by the two women, more in a quizzical manner than a dogmatic one:

> Clarke: "...I know there's a difference between men and women and this is going to be revealed in our work as artists, filmmakers, and that this is going to be good. This is going to be a contribution of sensitivity and perception that is beyond what we've got right now...It will be actually a ridiculous discussion to discuss men and women filmmakers in the future, because it will be just such a common thing. At this point it's still not common."
>
> De Hirsch: "...to be a male director – even on a small scale – becomes a very glamorous kind of occupation; but with the woman, oddly enough, being an actress holds a great deal more glamour, even though she may have a very small part, than the position of being a female director. On the other hand, there's an indulgence toward the female which sometimes works to a great advantage in terms of getting things done."
>
> (De Hirsch & Clarke, 1977, pp. 231–42)

The productivity of women filmmakers, particularly in the documentary genre, rose markedly in the 1970s; in her contemporary survey, "Notes on Women's Liberation Cinema," Ruth McCormick described these "militant" films as "made expressly to educate, to raise consciousness, to help create the forces for change" (McCormick, 1977, p. 290). She went on to say: "We need women making films about themselves, and about the men and children in their lives. These films should have a lot of anger in them, and as much humor as possible" (ibid., p. 291).

So, can we say there is a difference in representation from the way that female filmmakers bring a female sensibility to the screen? Acker says yes: "Distinct uses of the camera; a focused eye and heart toward aspects of women's lives previously ignored or pooh-poohed by male cinema, because of a lack of shared experience – all this is what distinguishes a female gaze" (Acker, 1993, p. 287). To back up her assertion she gives examples of the work of Margarethe von Trotta (*The Second Awakening of Christa Klages*, 1977), Márta Mészáros (*The Girl*, 1968; *The Two of Them*, 1977), and Donna Deitch (*Desert Hearts*, 1985). The work of these filmmakers within the women's media community was supported and influenced through the 1970s and 1980s by feminist film theorists: Mulvey notes that "feminist use of the new theory and its application to popular culture grew directly out of the Women's Movement concern with images, their contribution to fixing the connotations of gender and circulating images of women as signifying a patriarchal mythology of sexuality" (Juhasz, 2001, p. 23).

A related issue when viewing women on the screen, it has been suggested, is how women can identify with a female image when patriarchal systems of narration and identification make it easy for a female spectator to feel distanced from the image. Theorist Annette Kuhn has suggested that once the film industry again sees a greater involvement of women in all roles behind and in front of the camera there may be a transformation in representation. Paradoxically, it has been suggested that when female roles offer strong, positive models of behavior, they play into the trap of creating phallic images of women that feature in patriarchal erotic fantasies. Claire Johnston makes this point with Mae West, saying that the fetishization of the movie star "indicates the collective fantasy of phallocentrism" (C. Johnston, 1977, p. 411.); although West seems aggressive towards men and even contemptuous of her sexy image, at the unconscious level she only reinforces, not subverts, the male Oedipal fantasy.

Mulvey's theory addressed sexual difference under patriarchy and how Hollywood film combines the masculine, defined as the active pleasure of looking, and the feminine, defined as the image, into the "male gaze." John Berger in *Ways of Seeing*, published and broadcast three years before, in 1972, foreshadowed the basic tenor of Mulvey's theory when he said:

Men act and women appear. Men look at women. Women watch themselves being looked at. This determines not only most relations between men and women but also the relation of women to themselves. The surveyor of woman herself is male; the surveyed female. Then she turns herself into an object – and most particularly an object of vision: a sight.

(Berger, 1972, p. 47)

A Century of Female Cinematic Representation

How the spectator negotiates her way into the film relates, then, to the essentialism debate, but also depends upon historical concepts of sexuality that find their way into filmic scenarios. For example, the decades of twentieth-century film history, during which cinema influenced and coincided with the "genesis of modern woman," show us a range of socially constructed trends in representation: the sexless "doll-objects" seen prior to World War I in the films of D. W. Griffith had little in common with the post-war vamp Theda Bara. Flappers and working girls were popular in the films of the 1920s; the Hollywood glamour machine cranked out films in the new genre of chorus girl movies. Marjorie Rosen says that "films of the 20s attempted to squash feminine self-determination" (Rosen, 1973, p. 101); this is borne out by the basic story-line, in which the ambitious girl with stars in her eyes is punished in her quest for success either by the loss of Mr. Right (which condemns her to spinsterhood) or by old age (which destroys her beauty).

The Depression movies of the 1930s, showing women working by their wits in detective, spy and gangster story-lines, were also vehicles for the blonde bombshell era of Mae West and Jean Harlow, and the femme fatale Greta Garbo, who combined fragility with toughness. In her 1992 publication *Celluloid Sisters*, Janet Thumin suggests that the trend in the 1940s was women and sacrifice: in *The Seventh Veil* (Compton Bennett, 1945), *Bells of St Mary's* (Leo McCarey, 1945), and *Brief Encounter* (David Lean, 1946), moral problems were experienced by the female protagonists in relation to contemporary social structures. For the first time film audiences were almost entirely female, and a theme of films in the 1940s was the career woman who reflected the change in culture. The post-World War II reintegration of men into American society in the 1950s led to a decade of films that explored a variety of models of masculinity. Thumin says that where they appear, women motivate or impede the progress of the central male character, and she points to *The Dam Busters* (Michael Anderson, 1955), *East of Eden* (Elia Kazan, 1955), *Rebel without a Cause* (Nicholas Ray, 1955), and *The Searchers* (John Ford, 1956), where the male character is central and the dominant theme is the relation between masculinity and the nation and national unity (Thumin, 1992, p. 57f.). The interesting contrast in that decade between Marilyn Monroe (male fantasy figure) and Doris Day (wholesome virgin) held a deeper significance, in that Monroe was playing a dumb blonde but

Day's roles usually were women who were clever, independent, and ambitious – quite unlike the bulk of the roles for women in the 1950s. It is also worth noting the anti-female thrillers made by Alfred Hitchcock, such as *Psycho* (1960), *The Birds* (1963), and *Marnie* (1964), that underscored female helplessness. Films of the 1960s emphasized personal freedom, pleasure, and liberation, and the privileging of youth, as seen in such films as *A Hard Day's Night* (Richard Lester, 1964), *Bonnie and Clyde* (Arthur Penn, 1967), and *The Graduate* (Mike Nichols, 1967). The last of these not only exposed audiences to frank sexual content but also "broke with a whole genre past that upheld the sanctities of the marriage vow above everything else" (Quart & Auster, 1991, p. 90). The radical impulse that powered both mainstream and experimental filmmaking in this decade exposed social hypocrisy and political folly, setting the tone for a disillusionment with authority that would only be deepened in the next decade with the Watergate scandal and the tragedy of the Vietnam war.

In the 1970s, a wide variety of roles for women emerged, both in the sense of a shift from women as relationship-centered to career-oriented (*The Turning Point* [Herbert Ross, 1977]; *Kramer versus Kramer* [Robert Benton, 1979]) and in an increase in the aggressiveness of women, as in *Norma Rae* (Martin Ritt, 1979) and *Looking for Mr. Goodbar* (Richard Brooks, 1977). Not all of these films featured female characters who lived happily ever after – Joanna Kramer has to give up her son, even though she wins the court battle, because she realizes that her son is happiest with his father. *Looking for Mr. Goodbar* shocked American audiences with its frank portrayal of a promiscuous lifestyle and the implied just desserts Theresa Dunn receives for experimenting with her sexual freedom. *Klute* (Alan J. Pakula, 1971) and *Coming Home* (Hal Ashby, 1978) established Jane Fonda as an actress who specialized in roles in which women began to question their sense of identity, foregrounded by controversial social contexts – in the former, prostitution; in the latter, infidelity, Vietnam veterans, and anti-war sentiments.

Although the popularity of male "buddy" movies dominated the first part of the 1980s, Hollywood began to pay attention to women in the film industry who were popular actresses (such as Jane Fonda and Barbra Streisand). Two films, *Silkwood* (Mike Nichols, 1983), which profiled a political heroine, and *The Color Purple* (Steven Spielberg, 1985), which introduced the oppression of black women and lesbianism, came out of a Hollywood worried by Ronald Reagan's conservative policies (primarily by what effect they would have on the economic health of the studios). In the 1980s, women achieved real power in the film industry as directors, writers, and producers, but the latter part of the decade saw a backlash against feminism with the making of films such as *Fatal Attraction* (Adrian Lyne, 1987) and *Working Girl* (Mike Nichols, 1988). Quart and Auster describe the former as a well-made thriller that conveys the image of "the unmarried, professional woman as pathetic and mad and reaffirms the value of marriage and home as havens of warmth and stability and acts as a warning to women of the unnaturalness of living independent, solitary lives" (Quart & Auster, 1991, p. 171).

In the early 1980s, issues of masculinity, the male body as spectacle, and gay politics broadened the critical film theory field. Within the context of lesbian film, Chris Holmlund, writing in 2002, spots a sub-genre arising in the 1980s of the "femme" movie, where films such as *Lianna* (John Sayles, 1983), *Desert Hearts*, and *Personal Best* (Robert Towne, 1982) invited mainstream audience reception through filmmaking that was non-voyeuristic by following the conventions of the woman's film or "chick flick." It is to this genre we now turn.

The "woman's film" of the 1930s and 1940s tended to be a melodrama in which women could both rebel and be submissive. Christine Gledhill, Mary Ann Doane, and Annette Kuhn have all written about the critical framework within which to best analyze the woman's film: woman as subject, as spectator, as patriarchal fantasy object. How does the legacy of melodrama and romance influence the way women see themselves in contemporary film? Is the chick flick of today any different from the melodrama, with its roots in the nineteenth century? Can women be empowered by Bridget Jones? Do female audiences negotiate their way through the film, knowing that they might be projecting their own desires and fantasies onto the screen, and simultaneously receiving affirmation in their own experiences of romance and relationships? Margaret Gallagher says that "popular" forms of mass entertainment that were previously considered unworthy of critical media analysis, such as the soap opera, romance, and melodrama (traditionally tagged "women's genres"), have now been "reclaimed" (Gallagher, 1992, p. 7) by feminists. The theory of resistance, proposed by scholars such as Janice Radway – which suggests that audiences are active in their viewing, resisting, or even subverting socially constructed meanings from the films they are watching – is summed up by John Fiske, who says that women are not "cultural dopes" (Gallagher, 1992, p. 8). Women may be making pleasure for themselves and playing with notions of identity as they consume chick flicks, and are competent in negotiating their own meanings and even accepting escapist cinema for what it is without engaging in critical analysis. In other words, instead of asking whether representations of women in chick flicks are true, scholars might do better to ask what women who view these images do with them.

In the 1990s, feminist film theorists began to apply the feminist critique to the fine arts, and at last took seriously the pluralism of women's cinema, especially films addressing women of color. The black feminist critic Gloria Hull observed in the 1990s that circumstances for her have changed since the 1970s: "Women's studies – though still vulnerable – and feminist scholarship have been institutionally recognized. There is now a generation for whom feminism is largely intellectual. There is no longer the same precise need for the consciousness we carried of being infiltrators and subversives" (in Juhasz, 2001, p. 11). Avant-garde cinema became culturally marginalized in the 1990s, and films made in that genre received very limited viewing compared to previous decades; however, community video is a movement that spun off from feminist political filmmaking. The idea that feminist ideas can carry more weight in mainstream media, reaching a wider audience, increasing influence, and therefore provoking social change, has also convinced many feminist filmmakers, such as Michelle Citron (*Daughter Rite*, 1978), to try to work within the system today. However, the system has undergone tremendous change since the early days of feminist filmmaking: studios are still powerful, but the independent film sector of the world market has provided opportunities for many filmmakers who stood no chance of commercial success or who refused to play studio politics. Some filmmakers now refuse to even accept the designation "feminist," preferring instead to broaden out identity politics and recognize many sources of empowerment in their work. In Juhasz's *Women of Vision*, African American lesbian filmmaker Cheryl Dunye explains: "I am not going to say I am feminist or I am not feminist. I am as much feminist as I am a tennis player as I am a dog owner. It's a shifting identity. We have to embody all that in order to really 'be'" (in ibid., p. 299).

The maturity of feminist film theory has come with the realization that criticism and theory are subject to history and context – film as cultural text, with its dominant, oppositional, and negotiated readings, has provoked an ongoing torrent of discussion and debate within feminist discourse. As Deidre Pribram observes, "The relationship between history and so-called subjective processes is not a matter of grasping the truth in history as some objective entity, but in finding the truth of the experience. This...has to do with women's own history and self-consciousness" (Pribram, 1988, p. 184).

Parallel Paths

Summarizing the parallel paths that film theory and theology have taken in their evolution as areas of feminist critique, they:

- primarily both arise out of the women's liberation movement. The first wave of feminism – claiming a voice – had an impact on biblical interpretation and the abolitionist and suffrage movements, while the second – constructing a voice – was the more directly influential and creative in terms of theology and film. The third wave of feminism – the enabling of voices – builds upon and is impacted by the reality of multiculturalism and diversity of race, culture, and sexuality.
- using feminist critique, stimulate an awareness of male authorship of narratives and control of structures, contributing to the debate over whether to remain in the "malestream." In both disciplines of theology and film, feminists had to make the choice of whether to remain within the male-dominated cultures or whether to strike out as an alternative voice of protest. One attempt to introduce an experiential element to serious theological writing by Rebecca Parker and Rita Nakashima Brock (*Proverbs of Ashes*, 2002) has offered a powerful critique of traditional theology, such as the doctrine of atonement framed by "malestream" concepts of violence and sacrifice. Carol Christ and Mary Daly stepped away from traditional Christian theology to develop a Goddess thealogy and radical feminist theology, respectively. The same dilemma of remaining inside the system faced the female filmmakers of the 1960s and 1970s, many of whom continue to work outside the studio system to contribute feminist ideas through documentary and short film.
- provoke a critical examination of the portrayal of women's roles within texts. The valuable work done by feminist biblical interpreters, such as Elisabeth Schüssler Fiorenza, Phyllis Trible, and Sharon Ringe, has provided fresh insight into stories of women in the Bible and also in extracanonical texts. The work done by feminist film scholars, such as Annette Kuhn, Laura Mulvey, Yvonne Tasker, and Barbara Creed, has framed the discussion of the female presence in the filmic text.
- witness to a profusion of research and writings focused on and aimed at women. In such disparate categories of careers, whether it be faculty in education, professional and technical roles in the film industry, critical theorists, authors and editors of academic texts, or

theological and ministerial training, women have become a major force in the past four decades.

- encourage the recovery of women's contributions to tradition and history. Without the work of Schüssler Fiorenza, Brock, Carol Christ, and Karen Jo Torejesen, among many others, the fuller picture of theology and religion would never be realized. The recovery undertaken by cinema historian Ally Acker in *Reel Women* interestingly includes women who, far from seeing themselves as feminist, were dedicated to maintaining the film industry status quo. Among them were women like Anita Loos, who wrote over 200 screenplays during her career – her first in 1912 – and who reflected in her writing her real-life preference for a subservient role in relation to men. Dorothy Arzner, who directed 17 features from 1927 to 1943, saw her main task as conforming to the studio system; her prime objective was "making entertainment. Stories were light and theatrical. We did not know the word social significance" (in Rosen, 1973, p. 377). Even Ida Lupino, an actress who stumbled into directing when the director of a film she had co-written and produced fell ill, rejected the notion that her films have a feminist sensibility (Acker, 1993, p. 77), despite the fact that they dealt (uniquely for Hollywood productions) with relevant social issues, such as unwed mothers, adoption, and the psychological effects of rape on women. However, of these women Acker says that they still should be heralded as pioneers who were steadfast in establishing film as an innovative art form (Acker, 1993, p. xxvi).
- offer opportunities for women to study and research, critique and interpret in a traditionally male-dominated discipline. Harvard Divinity School began accepting women in the program only in 1955. Feminist scholars of theology and religion across the world have had only a short while to take up the academic life compared to men. Equivalent brevity exists in feminist film theory, which began to make its voice heard in the early 1970s within the also relatively new discipline of film studies.
- have increased women's influence in and setting of the mainstream ("malestream") agenda of film studies and theology. The value of being engaged in the effective "influencing and shaping of the discourses of malestream [biblical] scholarship" (Schüssler Fiorenza, 1993, p. xiii) comes not only from correcting distorted meanings but from framing new ones. The major issue of sexual power and the gaze, made famous by Laura Mulvey's essay, led the assault on dominant cinema and remained the theoretical topic of choice for the following decades.

- have made it easier for the spread and application of feminist perspectives to other areas within and allied to theology (ethics) and film (fine art, media). Diana Tietjens Meyers writes about the encoding of gender stereotypes within cultural imagery; she says that women cannot rely on men to break these stereotypes, that women instead "must speak their own lives" (Tietjens Meyers, 2002, p. ii). Alison Butler, writing in 2002, predicted that the experimental new media would have the effect of dissipating feminism's radical perspective, and so women who are using the new media and working within the contemporary fine arts will present less challenging images of women to society than in the past. It can only be up to those women to be informed about their feminist heritage and carry on the ideal of authentic representation of humanity within an increasingly complex cultural context. Woman-centered approaches to ethics link women's moral experience to equality in terms of human dignity and rights. Resisting entrenched, deeply held assumptions of dualistic behavior and cognition between the sexes has been a common thread within feminist theology and feminist ethics. Mary Grey explores right relation in her 1989 book *Redeeming the Dream*, setting ethical dilemmas within the framework of connectedness and community.

- have been affected by the organic pluralism of movements within feminism that move it away from homogeneity, recognizing differences among women. The emphasis on the "politics of location," in which cultural difference is respected, has been blamed for an increase in bland relativism. Alison Butler says that "feminism is bound to respond to globalization, or else wither away in decadent and willful blindness to the new forms taken by women's oppression in the 'new world order'" (Butler, 2002, p. 120). Butler goes on to mention the hybridity of filmmakers like Mira Nair and Gurinder Chadha, who "have used their own experience of hyphenated identity or mobility between cultures as the basis of dramas of cultural difference which insist on its presence within communities, families and individuals" (ibid., p. 109); in other words, unity in diversity. The pessimistic-sounding warning given by Butler is not echoed in the writings of feminist theologians contemplating the future of their discipline. Rosemary Radford Ruether states that the most significant development of feminism is "the contextualization of feminism across global communities: women in Latin America; the Philippines; Africa; Christian; Jewish; Buddhist and Muslim" (in Hinton, 2002).

Even with the changes to the theological and filmic landscapes through which these parallel paths have led, some would say that there has still not been enough evidence of transformation of patriarchal power into a gender-inclusive or even gender-neutral vision of the future. The creation of women-only communities, projects, and initiatives seems to many nowadays to be as lopsided and restricted in its vision and potential as the old way of doing things. Where feminism goes from here is not a question that can be addressed within these pages, but Charlene Spretnak urges women to avoid being overwhelmed by the work that is still ahead by understanding that the "feminist process...involves living the new possibilities now, as we struggle" (Spretnak, 1982, p. 539).

Embodiment and Women in Cinema

Alison Butler quotes Inderpal Grewal and Caren Kaplan in their insistence on the need for located feminist theory that "address[es] the concerns of women around the world in the historicized particularity of their relationship to multiple patriarchies as well as to international economic hegemonies" (Butler, 2002, p. 90). In looking at national cinema, Butler claims it is often the case that women are identified primarily by their affiliation to family rather than to any larger social structure; to quote E. Ann Kaplan, "Women do not inhabit a space of the state as home: women rather inhabit a space for their family as home, a space of much more local relations" (Kaplan, 1997, p. 45). Ursula King suggests that "it is much more difficult for women to keep their thoughts neatly and separately apart from their bodies as much of their experience is closely intermingled with bodily functions and events" (King, 1993, p. 70). Menstruation, conception, motherhood, menopause – all these and more, long connected with negative concepts of flesh, the earth, physicality that subordinate women in religious, cultural, and social contexts – are what make women more organically interconnected to the experience of life. The recent discovery in Hollywood of the menopausal woman as lead role in a feature film presents an opportunity to analyze the representational qualities that might convince film industry decision-makers to back such a film as a money-maker (in a market dominated by the 14–24-year-old male). The actress Meryl Streep has led the way in this type of role as she herself grows older (*Bridges of Madison County* [Clint Eastwood, 1995] and *The Devil Wears Prada* [David Frankel, 2006] being two very different representations of the "mature" woman!).

Something's Gotta Give (2003), written and directed by Nancy Meyers (whose 2000 film *What Women Want* is the highest-grossing film made by a woman director) is a case in point. It stars Diane Keaton (figure 2), who has ridden the baby-boomer generational wave of stardom: as a young woman in the 1970s she was Woody Allen's muse (*Sleeper*, 1973; *Love and Death*, 1975; *Annie Hall*, 1977; *Manhattan*, 1979); in the 1980s the proto-feminist working mother (*Baby Boom*, Charles Shyer, 1987); and in the 1990s the loyal wife at a time of cultural shifts and the shedding of domestic roles and traditions (*Father of the Bride I* and *II*, Charles Shyer, 1991, 1995; *The First Wives Club*, Hugh Wilson, 1996). The transition for Keaton into the older woman has come with the Meyers film, which also stars Jack Nicholson as Harry, a man in his sixties who refuses to "act his age" until he suffers a heart attack and falls in love with Erica, not only the mother of his current girlfriend but also a famous divorced playwright who then uses the real-life material of their romance and break-up to craft a hit play on Broadway. Much of the humor of the film is predicated upon the physical limitations of age upon romance, specifically passionate lovemaking: after taking Harry's blood pressure (which Erica cannot read without the aid of reading glasses), it is safe for them to make love. Also addressed by the film is the double standard society

Figure 2 From *Something's Gotta Give* (Nancy Meyers, 2003). Diane Keaton's cinematic success has spanned four decades.
Photograph: Columbia/Tri-Star/The Kobal Collection/Bob Marshak

imposes on single older men who date younger women and on older single women – nicely encapsulated by Erica's feminist sister:

> Here's the rub for women. Look at what we have here with you and Erica. Harry, you've been around the block a few times, right? You're what? Around 60. Never been married, which, we all know, if you were a woman, would be a curse, you'd be an old maid, a spinster. Okay, instead of pitying you, they wrote articles about you, celebrate you never marrying. It makes you elusive and ungettable. You're a real catch.

The romance is complicated by the ardent attention paid to Erica by Harry's young doctor (played by Keanu Reeves), who sees nothing wrong with a relationship with Erica despite the disparity in age. Erica is a professionally confident but sexually uptight woman who has given up on having a man in her life, so the attentions of two men – and her resulting rediscovery of the joys of sex – are overwhelming. When Harry calls off their budding relationship she reacts with episodic teary outbursts but channels her heartbreak into cathartic writing. On the brink of engagement to the young doctor Harry reappears in her life; he has reflected on his preoccupation with young women and now repents of his old ways. With the rather overt message that the two old folks belong together, the film leaves them living happily ever after. *Something's Gotta Give* might be saying that the cultural obsession with youth wrongly makes older people feel undervalued, or it could be warning that romance may rear its unexpected head at any stage of life. It is, in any case, recognition of the enduring star power of one of America's cinematic sweethearts as she boldly and publicly undergoes the archetypal transition from maiden to crone, proudly displaying wrinkled neck and sagging bosom to the camera.

Feminist Issues in French and Iranian Cinema

The functions of women's bodies in no way have necessarily to be linked to privileging the male in culture, religion, or society. As far back as Socrates, who identified only one enduring difference between men and women – "the male begets whereas the woman bears" (in Canto, 1986, p. 343) – the personal and political meaning of women has been debated. If we examine the shaping of gender identities by sexuality and religion it is instructive to compare and contrast two filmmaking cultures, those of France and Iran. Filmmakers from these two countries address the limitations imposed upon the representation of women in film as well as the religious and cultural values within which they operate as visual artists.

In the long history of filmmaking in France, women have played an important role: the most obvious of note is the first woman filmmaker, Alice Guy Blaché, who directed over a thousand films in a career that spanned three decades (1896–1920). There is a distinguished legacy of French women in documentary filmmaking, especially as a result of the revolutionary events of 1968, as well as the avant-garde work of Agnès Varda and Marguerite Duras. Since the 1980s popular film has had its share of women directors, such as Colline Serreau, Diane Kurys, and Claire Denis.

In representational terms, because of the relaxation of censorship in the late 1960s pornographic film has been a part of mainstream French cinema, notably in the soft-porn *Emmanuelle* (1974) which was the best-attended film of the 1970s, with nearly nine million spectators (Austin, 1996, p. 46). Woman as sexual object is common to the films of both Jean-Luc Godard (*Sauve qui peut (la vie)*, 1975) and Jean-Jacques Annaud (*L'Amant*, 1992). French actresses primarily identified as sex symbols, such as Brigitte Bardot, have been immortalized in another artistic medium: the idealized woman fetishized in the busts of the Republic called Mariannes, which have been modeled since World War II on actresses such as Catherine Deneuve and Bardot. Displayed in town halls across France, the Marianne symbolizes the values of the Republic – liberty, equality, fraternity – as well as embodying the Motherland. The "ideal" woman has also been portrayed on screen by Audrey Tatou (*Le Fabuleux destin d'Amélie Poulain*, Jean-Pierre Jeunet, 2001; *A Very Long Engagement*, Jean-Pierre Jeunet, 2004), who is not only beautiful but exudes a naïveté and optimistic confidence. She has been described as a "child-woman" in the early cinematic tradition of the melodrama waif. More like Audrey Hepburn's pixie ingénue than Bardot's sex bomb, Tatou has proved to be an unparalleled box-office draw (32 million people worldwide saw *Amélie*; in France *A Very Long Engagement* was seen by 4 million people in five weeks). Ginette Vincendeau speculates on the reason for this remarkable success, suggesting that Tatou's on-screen innocence "came as a relief in a French context of explicit reality television, arthouse fare and literature" (Vincendeau, 2005, p. 15).[4] Although portraying in both films a determined figure, Tatou offers a submissive, reassuring feminine (fantasy) character who counteracts the more challenging images of women in contemporary French cinema.

However, it is instructive for our purposes to examine such films, and here we will explore the most recent works of the filmmaker Catherine Breillat, who began making films in the late 1970s. She attempts to portray women who control their own sexuality and even, in some instances, the male gaze. She does this with graphic, sexually explicit images that she denies are pornographic because they explore sex from the perspective of the "female gaze." *Romance* (1999) is certainly ironically titled; a woman in a relationship with a man who has no sexual drive feels dishonored because he will not make love to her. She goes in search of sexual fulfillment and in the process displays a laconic self-hatred, submitting to sadistic domination and even rape by a man passing on the stairs. Her revenge on her boyfriend for being dishonored is complete when she at last becomes pregnant by him; as she is giving birth, he is killed in a gas explosion in their apartment, instigated as she was leaving for the hospital by turning on the gas range while he slept. Thus death and birth occur simultaneously, illustrating, one might suppose, the cycle of life that women control. This is a bleak picture of "romantic" relationships, the excitement and sexual thrill of first encounters giving way to predictable domestic gender roles, from which the woman breaks free but to which she then submits – however, with a vengeful purpose in mind.

Breillat's next film, *Fat Girl* (2001, also known as *À Ma Soeur*) begins with Anaïs, the eponymous teenage girl, on vacation with her family, singing a listless song about being bored. She indulges in a fantasy life of romantic ideas while her pretty and naïve older sister meets a young law student, who presses her to yield her virginity to him, even stealing a ring from his mother to present as an engagement ring. The girls share a room but that does not stop the student from sneaking in; the couple consummate their relationship while Anaïs watches from her bed. The film deals with issues of fidelity and deceit as the sisters experience this new phase in their relationship. Insisting to her sister at the beginning of the film that she would prefer to lose her virginity to a stranger rather than be disillusioned by a boyfriend who promises much and then breaks her heart, Anaïs proves to be eerily prescient, as the film climaxes with a scene of murder and rape. But it is her unrelenting gaze at the camera that subverts any conventional eroticism implied through a "male gaze," at its most unsettling when Anaïs is crying as the seduction scene unfolds: she turns away from the couple and stares into the camera while the sex scene in the background occurs in "real time" (one of the identifying features of Breillat's filmmaking). The final shot of the film also has Anaïs staring at the camera as she is taken from the crime scene.

Critics question whether Breillat's claim to subvert the male gaze is all that impressive if her characters are always engaged in joyless sex, rape, and death (see Vincendeau, 2001, pp. 18–20). The 2004 film *Anatomy of Hell* goes further than previous films in exploring sexuality, in that a gay man is invited to freely and perhaps even brutally explore a woman's body, an exercise in scrutiny without any erotic tension. The dialogue between the two characters is predicated on the hate and disgust that men feel for a woman's body: "I bless the day I was born immune to you and all your kind." The woman pays the man for his task, which evolves from sadistic humiliation to tender emotion over four nights. Breillat introduces explicit and disturbing images, including close-ups of the woman's genitals (a body double was used) and the dunking of a tampon in a glass of water for the man to drink (suggested by the woman as analogous to drinking the blood of one's enemies). The film will evoke visceral reactions in viewers – Breillat says the film "is about showing what is unwatchable" (in McNab, 2004, p. 22) – and especially in the scenes involving menstruation remind us of the taboos that religion and society have imposed on acceptable artistic representation. There is violence only in a verbal sense, and the sexual imagery is paired with a sometimes surreal but philosophical voiceover, pondering the nature of purity and of desire, read by Breillat herself. Neither of the characters in this film "fits" the gender norm: the man is gay and the female clearly in control of her sexuality and of the male gaze. Breillat denies that a Freudian psychoanalytical reading of the film is appropriate, commenting that in Freud's time women were mistakenly accused of penis envy when in fact they envied the power and rights men had that were denied to them. Susan Rubin Suleiman articulates this when she writes: "Women, who for centuries had been the objects of male theorizing, male desires, male fears and male representations, had to discover and reappropriate themselves as subjects" (Suleiman, 1986a, p. 7). Breillat implicates religion squarely in the oppression of women, when she claims that "Religion would have us believe that sex is simply about the flesh when in fact it's something higher and more idealistic. Religion says our bodies can't be seen because they are ugly and dirty when in fact the taboo is more about rituals of initiation" (in McNab, 2004, p. 22). Breillat is proud of the fact that her film is not pornographic, in the sense of taking pleasure in seeing dehumanizing sex acts on screen, but rather mythic in nature; she says that "in our society pornography is written on every woman's body. But here the words give you a context in which to confront the images that arouse so much fear" (ibid.).

As in the French cinematic context, Gönül Dönmez-Colin claims that "women's place (or lack of it) in the cinemas of the Islamic countries is directly linked to social and political evolutions in which religion and religious customs play an important role" (Dönmez-Colin, 2004, p. 7). It is instructive to recall two film-related events, located in different parts of the world, that occurred in 2004: the release in Indonesia of the film *Kiss Me Quick* (Findo Poernowo), and the screening on Dutch television of the short film *Submission Part I* and the subsequent murder of its director Theo van Gogh. Both events involved Muslim reaction to cinematic portrayals of women and have implications for the freedom filmmakers have to make movies without fear of being silenced by censorship or, ultimately, death.

Kiss Me Quick seems to be a victim of inconsistent moral standards in the exhibition of television programs and films in Indonesia. Although Indonesian productions are subject to a strict national code seeking to uphold morals and to maintain public decency, the Indonesian public is allowed to view without censorship permissive soap operas from India and films from the United States. Another complicating factor is that regional censorship boards have the power to treat films in different ways: in the same year a film showing two gay men kissing was passed by a regional board for screening. The title of *Kiss Me Quick* was already provocative and offensive to the public, the Indonesian Islamic Council declared, because it encourages young people to commit an act that will lead to adultery; in Islam touching and kissing between the sexes are discouraged until after marriage. The kiss in the title comes about on screen 80 minutes into the film. However, an attempt earlier in the year to declare kissing in public illegal was rejected by the Indonesian public, 90 percent of whom are Muslim, albeit described by Anna Lay as only "moderately religious" (Lay, 2004). The film was withdrawn by the Board of Film Censorship but Multivision Plus Pictures released a toned-down version in 2005, retitled *Just One Kiss*, which met with no controversy.

More serious was the reaction to Dutch filmmaker Theo van Gogh's *Submission Part I* (2004), a 10-minute English-language short that cost van Gogh 18,000 Euros and his life.[5] Broadcast at the end of August, *Submission Part I* dealt with Muslim women whose stories of abuse and rape are interwoven with prayers to Allah for help; their bodies are visible through their dress and they have inscribed on their skin Qur'anic verses detailing the permitted punishment for misbehavior of women. Death threats were issued by Islamic extremists to both van Gogh and script-writer Ayaan Hirsi Ali, a Somali-born woman who has renounced her

Muslim faith. They both produced the film to bring attention to the "taboo" subject of domestic violence against Muslim women.[6] Reaction to the film in the Netherlands, where 1 million of the 16 million population are Muslim, was intense, and van Gogh was planning a second installment of the film portraying Muslim men's points of view on violence against women when he was murdered in November 2004. His murderer received a life sentence after confessing to the crime, saying that he committed the murder out of religious conviction.

Clearly, when artists are censored in their attempt to express creatively their view of culture and society it is a serious restriction, but the murder of a filmmaker out of religious conviction is transgression, no matter which religion one professes, of the sacredness of life itself and, ultimately, of the power of the Creator alone to take and give life. The upsurge in extremist religious violence across all religious boundaries in the past decade has been accompanied by a claim to be acting on God's behalf. The insult perceived in the actions of van Gogh, in drawing attention to the violence against Muslim women, is more rightly ascribed to a cultural, rather than religious, custom that is seen today as a human rights violation.

Common Thematic Elements in Islamic Film

It might come as a surprise to many readers to know how vibrant the filmmaking industry is in some Islamic countries. In 2003–4 in the Middle East, Iran produced 80 films, while Turkey produced 17; Saudi Arabia produced its first female director, Hafa'a Al Mansour, in that year. However, the United Arab Emirates was the big player; for its "Films from Emirates" film festival, 65 short or feature documentaries and short or medium fiction films were shown. That year in Africa Egypt produced 21 films. In Asia Pakistan released 48 films, Malaysia 10, and Indonesia 50 (Rosenthal, 2005).

There is no doubt a wide diversity in the politics and history of these countries but there are some common cinematic elements, identified by Gönül Dönmez-Colin in her book *Women, Islam and Cinema*. First, in the representations of women there are repeated themes, trends, and stereotypes driven by male visual pleasure. The prostitute or "fallen" woman has been present from the early years of Islamic cinema: Dönmez-Colin refers to *The Clutch* (Sedat Semavi, 1917), which showed the first "fallen woman" of Turkish cinema. The term "prostitute" is synonymous with other terms: vamp, seductress, fallen woman, courtesan, nymphomaniac – in other words, any type of woman not the wife. Dönmez-Colin identifies two motives for films that feature prostitution: first, they legalized women's naked bodies, where sex on screen was meant to satisfy male viewer fantasies; and second, these films sent moral lessons to chaste family women, because "bad" women in films were inevitably punished in the end.

The popularity of violence against women in film, especially of rape scenes, brings up the issue of audience voyeurism. It also promotes the idea of women as property, seen in real life with the trafficking of young girls sold in Indonesia for less than the price of a goat. Violence within the family also is tolerated or excused, Dönmez-Colin maintains, because Qur'anic permission for men to dominate women in their care is used as a license for abuse, even though the Qur'an also says it is unlawful for men to possess women by force (see Dönmez-Colin, 2004, p. 80). In central Asian film Dönmez-Colin identifies most women characters as victims, objectified for erotic purposes.

In Turkey, another trend, that of religious ideology in film, began as a reaction against secularism, and in 1990 fundamentalist intellectuals vowed to "Islamize" the arts and media.[7] The creation of an Islamic state in Iran in 1979 is where we begin to see the religious trend of censorship. Ayatollah Khomeini said his revolution was not opposed to cinema, only to obscenity. However, he claimed that Western or "colonial" cinema alienated Iranian youth from their roots and so had to be stopped; this resulted in more than 180 cinemas being burned down, and many filmmakers were arrested and their films banned. Film production ceased entirely. However, in the early 1980s the Islamic authorities advocated the creation of a distinctly Islamic cinema to pass on traditional moral values, while also formulating a set of highly restrictive censorship codes. These regulations dictated that, for instance, films had to have a happy ending – even if not justified by the narrative. The representation of women was discouraged, but they could be shown as obedient wives and dutiful mothers, as long as they were modest and chaste characters. This presented a challenge to filmmakers: some decided to eliminate women characters altogether, as in *The Spell* (Dariush Farhang, 1986), about a princess disappearing in a castle hall of mirrors. Stories about children instead dominated the screen: Jafar Panahi and Abbas Kiarostami began their careers making films with child heroes. The language of Iranian cinema dictates the portrayal of women only as veiled; women characters must not have the direct gaze of any man seated in the cinema, and no emotive interactions between sexes are allowed on screen. Abbas Kiarostami's 2002 film *Ten* cleverly tells the story of a young divorced woman who is driving other women and her small son around Tehran, but whose life is constricted as much as her seat-buckled body is inside the car. Dönmez-Colin calls it an allegory of Islamist society and cinema, because both "try to relegate women to identities constructed by religious ideology or its dogmatic interpretations, undermining the evolution of women in a world constantly in motion" (Dönmez-Colin, 2004, p. 102). Panahi's *The Circle* (2000) not only shows the restrictions placed on women by institutional patriarchy (law and religion) but the invisibility in society that women seek in order to survive.

New Iranian Cinema

Almost thirty years on, post-revolution women are actively involved in the Iranian cinema industry, and a few have received international recognition (for example Samira Makhmalbaf). There has been a period of transition, in which filmmakers have tested the freedoms allowed by the authorities, who are still under the influence of conservative Islamist clergy: some women filmmakers tackle issues concerning Iranian women today, none more courageously than Tahmineh Milani, whose script for *Two Women* (1998) was finally approved after eight years by the Ministry of Islamic Guidance. Arrested in 2001 for making *The Hidden Half*, Milani was accused of slandering the Iranian revolution in it; she was released on bail when the Iranian president told the court her film was authorized by his Ministry of Culture.

The Day I Became a Woman (Marziyeh Meshkini, 2000) is an example of a film moderately successful outside of Iran, made by the powerful Makhmalbaf Film House group. Its production quality is high, with characteristic Makhmalbaf elements of strong colors and vivid cinematography. Meshkini is Mohsen Makhmalbaf's wife but a filmmaker in her own right, who is very outspoken when asked about the place of women in Iranian society: "As a woman, naturally I am more affected by problems that face women. Also, I believe we should help gain equal rights for woman [sic] through cultural activities" (Makhmalbaf Film House (n.d.)). The film comprises three short films in one, and portrays women in three different stages of life: Dönmez-Colin calls it "a sequential triptych that charts the kind of life a woman born in a traditional culture can expect" (Dönmez-Colin, 2004, p. 182).

First shown is a young girl, Hava (meaning Eve), whose ninth birthday changes her life forever as she puts on the hijab. The second segment is about a young married woman, Ahoo (whose name means "deer"), who risks the wrath of her husband, father, and religious elders for insisting upon finishing a bicycle race. And the final story features Hoora, an old widow, who goes on a buying spree so she can have all the material goods she could never own while her husband was alive. The film hints at a pessimistic inevitability in the young girl's life, which up until her birthday has been a carefree existence playing with her male friends. However, the fate of the young woman on the bicycle is ambiguous – the story is carried over into the final segment through a pair of other cyclists who appear on the beach, discussing conflicting interpretations of what happened to Ahoo at the end of the race. The old widow takes her purchases to the seaside and sets off with them all perched on a raft for a sea voyage. Despite the apparent message of bleak existence without hope, Meshkini says that her film offers a promise of change: "The situation [in which] one is trapped can be changed by movement... I want to say that a movement has started and should continue – like a river that flows non-stop. The movement of the women is the movement of the river. It is a metaphor. They are progressing to reach their final goal which is freedom" (Dönmez-Colin, 2004, p. 185).

Conclusion

Dönmez-Colin says that the Islamic revolution in Iran and the compulsory veiling of women "pushed women into the shadows, but eventually stimulated a movement among women to go behind the camera to have their voices heard" (Dönmez-Colin, 2004, p. 7). We can learn, through examining the way Muslim women are spectators, images, and constructors of images, how troubled the relationship is between women, Islam, and cinema. It is no less problematic in the filmmaking industries of France, or the United States or Great Britain, as the movement that began with women's liberation continues to produce change in cultural, religious, and social milieus across the globe. It is impossible, with such a dynamic industry, to give an accurate estimate of how many women are now involved in all levels of filmmaking. However, "The Celluloid Ceiling," a report in which Dr. Martha Lauzen compiles yearly statistics on women employed on the top 250 US domestic grossing films, found that "the percentage of women working as directors, executive producers,

producers, writers, cinematographers, and editors...has declined from 19% in 2001 to 16% in 2004" (Lauzen, 2006).[8] In anything other than historical terms, it is difficult to compare or contrast these figures with the "golden age" of early American cinema for women that Ally Acker extols, but we can point to another source of information about women in filmmaking, that of Gwendolyn Audrey Foster, whose international dictionary of women filmmakers features 200 women from 37 countries (Foster, 1995, p. 2). This text charts an expansive horizon of women directors alone, and is a useful reminder that filmmaking is a global enterprise, not the exclusive domain of Hollywood. Perhaps we can end this chapter with an optimistic view of the effects of the women's movement by reflecting on the words of Ursula King: "Contrary to some western critics who decry the feminist movement as a middle class, white, western phenomenon, it is clear that more and more women from all social and religious backgrounds around the world are speaking up and making their voices heard" (King, 1993, p. 223). When put into a global context, the experience of woman as spectacle – not simply in film but in life – provides a powerful incentive for women who are now in a position to reinvent storytelling.

Notes

1 According to Jenn Frederick, the first wave was from 1848, with the first Women's Rights Convention in Seneca Falls, to 1920, with the ratification of the 19th amendment (women's suffrage); the second was from the 1960s into the early 1970s; and the third wave designation appeared in the mid-1980s (Frederick, n.d.).

2 "For we have, built into all of us, old blueprints of expectation and response, old structures of oppression, and these must be altered at the same time as we alter the living conditions that are a result of those structures. For the master's tools will never dismantle the master's house. They may allow us temporarily to beat him at his own game, but they will never enable us to bring about genuine change" (qtd in Schulman, 2004).

3 *Christianity and the Making of the Modern Family* (2001), *Today's Woman in World Religions* (1994), *Sexism and God-Talk* (1993), *Women and Redemption* (1998), and *Goddesses and the Divine Feminine* (2005) are some of her works.

4 Vincendeau says that these types of films "pushed the limits of on-screen sex and violence further" and that the success of the two Tatou films "shows the hunger for images of child-like femininity to counter both the deluge of sex

and nudity in the media but also the increased (and, to some, threatening) visibility of French women in the workplace and public life" (Vincendeau, 2005, p. 15).

5　The film can be seen online at www.ifilm.com/video/2664111.

6　Hirsi Ali is described as one of a growing number of women "who say they want to spread the message that the Muslim faith can be practiced without what she calls 'savage medieval customs' like genital cutting, beatings or confining women to their homes" (Simmons, 2004).

7　Journalist Abdurrahman Sen coined the phrase "white cinema" for on-screen religious propaganda. See Dönmez-Colin, 2004, p. 88.

8　In a survey of genre, women were most likely to work on documentary and romantic comedy films, and least likely to work on horror features.

The Green Screen: Theological Perspectives on the Environment and Film

> God said, "This is the sign of the covenant that I make between me and you and every living creature that is with you, for all future generations: I have set my bow in the clouds, and it shall be a sign of the covenant between me and the earth. When I bring clouds over the earth and the bow is seen in the clouds, I will remember my covenant that is between me and you and every living creature of all flesh; and the waters shall never again become a flood to destroy all flesh."
>
> Genesis 9:12–15

Creation care is an ethic present in every major faith tradition. Across the globe, however, fear is growing that humanity is contributing to the environmental endangerment of the earth: one articulation of that fear is the 2006 documentary *An Inconvenient Truth* (Davis Guggenheim, 2006). Guggenheim's film features former US vice-president Al Gore (figure 3), who warns of the dangers that humanity faces when it ignores the power of nature or attempts to subvert the natural world for its own convenience and financial gain. Yet, in the United States, the film was greeted with the same polarizing attitudes that have gripped the country ever since the election of 2000. Those who support Bush were contemptuous of Gore, the film, and its exposition of the dangers of global warming. Many other Americans seemed to be in a state of denial that anything is wrong with the environment, an attitude cleverly

 Gaye Ortiz

114

Figure 3 Nobel Peace Prize 2007 nominee Al Gore in *An Inconvenient Truth* (Davis Guggenheim, 2006): "I don't really consider this a political issue, I consider it to be a moral issue."
Photograph: Lawrence Bender Productions/The Kobal Collection/Eric Lee

portrayed in a Bennett cartoon in the *Christian Science Monitor*: two cinema marquees, one displaying the title "An Inconvenient Truth" drawing no foot traffic, while the one next to it, "A Reassuring Lie," is packing in the crowds (Bennett, 2006, p.19). Many film reviewers gave the film a favorable review, with Roger Ebert being particularly effusive. In his words, "In 39 years, I have never written these words in a movie review, but here they are: You owe it to yourself to see this film. If you do not, and you have grandchildren, you should explain to them why you decided not to go" (Ebert, 2006). Further, leaders of numerous faith communities urged Americans to see the film so that a dialogue about the environment could begin across the country.

Among the questions this chapter will address is: can film be a stimulus for bringing the environment into the public consciousness? This question reintroduces the debate about spectatorship and whether audiences receive the filmmaker's meaning or whether they negotiate and construct their own meanings. Is there an awakening in the religious community to environmental issues, thus contributing an evangelical bent to the promotion of environmentally aware films that are being made today?

Or is the film industry simply taking advantage of the growing concern about the environment and looking to profit from the draw of sensational special effects in the eco-disaster genre?

Defining the Genre

One of the most important influences on filmic considerations of the environment is the classic book *Silent Spring* by Rachel Carson, published in 1962. The book is dedicated to Albert Schweitzer, who said "Man has lost the capacity to foresee and to forestall. He will end by destroying the earth" (Mahon, 1996).

Carson's observations of the disappearance of wildlife and the connection she makes with the insecticide-spraying campaigns at that time were seminal in the raising of environmental consciousness in America. Conservation had never raised much broad public interest in the decades after World War II, for few people really worried about the disappearance of wilderness. But the threats Carson had outlined – the contamination of the food chain, cancer, genetic damage, the deaths of entire species – were too frightening to ignore. For the first time, the need to regulate industry in order to protect the environment became widely accepted, and environmentalism was born (National Resources Defense Council, 1997). Carson was recently named as the top "eco-hero" by Britain's Environmental Agency in their list of "the top 100 green campaigners of all time"[1] (Adam, 2006).

Another influence in bringing the environmental threat into public consciousness was science fiction suddenly made real: "Science fiction was scorned as 'that Buck Rogers stuff' for its allusions to fictitious rocket ships and atomic weapons. Then V2 rockets whizzed across blitzed cities and an atomic bomb ended the war" (in Casselman, 2006). As the veteran science fiction author and director of the Center for the Study of Science Fiction, James Gunn, sees it, after World War II the visions of science fiction were validated "and people began to look at it as a fiction which deals with impending problems" (ibid.). One of those problems became climate change. Gunn believes that science fiction writers are doing humankind a favor by creating fiction about environmental threats to the earth: "They're trying to dramatize the human potential of what we now only see as scientific possibilities . . . because, as humans, we don't really see how it's going to affect us unless we see it enacted in fiction and in film" (ibid.).

Although to date there have been few feature-length documentaries about the environment, fictional motion pictures featuring environmental themes have been made for decades. David Ingram, in *Green Screen: Environmentalism and Hollywood Cinema*, defines an environmentalist film as one "in which an environmental issue is raised explicitly and is central to the narrative" (Ingram, 2004, p. vii). Not only that, he suggests that there might be identifiably differing attitudes to the environment detected in these films: "the 'conservationist' approach attempts to reconcile the environment with human commercial exploitation, the 'preservationist' approach prefers to set aside areas of the environment from human contamination, and the 'ecological' approach (including eco-feminism) sees nature as a well-balanced machine which is tampered with at our peril" (Bertrand, 2005). An interesting definition, but these distinctions, especially the last two, become quite difficult to separate when analyzing films that deal with environmental themes.

A different and much more activist definition of an environmental film comes from Mark Haslam, the director of Planet in Focus, an environmental film festival in Toronto. His definition of the environment is said by Candida Paltiel to consist of " 'contested terrain,' whether it is the natural, the social, or the political ... [s]o we don't feel restricted" in choosing films to screen in the festival (cited in Henderson, 2006). Since the films screened at the festival are inclusive of issues such as women's rights or genocide, in addition to "typical" themes of pollution or deforestation, this idea of the environment as contested terrain certainly broadens the scope for film beyond nature alone to, perhaps, the extent envisioned by the Genesis quotation at the start of the chapter: whatever threatens to destroy the God-nurtured environment of created life needs to be challenged through the rhetoric of advocacy that cinema provides.

Given the widely referential nature of the genre, it is interesting to examine how the environmental threat to life on earth has been visualized. The list of Hollywood films with an environmental theme really does not stretch back much further than the 1950s, when science fiction films foretold not only the effects of aliens landing from outer space but also the threat to the earth from environmental accidents caused by its inhabitants. One of the earliest examples is *Them!* (Gordon M. Douglas, 1954), which dramatized the effects of radiation on the earth's creatures when giant ants plague Los Angeles. An image poem representative of a totally different genre decades later, *Koyaanisqatsi* (Godfrey Reggio, 1982) has no characters and no plot but is a visually stunning film about the wonder of nature; music and the visual image dominate the film. Yet another genre, the children's animated film, came to grips with logging in the rainforests with *Ferngully: The Last Rainforest* (Bill Kroyer, 1992). Dramas that feature legal and corporate wrangling over the responsibility for the pollution and misuse of earth's resources became more prevalent in the late 1990s with *A Civil Action* (Steven Zaillian, 1998), and Steven Soderbergh's *Erin Brockovich* (2000). A cyclic rash of films that dealt with freak weather conditions – *Earthquake* (Mark Robson, 1974) and *Avalanche* (Corey Allen, 1978) in the 1970s, *Twister* (Jan de Bont, 1996) and *The Perfect Storm* (Wolfgang Petersen, 2000) – are not truly concerned with the environment. On the contrary, Benjamin Chadwick says that "these films teach one primary lesson: fear nature" (Chadwick, 2005, pp. 56–7). One film that does deal directly with climate change is *The Day After Tomorrow* (Roland Emmerich, 2004). With the help of special effects, the earth's polar icecaps melt in spectacular fashion, rapidly flooding and freezing a large part of the United States, but, according to Jacob Park, the film "simply isn't subtle enough to show the complexity of the dilemmas posed by an issue like global warming, with all of its social-political, economic, and ecological dimensions" (Park, 2006).

Entertainment or Education?

Perhaps the less cataclysmic the visual effects, the better the chance of a film capturing the real threat to human existence that ignoring the environment can bring. In the 1970s films such as *Silent Running* (Douglas Trumbull, 1972), *Soylent Green* (Richard Fleischer, 1973), and *The China Syndrome* (James Bridges, 1979) brought an unprecedented awareness of environmental hazards to film audiences. Their strengths were excellent acting and good plots with thoughtful scenarios. Roger Ebert in particular gushes about *The China Syndrome*: "the movie is, above all, entertainment: well-acted, well-crafted, scary as hell" (Ebert, 1979a). But, perhaps most importantly, these films were released at a time when moviegoers were receptive to the subject matter: space travel was a reality – the first Skylab space station was launched in 1973 (NASA Facts, 1997); nuclear plant accidents were starting to be reported; and population control was also in the news as the exploding birth rate in China was being dealt with by the implementation of a radical family planning program (Gu, 1994).

Silent Running stars Bruce Dern as Lowell, an astronaut aboard a spaceship housing the remnants of the earth's forests, heading for a new home on Saturn because there is no more room for them on earth. Upon discovering that the spaceship will not be recalled to earth until the forests are destroyed by the crew, Lowell takes command of the spaceship and determines to save the forests with the help of the three drones Huey, Louie, and Dewey (named after Donald Duck's nephews). *Soylent Green* is a science fiction film set in 2022 in New York, a dystopian city, overcrowded and polluted, with air unfit to breathe and tap water made available only to the rich. Said to be a product of soybeans, Soylent Green is one of the main sources for food. Charlton Heston stars in the film as the policeman who, "while investigating the death of a rich corporate executive, discovers the chilling source of Soylent Green" (Alexander, 1999). The theatrical release of *The China Syndrome* seemed prescient when, days later, a real-life nuclear accident occurred at Three Mile Island in Pennsylvania.[2] Corporate greed and wrongdoing underpin the story of environmental catastrophe in *The China Syndrome*, which occurs when television reporter Jane Fonda and cameraman Michael Douglas are filming a documentary about a nuclear power facility. When an accident happens in the plant, corporate attempts at a cover-up (while pressuring staff to bring the facility back online as soon as possible for financial reasons) clash dramatically with the actions of Jack Godell, a dedicated plant executive who tries to implement safeguards. Jack Lemmon was nominated for Best Actor by the American Academy Awards and won the Best Actor Award at the Cannes International Film Festival in 1979 for his role as the tragic hero Godell.

All three of these films seem to share a suspicion of institutional motives in the pursuit of financial or political gain over the good of the human race or even the planet itself. Yet Louis Alexander cautions us as viewers against assuming that Hollywood is supporting the cause of environmentalists when the industry produces these films: "Hollywood is an entertainer and rarely an educator. In real life, there is a public responsibility to seek an informed debate that will avoid mischaracterization, promote responsible advocacy and offer reliable evidence – while leaving dramatic license to the silver screen" (Alexander, 1999). His attitude is supported by Benjamin Chadwick, who says, "Conservation activism may be dramatic, but it makes poor entertainment for the general audience" (Chadwick, 2005). Neither critic considers the possibility that perhaps Hollywood can be both entertainer and educator.

An Inconvenient Truth

Should people of faith who are concerned about the environment not look to Hollywood for support, let alone for an ethical stance? As Neil Hurley has noted, "movie watchers are often exercising transcendental faculties of insight, criticism and wonder that come remarkably close to what religion has traditionally termed faith, prophecy and reverence" (qtd in R. Johnston, 2000, pp. 57–8). Such a theological approach to the cinematic experience respects the opportunity film provides for people of faith to encounter what they see on the screen in a way that both informs and enriches their understanding of the world around them. Indeed, Johnston claims that seeing films often helps him to see biblical verses or stories in a new light (see, e.g., ibid., pp. 85–6). Could it be the case, therefore, that a film like *An Inconvenient Truth* compels viewers to re-examine their understanding of what is expected of them as stewards of the earth? Might they come to a new appreciation of the verses from the prophets urging humans to follow God's commandments because of the intimate connection between the spiritual and natural worlds: "Is it not enough for you to feed on the good pasture? Must you also trample the rest of your pasture with your feet? Is it not enough for you to drink clear water? Must you also muddy the rest with your feet?" (Ezekiel 34: 17–18). The American organization Interfaith Power and Light (IPL) hoped that this would indeed be the case when it promoted the screening of *An Inconvenient Truth* in church congregations across the United States in October 2006. True to its mission statement, "Deepen the connection between ecology and faith" (IPL, 2006b), IPL sponsored "Spotlight on Global Warming," a nationwide religious screening of educational films including *An Inconvenient Truth*; over 4,000 congregations participated. Paramount Pictures sent out copies of the film on DVD to each of the film-screening hosts.

According to IPL, the issue of global warming requires a religious response, "motivated by love for our neighbors and the call to be responsible stewards of God's creation" (IPL, 2006a). One of the faith leaders involved in the campaign, a rabbi whose synagogue is the oldest in Pennsylvania, promotes raising awareness through movies: "With these screenings and discussion, we hope to inform and inspire people of faith to take personal and collective action to reduce global warming emissions" (Swartz, 2006). This expression of hope – that of an informed call to action – should be examined more deeply, and assisting in this examination is Clive Marsh, who, in his book *Cinema and Sentiment*, questions what kind of meaning-making is going on when people watch films: "what films do to people and what people do with films" (Marsh, 2004, p. ix). What is interesting about the IPL screenings across the United States is that the hosts of the presentations were encouraged to have a discussion with the audience after they watched *An Inconvenient Truth*. Discussing films after watching them is a habit that friends or family often practice; indeed this is reminiscent of the opening vignette of *Explorations in Theology and Film*, which describes a lively discussion at a table in a North London pizza parlor in the late 1980s as "an informal theology seminar...in progress" (Marsh & Ortiz, 1997a, p. 1). Marsh in *Cinema and Sentiment* makes the point that "films are watched within diverse religious frameworks" so that "At its richest...theological reception of, and conversation with, film would entail discussion of film within an explicit awareness of diverse possible responses" (Marsh, 2004, p. 136). Screenings open to the public but situated in a church might well cultivate an air of religious meaning for the audience already: in my own case, the film was screened in the sanctuary of our local Unitarian Universalist church (where, indeed, we often have film screenings and even film festivals held in the worship space), so the setting, for the audience, was redolent of worship. Marsh says the challenge is for churches to become cultural centers so that " 'being church' interweaves with the practice of film-watching" (Marsh, 2004, p.141).

For screenings of *An Inconvenient Truth*, the IPL guidelines for the host church included a suggestion that the evening should begin with prayer; the discussion materials included quotations from the major faith traditions, some from sacred texts, framing environmental crisis and creation care within a religious context. The way was prepared for offering a safe and respectful arena for diverse opinions and reactions to the film and to the topic of global warming, especially as audience members might come from further afield than from simply the host congregation (which often already has a notably diverse range of religious philosophies and practices held in creative tension within its walls). A discussion evening held after the screening invited people to explore ideas for making the film's message relevant to their local situation. The group, dubbed the "Gardeners of Eden," drew up a list of projects, some to be introduced to the congregation and others to the wider community, as well as planning to create a website and email listserve that would communicate ongoing news and information about creation care. If all 4,000 Christian, Jewish, Muslim, and Hindu congregations that participated in the screening of

An Inconvenient Truth keep the issue of the environment as a focus for their faith community, that would indeed carry forward the call to action that the film so urgently presented. The momentum that IPL hope will be sustained beyond the month of screenings across the United States by religious communities now depends upon how involved and active its audience members remain, with eco-friendly projects spinning off from the film-watching experience. In this instance, "film's challenge to theology" (to use Marsh's subtitle) is a clear one: audiences have been asked to find their theological and spiritual motivation to address one of the most compelling issues of our time.

Conclusion

Unlike, perhaps, any other film genre, the environmental film may be a sign of the times. It might prompt the film industry to assume (possibly unwillingly) the role of prophet, although how much longer humanity can afford warnings instead of action is unclear. Certainly, if nothing else, the environmental film demonstrates that compelling issues that affect the very survival of the planet are being addressed by the entertainment industry. The relationship between the "reel" and the "real" (to quote Rob Johnston, 2000, p. 195) has never been more integral to theology than when we consider the future of creation.

Notes

1 Al Gore was placed ninth, and at the bottom of the list Father Christmas was recognized for carbonless delivery.
2 As Chadwick puts it, this is "one of history's most disturbing examples of life imitating art" (Chadwick, 2005).

A Time to Kill?
Theological Perspectives
on Violence and Film

A useful introduction to this topic comes in the form of Bryan Stone's article, "Religion and Violence in Popular Film," which appeared in the April 1999 edition of the *Journal of Religion and Film*. Stone's premise is that, having surveyed the top 20 highest grossing films in America for each year from 1990 to 1998 – a total of 180 movies – he found 62 of these films "contained some representation of religion," albeit in the superficial sense in many cases of a Christian minister performing a marriage or funeral service, and that, of these films, as many as 44 "featured religion in some direct relationship to violence" (Stone, 1999, ¶6). While acknowledging that there are "those rare films that feature a glimmer of the power of religious faith to transform human life and challenge both personal and structural violence," Stone attests that such pictures "tend to minimize or even shun Hollywood film conventions and thereby risk their own popularity" (ibid., ¶43). It comes as no surprise, therefore, to find that, in his list of the most commercially successful films of the 1990s, very few such pictures feature – a state of affairs that he clearly laments. Rather, when religion is portrayed in connection with violence, Stone contends that religion is not sufficiently taken seriously as a motivating force for the rejection of violence, but tends instead to serve the paradoxical purpose of justifying and legitimating violence "or as a device for enhancing the entertainment value of violence" (ibid., ¶1).

Although he does not give these specific examples himself, films that feature crusaders or spiritual warriors are a case in point, along the lines

 Chris Deacy

123

of Clint Eastwood's Preacher in *Pale Rider* (Clint Eastwood, 1985) or Balian (Orlando Bloom) in *Kingdom of Heaven* (Ridley Scott, 2005), both of whom undertake violent acts in order to emancipate an oppressed people. In the case of the former, an enigmatic preacher arrives in a small Californian mining community in the nineteenth century to dispense judgment when the town falls victim to an avaricious and acquisitive strip-mining company that endeavors to drive the townsfolk from their land. Using force where necessary, the Preacher single-handedly manages to outwit, and outfight, the mining baron and his minions, to the point that he returns unscathed from a gunfight with five of his adversaries, all of whom are violently killed. In the latter, Balian takes up the sword in Jerusalem in the Middle Ages, at the time of the Crusades, for the sole purpose of protecting the helpless, maintaining peace, and insuring that the kingdom of heaven can take root on earth. Other examples include George Lucas's *Star Wars* (1977) and Quentin Tarantino's *Kill Bill: Vol. 2* (2004), where Luke Skywalker (Mark Hamill) and The Bride/Beatrix Kiddo (Uma Thurman) are trained by their respective spiritual masters – Obi-Wan Kenobi (Alec Guinness) in the case of the former, and Pai Mei (Gordon Liu) in that of the latter – in how to harness the correct use of mystical force in battle. In such instances, the "ultimate victory of good over evil always boils down to firing laser blasters, detonating bombs, or slicing through one's enemies with a light saber" (ibid., ¶21) in the case of *Star Wars*, or a Samurai sword in the case of *Kill Bill*.

Violence as an Anathema to Christianity

Stone concedes, however, that this is not representative of all Hollywood films. In some pictures, for example, a priest may appear for the express purpose of providing spiritual counsel or comfort in the face of violence. Although Stone does not refer to *Dead Man Walking* (Tim Robbins, 1995), this film provides a good example here, as it concerns the spiritual ministrations provided by a Roman Catholic nun, Sister Helen Prejean (Susan Sarandon), to a convicted murderer, Matthew Poncelet (Sean Penn), sitting on Death Row. Poncelot is a perpetrator of violence and, in Lloyd Baugh's words, "a nasty character with few redeeming features," who not only committed an appalling crime – he raped a young woman before murdering her and her lover – but, even in the present, "remains an arrogant and brutish young man, persisting in his racism, his self-pity and his aggressive and vulgar sexism" (Baugh, 1997, p. 151). Nevertheless, Prejean's role is to prepare him spiritually for his impending violent death by lethal injection, as well as empathizing with, and attempting to befriend, the families of Poncelot's victims. In more superficial instances, we could also cite in this regard films such as *Sister Act* (Emile Ardolino, 1992), where a sacred space, in the form of a convent, is established as a source of protection for a lounge singer whose life is in jeopardy after she witnessed a mob murder – thus making her a victim of impending violence – and *Sleepers* (Barry Levinson, 1996), in which a Catholic priest decides to commit perjury on the witness stand in order to help protect two abused boys, who are standing trial for murdering their oppressor, from being subjected to yet more violence and abuse.

Stone also gives the example of films in which religion is seen to be instrumental in the *rejection* of violence, although only two films out of the 180 examined adequately fulfill this criterion. One is the Disney animation *Pocahontas* (Mike Gabriel & Eric Goldberg, 1995), in which the deep spirituality of the protagonist, the daughter of a Native American tribal chief, advocates a strategy of non-violence toward the warmongering European invaders. The other is, paradoxically, a film that is "generally perceived as one of the most violent" (Stone, 1999, ¶33) of the decade, *Pulp Fiction* (Quentin Tarantino, 1994). This is a film that is ostensibly concerned with the interconnected lives of a series of gangsters, mobsters, hit men, and bandits in four short stories set in Los Angeles, but which nevertheless contains a rich treatise on the incompatibility between leading a "religious" life and working as a contract killer. Having witnessed an apparent act of divine intervention, whereby a stream of bullets, fired from a gun that is just inches away, completely misses its intended targets – "This was divine intervention...God came down from heaven and stopped these...bullets...What happened here was a miracle" – Jules (Samuel L. Jackson) is convinced that this is a sign that his mission in life is go straight: "I'm just gonna walk the earth...until God puts me where he wants me to be." As Adele Reinhartz puts it, "Jules has been transformed into a pious, born-again Christian, just waiting for God's personal word" (Reinhartz, 2003, p. 105).

Of course, this is all carried out rather playfully, even comically, with both the violence and purported conversion in the film meant to be distanced, rather than taken seriously. Whenever I show excerpts from *Pulp Fiction* to my students, in particular the scene that immediately follows this one, when Vincent Vega (John Travolta) inadvertently shoots Marvin (Phil LaMarr) in the face after the car Jules is driving goes over a bump in the road, the response is invariably one of laughter rather than recoil from fright or horror at the gruesomeness on display, thus drawing attention to the artifice and self-referentiality that lie at the film's core. As Roger Ebert said of Tarantino upon the film's release in 1994, "Here's a director who's been let loose inside the toy store, and wants to play all night" (Ebert, 1994). Similarly, writing in 2001, Ebert observed that "It is Tarantino's strategy in all of his films to have the characters speak at right angles to the action, or depart on flights of fancy" (Ebert, 2001). Tarantino's is a filmic universe where "there are no normal people and no ordinary days" (Ebert, 1994), and even Reinhartz acknowledges in an article on the picture in the *Journal of Religion and Film* that "the overall tone" of *Pulp Fiction* and "its playful subversion of standard Hollywood tropes . . . make it difficult to believe wholeheartedly in Jules' transformation," not least in view of the fact that *Pulp Fiction*'s "movie images, plot, characters, and dialogue owe far more to the corpus of Hollywood flicks" (Reinhartz, 1999) than to the world of the Bible (and, specifically, the book of Ezekiel, which is referenced throughout). Nevertheless, the film does place the existence of some form of transcendental or theistic framework, albeit allusively, at the heart of one of its leading character's trajectory, and it is certainly intrinsic to the narrative that unfolds. It is, therefore, ironic that *Pulp Fiction* should be one of the few films in Stone's study to feature "an explicit rejection of violence out of a clearly religious motivation" (Stone, 1999, ¶33) when it features – whether gratuitously or otherwise – the perpetration of criminal, and violent, acts.

However, seeing the likes of *Pocahontas* and (if we accept Stone's reading) *Pulp Fiction* as mere aberrations, Stone argues that many films are inclined to juxtapose and intercut, rather than set up a distinction between, religion and violence (let alone repudiate the latter altogether, as in the case of *Pulp Fiction*). Stone refers in this regard to *The Godfather* (Francis Ford Coppola, 1972), where, in the final scene, a mafia killing spree is juxtaposed with the scene of an infant baptism, and *Face/Off* (John Woo, 1997), where, again at the end of the picture, a violent shoot-out between the film's protagonists takes place inside a Spanish church and is intercut with "depictions of crucifixes, the Madonna, religious flowers, votive candles, and flying doves" (Stone, 1999, ¶36). The fact that John Woo is a Christian filmmaker appears to be lost on Stone, who merely contends that "the violent is made to appear all the more violent by its intrusion into sacred space" (ibid.). Woo is on the record, however, as saying "I like doves. They look so beautiful . . . For me they represent peace and love and purity. And sometimes they're seen as the messengers of God, so they're important to me because I'm a Christian" (qtd in Brooke, n.d.). It may well be the case that, in *Face/Off*, religion and violence are inextricably interlinked, but this is a serious problem, rather than a blessing, in Stone's eyes, and there is no suggestion that some kind of spiritual raison d'être may lie at the kernel of this action film. Noting that as a society we are deeply shaped by visual media, Stone bemoans the fact that we are increasingly desensitized to violence in film, not least in terms of the way in which it is repeatedly depicted by filmmakers as "natural" and "right" (ibid., ¶4). Accordingly, so accustomed are we to being bombarded with images of violence – which he defines as going beyond merely physical acts of destruction and physical abuse to include psychological manifestations, whereby if one person violates another's personhood then violence is being perpetrated – that we are increasingly unable to associate on-screen violence with anything other than entertainment value. Perhaps, to borrow the wording of Neil Postman's critique in this regard, we are literally amusing ourselves to death! So inextricable is the link between violence and entertainment that "a film cannot use violent images to communicate a different message" (ibid., ¶40), not even when religion plays a discernible role in that picture. Stone's hypothesis is that, barring the odd exception, popular film is unable to deal with the complexity and seriousness of religious experience and faith with regard to the treatment of violence, enslaved as it is to what he refers to as "standard film conventions that truncate depth and abbreviate complexity in the service of entertainment" (ibid., ¶38). To give an example, Stone argues that "a film that employs an adventure film's scenes of sex and violence cannot communicate anything but voyeuristic exploitation of suffering people," in which the "pain of the oppressed is ultimately used for the entertainment of comfortable spectators" (ibid., ¶40).

This is no less the case in explicitly religious films. Regarding *The Passion of the Christ* (Mel Gibson, 2004), for example, I have written elsewhere that Gibson's biopic of the last 12 hours in the life of Jesus is more interested in depicting the brutality and viciousness of Good Friday than in the majesty and exuberance of Easter Sunday, in which the resurrection takes up just a few seconds of screen time in an otherwise relentless and violent assault on the senses (Deacy, 2005, p. 107). Writing in *USA Today*, Claudia Puig referred to the film upon its release as "one of the most unrelentingly graphic and blood-drenched films ever made," and claims that its "ascendance to the ranks of the definitive Jesus movies may be hampered by its unrelenting, almost orgiastic violence," in which Jesus systematically has violence inflicted upon him "to the point of cinematic overkill" (Puig, 2004). Similarly, all seven contributors to "Table Talk: Reflections on *The Passion of the Christ*," which comprises the epilogue of *Cinéma Divinité*, are identified as having been "numbed by the relentless violence of the film," to the extent that "the point and purpose of depicting such excessive violence" (Aitken et al., 2005, p. 311) is not demonstrably clear. It may be the case that, for more conservative viewers, Gibson's picture comprises a noble and devotional rendering of the sacrifice and martyrdom that Jesus experienced on his path to Calvary, but it is a moot point as to whether the violence on display is as theologically fecund as many Christians have alleged. As Michael Wilmington of the *Chicago Tribune* sees it, what Gibson delineates on screen is so visceral and graphic that "some audiences may emerge from the experience more drained or enraged than elevated or vibrant with Christian love," with the film containing "more power and gore than power and glory" and "more blood and guts than blood and redemption" (Wilmington, 2004). British journalist Anthony Quinn is similarly concerned that "Anyone even vaguely acquainted with Christ's teachings in the Gospels will know that His was a message founded on love, humility and compassion, qualities conspicuous by their absence in a film that amounts to an appalling pageant of blood-splattered cruelty and sadism" (Quinn, 2004). There is a danger, indeed, that for anyone not already familiar with the Christian story, there is something inherently alienating about a film whose incessant and unmitigated depiction of violence never adequately explores the theological raison d'être behind the carnage on display. The film's success ultimately depends on what beliefs and values one holds before one sets foot in the auditorium, and to this end it could be argued that Gibson is merely preaching to the converted and taking the faithful on a tour.

That religion and violence are interwoven cannot therefore be denied. However, whether we are talking about ultra-orthodox and evangelical Jesus films or mainstream Hollywood products, along the lines of the 180 films from the 1990s explored by Stone, there would appear to be no distinction between them when it comes to using violence as a vehicle for the "entertainment of comfortable spectators" (Stone, 1999, ¶40). The debate is thus much more complex than commentators and theologians often acknowledge. It may be the case that violence is seen as a threat to Christian values – and Stone himself would seem to go down this path, particularly as he extols only the virtues of that minority of films that portray religion "as a force in personal, family, or social life" that moves us "away from violence and toward nonviolence" (ibid., ¶38) – but Gibson's *Passion* is a good illustration of a film that endeavors to commingle the two as a way of bolstering and even sanctifying the Christian message. Ironically, though, the same critics who have lauded *The Passion* have also been instrumental in identifying violence as a demonstrable threat to Christian values. Following the Columbine High School Massacre in 1999, it is significant that, in an article for the *International Herald Tribune*, John Broder and Katharine Seelye reported that whereas "Democrats tend to finger guns and their powerful lobby, the National Rifle Association," as responsible for the violence that was perpetrated in a school playground, "Republicans are more inclined to blame Hollywood and the glorification of natural born killers in movies, music and video" (qtd in R. Johnston, 2000, p. 146). Michael Moore's provocative, Oscar-winning documentary *Bowling for Columbine* (2002) epitomizes this fissure between liberal and conservative wings, with Moore unapologetically blaming the massacre on America's fanatical obsession with gun ownership, while conservative critic Michael Medved takes the opposite view. Commenting on allegations that the high-school killers were "highly influenced" by the mass media, Medved told an audience of Christian students in March 2000, at the Wesleyan-based Greenville College in Illinois, that "even if you don't decide to be influenced by [popular culture], you can get hit over the head by someone who is" (*Greenville Advocate*, 2001). Medved, who was cited in chapter 1 of this book as lamenting the fact that the tendency in movies (as well as music and TV) is to "revel in graphic brutality, glorifying vicious and sadistic characters who treat killing as a joke" (qtd in Lynch, 2005, pp. 84–5), also affirmed that "The academic connection between violence in real life and violence in the media is a stronger connection than that between smoking and lung cancer" (*Greenville Advocate*, 2001). In his words, "Movies and TV do not reflect any reality in this universe or any universe yet discovered. What you see is basically a reflection of nothing other than people's warped imagination" (ibid.). Medved argues, for example, that every night on prime-time television, the four major television networks in America (ABC, CBS, NBC, and Fox) feature an average of 350 characters, of whom seven will be murdered – "How many nights will it take before everyone is dead? . . . If the world looked like it does on TV, you wouldn't have to worry about population problems, because everyone would be dead in 50 nights, and the last one alive could turn off the TV!" (ibid.).

The fact that Medved also unreservedly defends *The Passion of the Christ*, which, he wrote in January 2005, "still plays with the same fiery immediacy it brought to its explosive Ash Wednesday release" in the previous year and which it is "easy to imagine church groups (and cinema students) still watching...with avid attention 50 years from now" (Medved, 2005) would suggest that it is not violence *per se* that is at issue here, but, rather, the *context* within which it is used. Curiously, in all of the articles Medved has written about *The Passion* for such publications as *Christianity Today* (Medved, 2004a), *USA Today* (Medved, 2004b), *Beliefnet* (Medved, 2004c), the *Christian Science Monitor* (Medved, 2004d), and *American Enterprise Online* (Medved, 2004e), the film's violence is conspicuously overlooked, with the bulk of his attention paid to the film's supposed anti-Semitism, a charge that Medved, an Orthodox Jew, is keen to play down. One of his few specific references to the charge of violence appears on the Religious Tolerance website in the context of whether the film is suitable for children to see, in light of Gibson's own recommendation that *The Passion* is unsuitable for audiences who are younger than 13 years of age, in which Medved is quoted as saying that the film is comprised of "two hours of almost uninterrupted and unendurable pain" (Robinson, 2004). However, this is cited somewhat out of context, as Medved has written elsewhere that, "When I watched the rough cut [of the movie] at the offices of Gibson's Icon Entertainment International, I also felt overwhelmed by its lyrical intensity and devastating immediacy: the suffering of Christ (superbly played by the haunted and haunting Jim Caviezel) becomes almost unendurable" (Medved, 2004e). Rather than see the level of violence as extraneous or sacrilegious, Medved believes that *The Passion* constitutes "an audacious work of art that represents by far the most compelling cinematic adaptation of a Biblical story ever attempted by Hollywood" (ibid.). Medved may be quick to target most of Hollywood's output for its penchant for delineating excessive (and immoral) images of violence, but when Paula Fredriksen of Boston University argued in an article for the *New Republic* in 2003 that Gibson's *Passion* was set to unleash anti-Jewish violence, and that when (not if) "violence breaks out, Mel Gibson will have a much higher authority than professors and bishops to answer to" (Fredriksen, 2003), Medved's response was to label this as one of many "hysterical pronouncements, all too typical of the current storm," which, he claims, has "emerged out of a poisonous combination of mistakes, misunderstandings, and sheer malice" (Medved, 2004e) on the part of the film's detractors.

Down the Slippery Slope: The Commingling
of Religion and Violence

A similar paradox arises in the case of action films that contain ostensibly Christ-figure protagonists, along the lines of John McClane (Bruce Willis) in *Die Hard* (John McTiernan, 1988) or Martin Riggs (Mel Gibson) in *Lethal Weapon* (Richard Donner, 1987), which are often very different in essence from, rather than functional equivalents of, the New Testament Jesus. Although action movies tend to feature selfless, heroic individuals who "do what they have to do in order to get the job done" – whether it is saving America from terrorists and hostage-keepers, as in the *Die Hard* movies, or medieval England from an iniquitous and corrupt law-and-order system, as in *Robin Hood: Prince of Thieves* (Kevin Reynolds, 1991), it is questionable, in view of the violent acts that these figures carry out in order to accomplish their goals, whether such figures may legitimately be designated as Christ-like. Irrespective of whether we call such figures "heroes" because of their capacity for "delivering salvation, enacting positive change, and bringing relief from suffering or oppression" (Fitch, 2005, ¶5) or anti-heroes because of their reluctance to answer the call to action, resulting from their fallible and flawed human nature, John Fitch rightly calls upon theologians to exercise caution before formulating parallels and analogies with the person of Christ. For, in so many instances, Fitch argues that the alleged cinematic Christ-figure is very different in nature from the Jesus of the New Testament, whose example of not doing harm to other people (Matthew 5:21–6, Romans 12:14–21) does not find too many obvious counterparts on the silver screen. Rather, although the cinematic hero may aspire to redemption, the difference is that, in the case of the likes of John McClane and Martin Riggs, their redemption is "marked by the blood of their enemies" (Fitch, 2005, ¶16) and not only is violence perpetrated, but that violence is no less vicious and barbaric in nature – it may even be more so – than that which is carried out by their adversaries. As Robert Ellis puts it, "while [Bruce] Willis' character risks himself, and even behaves selflessly, the 'deliverer' he portrays ultimately beats violence with more 'redemptive' violence" (Ellis, 2005, p. 17). Fitch's contention is that "According to the Christic example, to which all of his followers are subsequently called, a man should do no harm to any other man, which means actively denying a fundamentally flawed human nature" (Fitch, 2005, ¶16). Whereas Christ calls for surrender to a spiritual calling, with the concomitant need for self-sacrifice and spiritual reawakening, in so many films there is "always much spilling of blood," which is "justified as righteous action" (ibid., ¶23), conducted as it is by "men and women of violence, of revenge and reparation" (ibid., ¶16) who are "brought to a kind of 'holy aggression' by circumstances beyond their control" (ibid.). In the case of *Die Hard*, for example, the discovery that the hero's estranged wife has been taken hostage by international terrorists and that only he is in any position to rescue her and her co-workers who are being held against their will on the thirtieth floor of a Los Angeles hotel precipitates McClane – "a regular guy with typical character flaws" (Nolan, 2005, p. 37) – into becoming a savior-figure who "is enabled to transcend his defects, overcome the bad guys" (ibid.), and recover his marriage. As Fitch puts it, this is "certainly not Christ-like in the traditional sense, yet postures as a righteous stance by virtue of its dedication to a high ideal, coupled with the embrace of self-sacrifice" (Fitch, 2005, ¶17). The hero may very well be "absolved of past sins and indiscretions" and undergo a character transformation, but only by means of what Fitch calls "a resolute dedication to violence and vengeance" (ibid.).

The fact that *Die Hard* and its sequel *Die Hard 2: Die Harder* (Renny Harlin, 1990), together with a number of other action films, are set during the Christmas season – such as *Lethal Weapon*, *The Long Kiss Goodnight* (Renny Harlin, 1996), *Home Alone* (Chris Columbus, 1990), and *Kiss Kiss Bang Bang* (Shane Black, 2005) – has led Rowana Agajanian to make the similar claim that their portrayal of weaponry and violence, "whether slapstick or real," is "incongruous to the Christmas message of 'peace and goodwill to all men' with which we are so familiar" (Agajanian, 2000, p. 146). This is reiterated by Terrence Rafferty in the *New Yorker*, who wrote that one of the most prominent aspects of *Die Hard* "is the sheer joy it takes in destruction," and that, "In a strange way this picture's mixture of sentimentality and violence defines Hollywood's version of the Christmas spirit: you get a lot of expensive toys and smash them all to pieces, because you know there are a lot more where they came from" (qtd in ibid., p. 161). Tempting though it may be, therefore, to use Christian concepts and vocabulary to describe the trajectory that alleged cinematic Christ-figures may follow, the fact that any redemption that takes place involves "blood and retribution" rather than "spirit and conscience" prompts Fitch to categorize it as no more than a "faux moral redemption" (Fitch, 2005, ¶18). No authentic change or spiritual transformation takes place, as the likes of McClane and Riggs "frequently murder their way" to a kind of "nebulous spiritual freedom which may be culturally sanctioned by a social system that still seems to reward a sadistic response to danger or any kind of threat" (ibid.).

This underscores the very problem that Medved and others fail to take on board, since whatever pleasures more conservative Christians may find in *The Passion of the Christ* – and, to be fair, there are obvious differences in that Gibson's Jesus is never anything other than a tragic victim of relentless and malicious violence, rather than an active perpetrator in the manner of Riggs or McClane – Melanie Wright is correct to read *The Passion* as a "highly resonant" movie for contemporary American audiences inasmuch as it relates to "their post-September 11th sense of embattlement," both physically and spiritually, as well as to those conservative Christians who feel themselves "to be under 'attack' from liberalism" (in Aitken et al., 2005, p. 321). In other words, as what Wright calls "a muscular Jesus who is also embattled but wins through" (ibid.), Gibson's Jesus will have much to offer those audience members who look upon Christ as a triumphal figure who will defeat all enemies and secure an unconditional victory. That Wright found that the final scene, in which a restored and healthy-looking – indeed, incandescent – Jesus is resurrected from the dead and has thereby managed to emerge triumphant from the extreme violence and abuse meted out to him, "reminded me of *The Terminator*" (ibid.) is a case in point. Jesus may not take up the sword and eradicate his enemies in the manner of Arnold Schwarzenegger, but a similar pattern can nevertheless be discerned. Jesus has risen victorious over his enemies, giving sustenance to those in our culture who look upon Christianity as a crusading force that will quell its enemies – whether in the form of Middle Eastern terrorists or those more liberal forces who, it is alleged by Medved and others, erode the moral backbone of audiences by promulgating images on cinema and TV screens that revel in graphic and even orgiastic scenes of brutality, bloodshed, and violence.

It may be Fitch's hope that, amidst all of the violence that appears in action movies such as *Die Hard*, there may be a "point ahead, on the cinematic horizon, when filmmakers will give equal screening to the hero who achieves a non-violent transformation" (Fitch, 2005, ¶28), but, albeit paradoxically, it is conservative Christians as much as the "liberal" film industry who find the use of violence potentially efficacious. It is, of course, the case that, moved by the example of Jesus's life and teaching, many Christians, since the origins of the early Church, have been committed to a non-violent lifestyle. In a letter written by the US Catholic bishops entitled "The Challenge of Peace: God's Promise and Our Response," published in 1983, the point was made, for instance, that some have "understood the gospel of Jesus to prohibit all killing" or "affirmed the use of prayer and other spiritual methods as means of responding to enmity and hostility" (qtd in Gill, 2006, p. 247). However, that there is a close alliance between religion and violence cannot be overlooked. John Fitch and Bryan Stone may agree that Christianity, at least in its essence, does not require violence, and certainly does not need to promote it, but the situation is much more complex than that. As Mark Roncace sees it, "The same religion that has evoked loving and compassionate action toward other human beings is the same religion that produced the Crusades, the Inquisition, and the Salem witch trials" (Roncace, 2002, p. 299). Although, as Johnston reports, "Hollywood seems to be realizing that the public outcry about violence in Hollywood is growing" – following the dissemination in recent years of full-page advertisements in major newspapers across the United States "decrying the sharp escalation in violence and explicit sexual content in television, movies, music, and video games," in which it is claimed that "children are being robbed of their normal childhood innocence" (R. Johnston, 2000, p. 146) – the challenge that lies ahead is also for theologians, rather than simply the media, to confront. Aside from the somewhat distracting debate as to whether, as Lynch puts it, "children, who are often depicted as particularly susceptible to the effects of media violence, respond by simply imitating that violence" (Lynch, 2005, p. 88) – and the case in Britain in which, in 1993, two 10-year-old boys from Liverpool murdered two-year-old Jamie Bulger raises a number of questions about the alleged links between so-called "video nasties" and real-life violence, following unproven claims made at the time that the killers were re-enacting a death-scene from *Child's Play 3* (Jack Bender, 1991) – the onus on the theologian is to address wider and more complex questions concerning the efficacy and *telos* of violence.

A partial step in this direction is provided by Roy Anker. Whereas Bryan Stone sees *The Godfather*'s juxtaposition of violence and religion, as the baptism of Michael Corleone's (Al Pacino) son is intercut with a killing spree that Corleone has commissioned, as comprising a typical "filmic device for drawing attention to the violent" (Stone, 1999, ¶43) and enhancing its entertainment value, Anker suggests an alternative reading of the use of violence in film that does not see violence as a purely negative force that truncates depth and abbreviates complexity in the service of entertainment. In situating it within the context of Christian ritual and practice, Anker indicates that the violence on display in *The Godfather* serves the positive function of showing how violence "specifically transgresses the core theological and moral values of the western world's major religious tradition" (Anker, 2004, p. 60). Rather than constitute a corrosive force that will turn us into immoral beings with a proclivity for replicating in the real world the violence we witness on the silver screen, the suggestion here is that film can be a positive and effective agent that sets up a dichotomy between, and thereby draws attention to, the gulf between the values of Corleone and those of Christ. The eruption of violence at the end of *The Godfather* could thus be said to "oppose and desecrate a benign natural order and the redemptive purposes of Christian ritual" (ibid., p. 61) and to become a "defilement, desecration, and straight-out blasphemy of the innocence and festivity God intended for family life" (ibid., p. 62). This is certainly in keeping with Anker's more synthetic and sacramentally based understanding of the relationship between theology and culture, which ties in with Niebuhr's *Christ above Culture* model, and a prime example of how, as was mentioned in chapter 1, "grace befalls unlikely and unsuspecting people in surprising and unforeseeable ways that are quite beyond human prediction, conception, or charting" (ibid., p. 17). Although the violence in *The Godfather* is morally and theologically indefensible, comprising as it does "a violation that is never justified or regenerative" (ibid., p. 58), Anker would appear to be of the view that this is all the more reason to watch it, rather than abstain from it in the manner of Niebuhr's *Christ against Culture* approach. For, in keeping with those who see the values delineated in film as preparatory to Christian revelation, Anker does not believe that audiences will be predisposed to turn into immoral beings, but instead will come to see for themselves that "all violence invariably and essentially opposes the goodness of life" (ibid., p. 60). Indeed, Anker takes the line that "violence's ample measures of deceit, surprise, ferocity, and viciousness speak for themselves," appalling us in their extremity and allowing "the horrific cost of violence to seep into every violence-hungry viewer" (ibid.).

This is, however, at best, an extremely optimistic view that sees audiences as being able to cultivate their sense of what it is to be human, and to be capable of finding redemption in the most unlikely of places. At worst, it is hopelessly naïve, as it assumes that audiences will, having witnessed cinematic violence, instinctively recoil from it, albeit thanks to God's grace. A more creative approach for theologians to take would be one that sees violence as itself theologically profound, if not, indeed, justified or even necessary – and to do this in respect of "secular" films rather than merely in theologically conservative Jesus biopics along the lines of Gibson's *Passion*. Theologians must address the fact, for example, that, although the Hays Production Code in America attempted to prevent audiences from identifying or empathizing with violent films, along the lines of *Little Caesar* (Mervyn LeRoy, 1931), *The Public Enemy* (William A. Wellman, 1931), and *Scarface* (Howard Hawks, 1932), audiences found the criminally minded protagonists played by the likes of James Cagney and Edward G. Robinson "so much more appealing than the characters opposed to [them]" that they found themselves rooting for them "in spite of themselves" (Martin Quigley Jnr qtd in Christianson, 2005, p. 112). As I have written previously, it is significant, theologically, that in the 1930s and 1940s film audiences began to be influenced and inspired by such "rebels" and "anti-heroes" even though they were on the other side of the law or died for violating society's code (Deacy, 2001, p. 98), since it is the intrinsically flawed, fallible, and human nature of such film characters that makes a judicious correlation with the Christian tradition, and with the person of Christ, so compelling (ibid., p. 99). In marked contrast to the triumphant and all-conquering Christ of Gibson's *Passion*, if film heroes are seen as fully *human* rather than as overwhelmingly superhuman, transcendent, or even divine, then this has theological provenance, as Christian tradition – in particular the Antiochene school of the early Church[1] – holds that only a tainted and even sinful individual can speak to, and be in a position to address the needs of, a tainted and sinful humanity (ibid.). Accordingly, just as Christ can only perform the role of humankind's Redeemer if he has himself undergone what it means to be fully human, so films where the activities of criminals are "at the centre of the narrative" and whose actions are "brutally, vividly and even sympathetically portrayed" (Christianson, 2005, p. 112) can be christologically and theologically rich. Cagney and Robinson's gangsters may not be moral exemplars, in that they tend to die at the end of their films without imparting much in the way of a concrete model as to how we should orient and live our lives, but they nevertheless confront and wrestle with the key challenges and questions that lie at the heart of the human condition in a manner that Gibson's trans-human and celestial protagonist, with his superhuman ability to withstand and transcend unmitigated violence and abuse, is unable to attain. Paradoxically, therefore, the Jesus of *The Passion* is a more distant, alienating, and theologically deficient role model than those dysfunctional and often violent film protagonists whose penchant for wrestling with the age-old struggle between guilt and innocence, salvation and damnation, demonstrates that they embody and live out the very human struggles within which audiences at home are equally immersed.

Rather than suggest, as Medved, Stone, and Fitch are inclined to do, that the portrayal of violence, and violent protagonists, in film is counter-productive, and can only lead audiences to stray and be unable to discern any Christian or theological alternatives to violence, Eric Christianson makes the pertinent point with respect to *The Godfather* that, in portraying the life of Italian Americans "with some dignity and realism," and in its depiction of a "united, convivial and cosy Mafia family," Coppola has "created an inviting aura around criminal life" (Christianson, 2005, p. 114), and one which is not a million miles distinct from the world of the Bible. For, in a no less violent manner, "Lot is prepared to hand over his daughters to certain death to save his skin" and, when a "concubine is left for dead," the Levite "does nothing but gruesomely desecrate her body with a violence that would not pass the censors" (ibid., p. 114). Likewise, King David's promising beginning was "overshadowed and consumed by his violent rise through the echelons of power," in a story of "house against house, the defeat of one family by another" (ibid., p. 121). Christianson continues that David's story is one of

> loyalty, corruption and tragedy through moments of moral weakness. It is a story of Old World values moving inexorably towards an institutionalized form of power. And in the ignoble end (in bed with a concubine probably young enough to be his granddaughter), having lost his son, and lost any moral voice within his family, I am reminded of Michael Corleone's lonely and feeble demise.
>
> (ibid.)

Ironically, therefore, despite the concerns of more conservative critics that Hollywood should refrain from creating films that weaken or debase the moral standards of audience members (in keeping with the ethos of the Hays Code), Christianson asks whether, in the form of Michael Corleone, *The Godfather* offers us "a man that we want to be, or that we can't help being" (ibid., p. 118). Just as the Bible does not necessarily paint the likes of King David and Lot as unblemished or wholly sympathetic protagonists, so it is possible for audiences to empathize, even identify, with film characters precisely because of their intrinsic fallibility and humanity. As Sara Anson Vaux says in relation to the protagonist in *Unforgiven* (Clint Eastwood, 1992), a film which will be explored in more detail in chapter 6, the drawing of William Munny (Clint Eastwood) "is not that of a blameless hero or even a seamless villain but of a deeply conflicted person such as we are, struggling with the need to carry his religious convictions over into his everyday worlds of work and family" (Vaux, 1998, p. 445). In other words, he is just like "one of us," and "a man much like other persons who has tried to shake off his bloody past, admits his sins, clearly understands his past actions as wrong, and takes the consequences of his actions, even his final, bloody ones, on himself" (ibid., p. 446). Is it therefore surprising, in the words of Neil Hurley in the context of American gangster movies and *film noir* from the 1930s and 1940s, "How often we identified with gangsters, criminals, gun molls, and prostitutes in Hollywood films" (Hurley, 1982b, p. 67)?

Concluding Reflections: Christianity as Violence

A film such as *The Godfather* therefore poses an important challenge to theology. Not only can it be counter-productive when filmmakers are asked, in the manner of the Hays Code, to refrain from enabling audiences to sympathize with criminals and acts of violence, it also fails to understand the inextricable link between Christianity and violence, at the heart of which lies the explicitly violent symbol of the Cross. As David John Graham wrote in *Explorations in Theology and Film*, "With a strange irony, the means of redemptive atonement in both the Jewish and Christian traditions involves an act of immense violence," in the form of the "system of animal sacrifice in ancient Judaism, and the figure of Christ on the cross atoning for the sins of the world" (Graham, 1997, p. 91). The violence may have since been "dressed up and softened in church architecture," to the point that it now denotes "a religious symbol of comfort and hope" (ibid., p. 88) rather than the epitome of violence, evil, and suffering, but, as José Míguez Bonino, an Argentinian liberation theologian, sees it, violence can even be elevated to the ultimate principle of creation. In his words, "Only in the destruction of everything that limits him ... can man find his freedom, i.e. his humanity" (qtd in Gill, 2006, p. 259). Therefore, instead of comprising a negative force or a "rupture in harmony," Bonino suggests that violence may be "a positive manifestation of the situation which requires righting" (ibid., p. 260):

> Man is a creator, and creation is always, in some measure, a violence exerted on things as they are. It is an affirmation of the new against "that which is"; it is an eruption that can only make room for itself by exploding the existing systems of integration. Violence plays a creative role in this scheme as the "midwife."
>
> (ibid., p. 259)

In characteristically liberationist language, Bonino thus takes the line that conflict and violence are means by which we are enabled to be freed from those conditions, which might include "slavery, vengeance, arbitrariness, oppression, lack of protection" and "usurpation" (ibid., p. 260), that prevent us from being responsible and autonomous agents, in relation both to other human beings and to God. All attempts to domesticate and water down the violence that lies at the kernel of Christianity are thus theologically misguided, not least because they ignore the extent to which violence may be seen to comprise not simply a destructive and disruptive force but something that is potentially cohesive and redemptive, which – as I have argued elsewhere in relation to *Fight Club* (David Fincher, 1999) and *Raging Bull* (Martin Scorsese, 1980) – manages to reintegrate the alienated and aberrant individual (see Deacy, 2005, pp. 42–7; 68–78).

Despite John Fitch's earlier warning to theologians against formulating injudicious analogies between the New Testament Jesus and cinematic Christ-figures, on the grounds that the violence perpetrated by film characters is at variance with the non-violent proclivities of Jesus in the Gospels, it may actually be the case that the greater the violence on display in film, the greater the Christian parallels and resonances. For example, drawing specifically on *One Flew Over the Cuckoo's Nest* (Milos Forman, 1975), Nicholas Wood has recently argued that the scenes of violence that permeate this picture, in which Jack Nicholson's revolutionary anti-hero, Randle P. McMurphy, does to the inflexible and hypocritical regime of an Oregon mental asylum in the 1960s what Jesus did to the Jerusalem Temple in the first century, makes the analogy with the Christian tradition, and with the person of Christ, stronger rather than more remote. Seeing this as "a helpful corrective to the sentimental portraits of Jesus so beloved of our Victorian forebears who bequeathed to subsequent generations the notion of 'Gentle Jesus, meek and mild'" (Wood, 2005, p. 120), Wood argues that if McMurphy "seems to us an unlikely and even scandalous ideal as some sort of saviour figure, that was precisely how Jesus appeared to many of his contemporaries" (ibid.). Without going so far as to argue that both Jesus and Randle P. McMurphy "behave in identical ways," it is his contention that "there are strong parallels in the way that each in his own context is *perceived*" (ibid., p. 121) by their contemporaries. That is, just as Jesus resisted the narrow orthodoxy of his day, as epitomized in what he saw as the pettiness and double standards of the Pharisees, and challenged his followers to live a life that accorded with the coming Kingdom, "so McMurphy resists the inflexible rules of the institution and challenges the inmates to take their freedom and live life to the full" (ibid., p. 118). However, it is Wood's premise that because of what he terms "our Victorian inheritance," our "public sensibilities are easily shocked when stereotypical and innocuous images of Christ are challenged," and that "it is important to recognize that it is the strong characters, the charismatic personalities, and those people who are challenging, who are the ones who get noticed and who often fall foul of those with a vested interest in maintaining the status quo" (ibid., p. 121).

Rather than antithetical to the Jesus of the New Testament, as Fitch would believe, McMurphy may actually be closer in spirit to the violent and revolutionary Jesus that, for instance, S. G. F. Brandon delineated in his 1967 publication *Jesus and the Zealots*, in which a close association is drawn between Christ and the Zealot movement of the first century. This is also a perspective that strongly informs Martin Scorsese's *Last Temptation of Christ* (1988), in which Jesus is taunted by Judas (Harvey Keitel) over his role as a political Messiah, who will overthrow the Roman conquerors and expel them from Israel, and in which there is an overtly revolutionary dimension to Jesus's ministry. As Jesus says at one point in the film, following the cleansing of the Temple, "I didn't come here to bring peace, I came here to bring a sword." Likewise, knowing that his death is imminent, Jesus pleads with God in the Garden of Gethsemane to let him die not on the Cross but with an axe. In the New Testament, also, although the Jesus presented in the Gospels is what Mark Roncace calls a "socially, economically, politically and militarily powerless figure" who associates with those on the margins of society, in the Book of Revelation "Christ is an exalted, powerful, militant figure who is a conquering warrior-judge and who violently destroys his enemies and inflicts wrathful punishment on them" (Roncace, 2002, p. 282). Fitch's claim that, not least in the Sermon on the Mount, Christ set an example of doing no harm to any other person – "to which all of his followers are subsequently called" (Fitch, 2005, ¶16) – is thus only a partial picture of what is recorded in the New Testament, and overlooks the fact that Jesus is not only a figure of love, peace, humility, kindness, and creativity, but, in respect of Revelation, also embodies and dispenses judgment, violence, power, vengeance, and destruction. When we witness Clint Eastwood's Preacher in *Pale Rider* riding on a horse, tackling "evil" head-on, and administering justice by killing his enemies, what we see is remarkably similar in vision to Revelation 19:11, where the author rejoices that "I saw heaven opened, and behold, a white horse! He who sat upon it is called Faithful and True, and in righteousness he judges and makes war." Even the name "Pale Rider" comes from Revelation, and in the film a young girl reads aloud from a passage from the book that speaks of "a pale horse" and its rider, whose "name was Death," who is given "power over a fourth of the earth, to kill with sword and with famine and with pestilence" (Revelation 6:8). This may not be an interpretation with which Fitch, Stone, and Medved will concur, but it highlights both the political and revolutionary aspect of Christ and the possibility that movie heroes (and anti-heroes) may be Christ-figures precisely *because of* the violence and punishment they mete out.

In broader terms, René Girard has even maintained in his groundbreaking work *Violence and the Sacred* (1977), first published in French in 1972, that the history of religion *per se* is based on violence. The specific context of Girard's argument is that, in religious traditions, violence is characteristically directed against a sacrificial scapegoat, as internal violence and hatred within individuals is transferred by the community at large to an innocent victim. This is in keeping with the Jewish Day of Atonement in which, as we learn from Leviticus 16, the high priest would "lay both his hands upon the head" of a live goat "and confess over him all the iniquities of the people of Israel, and all their transgressions, all their sins," before then sending the goat "away into the wilderness" (Leviticus 16:21). This, then, has the effect of uniting the community and bolstering group solidarity, though at the expense of simply externalizing one's individual demons and "passing the buck." While this is not the place to look at this concept in more detail, it is significant that Lyden draws a link between Girard's ideas and how in many films – especially Westerns, horror, and action movies – this scapegoating motif is prominent, as characters become the scapegoat for our "own violent feelings that are projected upon [them]" (Lyden, 2003, p. 93). As our guilt is projected on to the protagonist, we feel their "guilt and pain as our own" (ibid., p. 92) and are enabled to "experience some sort of catharsis in seeing victims violently sacrificed" (ibid., p. 84). Violence may not be an intrinsically good thing on this reading, but it does show – in a manner which Fitch and Stone do not seem to acknowledge – that "violence" is not some external "other" that stands in stark opposition to the intrinsically "nonviolent" nature and orientation of Christianity, but is an inescapable part of Christianity's origins. Girard does believe, however, that Christianity was the first religion in the ancient world to challenge this concept of scapegoating and atoning violence, through its emphasis on the injustice of Christ's violent death. But there is little leeway here for more conservative-minded Christians, who are so critical of the dangers that violence can engender, to see Christianity as qualitatively different from all other religious traditions. Rather, as Girard points out, even though, as primitive society evolved, humankind gradually drew "away from violence" and eventually lost sight of it, it is not possible for "an actual break with violence" ever to take place – indeed, no sooner has it appeared to go

Figure 4 Sara Anson Vaux and Robert Jewett have offered competing readings of *Unforgiven* (Clint Eastwood, 1992). Is it a film about regeneration through sacrificial love or regeneration through violence?
Photograph: Warner Bros/The Kobal Collection

away than it will "always stage a stunning, catastrophic comeback" (Girard, 1977, p. 307). This may make for uncomfortable reading on the part of those theologians, such as Robert Jewett, for whom there is an innate dichotomy between Christianity's gospel of sacrificial love and the penchant in many contemporary films for preaching the gospel of regeneration through violence (see chapter 6) (figure 4). But, as Sara Anson Vaux sees it, American society itself is "a society born of violence, drenched in blood, and perpetuated by aggression that nonetheless struggles to fold into its body politic democratic ideals, peacemaking, and religious faith" (Vaux, 1998, p. 443), as the heritage of the American Civil War so glaringly testifies. Unless violence is therefore accepted for what it is – an elementary and integral part of theological and religious discourse – then all theological discussions on the theme of violence will continue to be no more than incomplete and devoid of real substance.

Note

1 For more on this, see Deacy, 2001, pp. 81–9.

The Final Verdict:
Theological Perspectives
on Justice and Film

In many respects, this chapter comprises a fitting counterpart to the conversation that was generated in the preceding chapter on violence. As the reference to movie Westerns has evinced, the boundary between the pursuit of violence and the dispensation of justice is often a delicate and permeable one, in which, to cite the example of *Pale Rider* (Clint Eastwood, 1985), a resolutely anti-heroic protagonist takes it upon himself to destroy a malevolent and oppressive federal marshal and his subordinates, as well as the buildings they inhabit, in order to insure that those who are unable to defend themselves are sufficiently recompensed and delivered from corruption, greed, malice, intimidation, and injustice. In the New Testament, also, we learn that St. Paul, prior to his dramatic conversion on the road to Damascus, had no scruples about administering intensive acts of violence in order to secure justice, as demonstrated by the reference in Galatians to his "former life in Judaism," in which "I persecuted the church of God violently and tried to destroy it; and I advanced in Judaism beyond many of my own age among the people, so extremely zealous was I for the traditions of my fathers" (Galatians 1:13–14). In other words, there was an inextricable link for the pre-transformed Paul (or Saul) between militant and violent action and the accomplishment of what is deemed to be a just cause. The fact that in his letter to the Philippians Paul even refers to how he saw his zealous persecution of Christians as "blameless" and as "righteousness under the law" (Philippians 3:6) goes some way toward highlighting the extent

Chris Deacy

to which violence was believed to be an acceptable means of safeguarding the integrity of God's law. The fact that, in the Western genre in particular, the violence that takes place is characteristically construed as having a laudable goal or *telos*, such as the protection of the weakest and most vulnerable members of society, suggests that it is not a million miles distant from the world of the New Testament.

In *Unforgiven* (Clint Eastwood, 1992), for instance, William Munny (Clint Eastwood) is a retired gunslinger and bounty hunter who reluctantly returns to his former life to oppose and root out the injustice that is perpetrated in the town of Big Whiskey, Wyoming, by a corrupt sheriff, Little Bill Daggett (Gene Hackman), a remorseless and sadistic former criminal who dispenses justice with a rod of iron and wreaks personal vengeance on those, such as English Bob (Richard Harris), who dare to challenge his authority. Munny's motives are somewhat ambiguous: having lost his wife to smallpox and struggling to raise his two children on their poverty-stricken Kansas farm, it is the financial incentive of a thousand dollars reward for the capture of two cowboys who mutilated a prostitute ("They cut up her face, cut her eyes out, cut her ears off, hell, they even cut her teats") that drives him to Big Whiskey, and his decision, once there, to fight Little Bill is born out of revenge for the brutal murder by the sheriff and his deputies of his partner, Ned Logan (Morgan Freeman), whose corpse has been ignominiously displayed for all to see in a box outside the saloon. We also learn that Munny's past life is far from noble or heroic. Upon being addressed at one point as "William Munny out of Missouri, killer of women and children," he replies not by rejecting the attribution but by acknowledging, "I've killed just about anything that walked or crawled." The film has also been taken by some theologians to suggest that, unlike the more clear-cut savior-figures that are foregrounded in more traditional Westerns, such as the Preacher in *Pale Rider* or Alan Ladd's protagonist in *Shane* (George Stevens, 1953), who, we are led to believe, are more at peace with themselves and have retired back into the sunset with some satisfaction at having achieved their valiant objectives, this film lacks a discernible moral vision. In Peter Francis's words, "There is no riding tall in this film, no noble cause and William Munny returns with the bounty money, not forgiven and redeemed but *unforgiven*" (Francis, 2005, p. 196). Nevertheless, there is a certain "moral balance, in which good eventually silences evil" (Ebert, 2002), that lies at the heart of *Unforgiven*, as betokened by Munny's warning to those who stood idly by and gave sanctuary to those responsible for the mutilation of the prostitute – "You'd better not cut up or otherwise harm no whore, or I'll come back and kill every one of you sons of bitches." No matter how ambiguous his motives or how limited the satisfaction he achieves at the end – as Francis sees it, "We can say that in the film he never finds redemption" (Francis, 2005, p. 197) – Munny's struggle to redeem a violent past is not without theological significance, succeeding as it does in raising vital questions about the compromises and limitations – even inadequacies – of human justice.

Justice and Regeneration through Violence

This is not to say, however, that all theologians and critics have interpreted *Unforgiven* in this way. Robert Jewett, for example, has presented a scathing indictment of Eastwood's film, which, he argues, invites audiences "to solve its problems by shooting down its sheriffs and placing truck bombs in front of its federal buildings" (Jewett, 1999, p. 149). Linking the ideology of regeneration through violence that permeates *Unforgiven* with the Oklahoma bombing of 1995, in which the federal building in Oklahoma City was truck-bombed by those who believed that an iniquitous political and economic system, with its brutal and corrupt governmental agents, was in need of violent redemption,[1] Jewett blames "the scenes of violence in popular culture" – not least in *Unforgiven* – for inspiring "contemporary militias and neo-Nazis" to carry out their activities in the same way that, in St. Paul's day, Jewish zealots "were following the heroic examples of Phineas and the Maccabees" (ibid., p. 156). Contemporary films are littered with this motif of regeneration through violence, from superhero movies such as *Batman Begins* (Christopher Nolan, 2005) to police dramas such as *CopLand* (James Mangold, 1997), whose portrait of a corrupt New York City police force that is obliterated in a violent bloodbath at the picture's denouement could be construed as a modern-day Western, even if instead of Eastwood's morally ambiguous bounty hunter we have Sylvester Stallone playing an honorable, albeit reticent, county sheriff who, after much prevarication, wipes out the unjust upholders of the law by gunfire and the shedding of blood. Jewett counters this, however, with the argument that Jesus's understanding of justice took a wholly different form, entailing love and the requirement to understand one's enemy and to submit to unjust authorities (such as Rome), rather than resort to the use of zealous force (which he believes Jesus has thereby rendered obsolete). The fact that God raised Jesus from the dead is sufficient proof for Jewett that Jesus's refusal "to play the role of the militant messiah" (ibid., p. 150), and his concomitant espousal of a non-violent form of justice, were sanctioned by God. Despite Clint Eastwood's own attestation, at the time *Unforgiven* won the Academy Award for Best Picture in March 1993, that the film "preaches that it isn't glamorous to kill people, it's not beautiful, and I think that's very current on people's minds today" (qtd in ibid., p. 159), Jewett feels that this apologia does not go far enough to allay the suspicion that, in *Unforgiven*, those who dispense justice by carrying out violence are "depicted as true heroes" (ibid.) all the same, since there is no ultimate conversion from the path of violence to non-violence.

In marked contrast, Sara Anson Vaux, in a dialogue with Jewett in the summer 1998 edition of the journal *Christianity and Literature*, suggests that the opposite of this may be true. Violence may be an anathema in Jewett's eyes to the ability to attain or dispense justice, but Vaux argues for a more nuanced interpretation of *Unforgiven* that exposes the horrors of violence and death while simultaneously celebrating the power of love to heal and restore. Rather than a glamorizing of violence and a pointing away from justice, Vaux suggests that a conversion experience lies at the heart of Eastwood's film. Munny may inflict violence at the end of the picture, in the shootout that conforms to what Jewett sees as the myth of regenerative violence – and the fact, moreover, that Munny shoots dead a number of unarmed men would certainly go some way toward bolstering Jewett's thesis – but Munny does so "in the name of a justice that transcends Little Bill's petty tyranny" (Vaux, 1998, p. 453). Impelled by the love of his late wife, Claudia, who, Munny explains, "cured me of drinkin' and wickedness," even the return to his old ways at the end of the film has as its goal not greed or the love of killing but the wish to provide financially for his two young children. As he explains to his friend, Ned (Morgan Freeman), "I seen the error of my ways ... the sins of my youth," and "Just cause we're goin' on this killing, that don't mean I'm going back to being the way I was." Despite his reputation as a "known thief and murderer, a man of notoriously vicious and intemperate disposition," as we learn from the caption that appears on the screen at the end of *Unforgiven*, Claudia continues to transform William Munny from beyond the grave and has instilled in him the ability to reflect on the value of a life that is cancelled out by death. In Vaux's words, "This is a film of great spiritual richness and physical beauty that dares to turn ideas about justice upside down, that asks again and again when if ever we need to kill, and that insists throughout that as flawed human beings we must and can be redeemed by love" (ibid., p. 455). The quest for purity and justice and the radical nature of forgiveness (in marked contrast to Francis's reading that Munny is ultimately unforgiven and unredeemed) that underscores what Vaux thinks about this film is not, therefore, one at odds with the Christian understanding of sacrificial love in the way that Jewett describes. Rather than continue the cycle of regenerative violence, *Unforgiven* raises the possibility that violence comes at a heavy price. The film gives rise to the possibility that violence, although it may be a precursor to the attainment of justice in a squalid, sinful, and unjust universe, has no ultimate or intrinsic value or worth.

In examining the theme of justice, therefore, it is apparent that a range of – often competing – theological perspectives are in play. On a superficial level, it might be expected that a chapter on this topic would be likely to concentrate on those films that explicitly delineate and wrestle with the theme of justice, in the manner, for example, of a courtroom thriller. After all, as the titles alone of such John Grisham adaptations as *The Firm* (Sydney Pollack, 1993), *The Pelican Brief* (Alan J. Pakula, 1993), *The Client* (Joel Schumacher, 1994), *The Chamber* (James Foley, 1996), and *Runaway Jury* (Gary Fleder, 2003) all suggest, films have long been in the business of grappling with questions of truth, justice, integrity, and the law-making process. The qualification must be made, of course, that many such films have arisen from popular law fiction, and so it may be stretching the point somewhat to imply that they were created specifically because Hollywood producers have or had an explicit interest in exploring justice in American society *per se*. But there are a number of notable instances where Hollywood has grappled sincerely and unpretentiously with this theme. Most memorably, the adaptation in 1962 of Harper Lee's Pulitzer Prize-winning novel *To Kill a Mockingbird* (Robert Mulligan), in which Gregory Peck's Atticus Finch defends a black man who is accused of raping a white woman in a racially divided Alabama town in the 1930s, together with *Judgment at Nuremberg* (Stanley Kramer, 1961), in which four German judges who used their offices to administer Nazi sterilization and cleansing policies during the Third Reich are put on trial for crimes against humanity, have, whether fictionalized or not, managed to touch on issues that have a strong social, political, and legal resonance. Moreover, they comprise earnest attempts to document on celluloid questions that are far from the province of the theologian, concerning as they do matters pertaining to human pride, prejudice, jealousy, sin, ignorance, intolerance, vindictiveness, and the concomitant limitations of obtaining natural justice. The same could even be said of the aforementioned Grisham adaptations, which characteristically portray materially obsessed, unscrupulous lawyers who are transformed by suffering and destitution into selfless, humble, and more responsible individuals who cherish the joys of the families and friendships they had hitherto spurned. However, a far wider scope is required if a judicious theological conversation is able to take place than one that merely runs through a check-list of films that ostensibly (and superficially) deal with the law, and this chapter will attempt in this regard to scrutinize the broader theological tapestry before focusing on one or two films that might best be found to illustrate some of the processes at work.

Theological Models of Justice in Film: *Mishpat* and *Sedakah*

In his 1994 novel *Disclosure*, which was turned into a commercially successful film later that year by Barry Levinson, starring Michael Douglas and Demi Moore, Michael Crichton depicts a sexual discrimination case between Tom Sanders, a happily married and high-flying computer engineer at Digicom Corporation, and his ex-girlfriend, Meredith Johnson, who has just joined the firm's Seattle-based operations as his superior. Upon discovering that Johnson's appointment is a ruse to get him fired, Sanders engages the services of a civil rights lawyer, Louise Fernandez, who sympathizes with his predicament, but advises him that his chances of winning the discrimination case are remote, and that, if he brings a lawsuit, "you'll never work in this industry again. I know it's not supposed to work that way, but as a practical matter, you'll never be hired for another job. That's just how it goes. It would be one thing if you were fifty-five. But you're forty-one. I don't know if you want to make that choice, at this point in your life" (Crichton, 1994, p. 168). Slumping back in his chair in despondency, Sanders responds, "But it's so unjust," to which Fernandez retorts: "Unfortunately, the law has nothing to do with justice, Mr. Sanders . . . It's merely a method for dispute resolution" (ibid.). While a work of fiction, Fernandez's almost throwaway remark – which is uttered between the acts of putting on a raincoat and snapping her briefcase shut while in the process of hurriedly leaving her office – gets to the nub of the matter: no matter how many films (or for that matter novels) address legal questions, there are wider issues at stake, which the theologian should overlook at his or her peril. Important though the theme of justice is in the Bible, not least in the following quotation from Micah 6:8 – "He has showed you, O man, what is good; and what does the Lord require of you but to do justice, and to love kindness, and to walk humbly with your God?" – it is apparent that the question of how to go about "doing justice," and applying this injunction in practice, is fraught with difficulties. In broad outline, there are two (Hebrew) words for justice in the Old Testament:[2] *mishpat*, which refers to particular and specific duties and responsibilities that must be adhered to within the context of a life lived in covenant in God, and *sedakah*, which looks at the overall picture of what a culture does (see Lebacqz, 1998, p. 167), again within a transcendent context. The former bears the closer resemblance to our modern understanding of the law, in that it tends to examine individual issues and the necessary rules and regulations, so that a specific action is either right or wrong, just or unjust. In the case of *To Kill a Mockingbird*, this understanding of justice would enter into the specifics of whether Tom Robinson (Brock Peters) was guilty or not guilty of raping Mayella Violet Ewell (Collin Wilcox). The fact that the justice system is portrayed in the film as defective, in that an all-white jury, even when presented with persuasive evidence that the black defendant is innocent of the crime, nevertheless sees fit to condemn him, would not be the relevant consideration here. Any wider issues about the inadequacies of the law to dispense justice would come under the remit of *sedakah*, which is seen to be the all-encompassing and ultimate fountain of justice, from which all particular judgments must derive, in the spirit of the prophet Amos, who issued the call to Israel to "Let justice roll down like waters, and righteousness like an everflowing stream" (Amos 5:24), thereby sweeping away all iniquities. The fact that injustices are perpetrated say more, on this theological understanding, about human frailty and sin than about any intrinsic fault in the ethical and legal framework that shapes and drives the universe.

The Two Cities: Heavenly vs. Earthly Justice

Accordingly, issues of good and bad, right and wrong, justice and injustice, are vitally important considerations, but, theologically speaking, there will always be a distinction (indeed, a fissure) between divine and earthly justice – that is, between the principles of justice and the imperfect ways in which justice is administered by humans on earth. This opposition can be found to lie at the very kernel of Augustine's *City of God*, which identifies the person of faith as akin to a "pilgrim in a foreign land, away from God" (Augustine in Gill, 2006, p. 117); earthly rules and justice have their place, but only in a transitory and ephemeral sense. Important though it is to avail oneself of earthly laws – in Augustine's words, the person of faith should "not hesitate to obey the laws of the earthly city by which those things that are designed for the support of this mortal life are regulated" (Augustine in ibid., p. 120) – only heavenly, or divine, justice possesses definitive and integral value. Divine justice does not annul earthly justice *per se*, but earthly justice only has value insofar as "no hindrance is presented thereby" to divine justice and to what Augustine calls "the religion which teaches that the one supreme and true God is to be worshipped" (Augustine in ibid., p. 121). Although the Church is in the world, it is not of the world, and, for Augustine, only at the Last Day will this tension be resolved. The downside here, however, is that, as Gill puts it, "The pilgrim status of Christians effectively means that they may simply have to endure injustice rather than attempt to change it" (Gill, 2006, p. 121). Indeed, individual Christians, on this interpretation, are not persuaded to oppose injustice, in any of its multiple manifestations, whether slavery, oppression, racism, intolerance, bullying, sexism, or any form of physical or mental abuse. Rather, they are expected to tolerate and suffer it, and simply "wait for the time when 'God is all in all'" (ibid.).

In more recent times, William Temple wrote in 1941, shortly before becoming archbishop of Canterbury, that

> it is sometimes supposed that what the Church has to do is sketch a perfect social order and urge men to establish it. But it is very difficult to know what a "perfect social order" means. Is it the order that would work best if we were all perfect? Or is it the order that would work best in a world of men and women such as we actually are? If it is the former, it certainly ought not to be established; we should wreck it in a fortnight. If it is the latter, there is no reason for expecting the Church to know what it is.
>
> (Temple in Gill, 2006, p. 165)

In keeping with Augustine's distinction between the "two cities," Temple distinguished between "men as they are" and "men as they ought to be" (ibid.), and was concerned that, as they are still on a journey toward "what they ought to be," any attempt to establish a political or legal system that assumes that human beings have already reached their end-goal, and are on the brink of living in the Kingdom, "will involve certain failure and disaster" (ibid.). For, without even going so far as to claim that "men are utterly bad" (ibid.) or even that "they are more bad than good" (ibid.), Temple affirmed that the bottom line is that "they are not perfectly good, and that even their goodness is infected with a quality – self-centredness – which partly vitiates it, and exposes them to temptations so far as they achieve either freedom or power" (ibid.).

The Vicissitudes of Earthly Justice

On this reading, the Church's primary aim may be to *be* the Body of Christ in the world and to uphold the dignity of all human beings, but, as Charlene Burns affirms, worldly institutions are necessarily "made up of individual human agents within a specific cultural matrix" (Burns, 2004, ¶17). As a consequence of this, there will always be occasions in which members of the Body of Christ will seek to "promote the aims of the societal environment" and to be "influenced by personal and societal agendas" (ibid.) instead of ushering in the Kingdom. Citing the example of *Mystic River* (Clint Eastwood, 2003), Burns suggests that as these secondary, human-oriented agendas "feed back onto the agendas" of the Church's "primary aims," it is possible for the institution of the Church – in the context of this film, the Roman Catholic Church in Boston – to "become complicit in social evil" (ibid.). In the film, we witness Jimmy and Annabeth Markum (Sean Penn and Laura Linney) attending Church as proud parents, when their youngest daughter, Sara (Jillian Wheeler), celebrates her first mass. For Burns, however, "Were the Church adequately manifesting its primary aims in the world," we would expect to see "the emotion attached to this spiritual event" spilling over into "a lived spirituality for these people" (ibid., ¶18), so that there would be a sense in which they were seen to be living out a Christian ethic. In reality, although Jimmy does appear to feel guilt at having committed murder, it is only guilt for having killed the wrong man rather than for murder *per se*, and Annabeth is even a willing co-conspirator, refusing as she does to let her husband feel any remorse for what he has done, and demanding, moreover, Lady Macbeth-style, that he must channel his energy into putting his family's vested interests over and above the stipulations of the law (and, by implication, those of the Church). As Burns puts it, "The Eucharist is for these people nothing more than a rite of passage," and thereby the primary aims of the Church in offering communion have been so infected with sin "that they no longer operate to make Christ a felt-presence" (ibid.).

On a superficial level, therefore, while it is demonstrably the case that Christian images and symbols have been adopted by our culture – and the fact that Jimmy has tattooed on his back a large Christian cross is further evidence that this is so – its *substance* has not, leading Burns to issue the warning that Christianity "verges on moral bankruptcy" (ibid., ¶19). This is not wholly distinct from the scenario in *Unforgiven* where the prostitutes who put up the reward money to avenge the mutilation of one of their number are required to seek justice outside of the inescapably corrupt lawmaking agencies of Big Whiskey, in the form of an external deliverer. Munny and his cohorts may not be able to offer even a partial embodiment, in Jewett's eyes, of Christian justice through self-sacrificial love, but since, as Vaux succinctly puts it, "Neither society nor the Church provides them with better rescue" (Vaux, 1998, p. 446), their desire for retributive justice is an inevitable (if not condonable) reaction to an existing structure of sin, suffering, and powerlessness. On the positive side, however, Burns takes some comfort from the end-scene of *Mystic River*, in which a police detective – "cultural symbol of the good" (Burns, 2004, ¶20) – and former schoolfriend of Jimmy, played by Kevin Bacon, is seen not only to suspect Jimmy of murder but, in squeezing the imaginary trigger of a gun that is pointed at Jimmy, to hold out the possibility of bringing him to justice. Whatever the violent connotations are of wielding a gun, this was the instrument used by Jimmy to torture and brutally murder his latest victim, and, in Burns's words, "We are left with the visual promise that striving for justice has not ceased" (ibid., ¶21). As with *Unforgiven*, therefore, the longing for justice ultimately transcends the specific means by which that yearning is manifest and understood. A solid ethical structure could thus be said to undergird both films, which delineate violence with the express intention of re-enforcing both the dignity and sanctity of human life, whereby the act of killing – though in itself an evil – can be a necessary, even inevitable, prelude to justice and to what Vaux refers to as a leaning "toward light and peace" (Vaux, 1998, p. 452).

Toward a Synthesis of the Two Cities:
Snow Falling on Cedars and *The Verdict*

Similar motifs are in evidence in *Snow Falling on Cedars* (Scott Hicks, 1999), a film set in the early 1950s in the aftermath of World War II on an isolated island in the Pacific northwest, and which, like *To Kill a Mockingbird*, addresses the issue of racism. With the memories of Pearl Harbor still fresh among this close-knit and mistrustful community, Kazuo Miyamoto (Rick Yune), a Japanese American soldier (a decorated American war hero, no less) stands trial for the murder of a local, well-liked, white fisherman, and – despite genuine ambivalence in the evidence against him – looks set to be found guilty by his white jurors. As David Guterson suggests in his 1995 novel on which the film was based, there are limitations to fathoming any form of justice within such an environment, constrained as it is by surrounding waters, which imposed upon islanders certain duties and conditions foreign to mainlanders... There was no blending into an anonymous background, no neighbouring society to shift toward. Islanders were required, by the very nature of their landscape, to watch their step moment by moment. No one trod easily upon the emotions of another where the sea licked everywhere against an endless shoreline.

(Guterson, 1995, p. 385)

For this world – "whose inhabitants walked in trepidation, in fear of opening up" (ibid.) – is one that, as Miyamoto's worldly-wise, septuagenarian lawyer Nels Gudmundsson (played in the film by Max von Sydow) attests in his powerful closing summation, is steeped in "the same human frailty passed from generation to generation... We hate one another; we are the victims of irrational fears. And there is nothing in the stream of human history to suggest we are going to change this" (ibid., p. 368). The film's courtroom, indeed, could be said to epitomize humanity's flawed attempt to discern right from wrong, to distinguish between justice and injustice, and to impose order and intelligibility within a universe where "indifferent forces... ceaselessly conspire towards injustice" (ibid.).

However, this need not be the end of the matter. A suitable analogy here is with the Book of Ecclesiastes in the Old Testament, whose author, Qoheleth, paints a picture of human history as an endless, predetermined cyclical process in which we are at the mercy of forces beyond our control – "What is crooked cannot be made straight, and what is lacking cannot be numbered" (Eccl. 1:15) – and in which "the fate of the sons of men and the fate of beasts is the same; as one dies, so dies the other... all are from the dust, and all turn to dust again" (Eccl. 3:19–20). Despite such a bleak and cynical perspective, however, which correlates with Gudmundsson's vision of life, Qoheleth believes that we need not thereby be entirely without hope. For, provided that we are free from all illusions about life's capriciousness and acknowledge the prescribed limitations of our existence, there is no reason why we cannot appreciate and enjoy our good fortune if and when it comes and to strive to make the best of this life in all its apparent inscrutability and lack of justice. Indeed, rather than withdraw from life, Qoheleth sees life as the only jewel that humans possess, and so the onus is on us to live as authentically as possible – only by living life can any value, transitory though that might be, be ascribed to it. In Qoheleth's words, "if a man lives many years, let him rejoice in them all" (Eccl. 11:8). Similarly, in *Snow Falling on Cedars*, despite all the signs to the contrary, Gudmundsson issues a plea to the 12 members of the jury that, although "There are things in this universe that we cannot control," their response should not be one of simply yielding and giving in "to a universe in which things go awry by happen-stance" (Guterson, 1995, p. 367). Rather, "in the face of such a world you have only yourselves to rely on. You have only the decision you must make, each of you, alone. And will you contribute to . . . injustice? Or will you stand up against this endless tide and in the face of it be truly human?" (ibid., p. 368).

No matter how much fate, coincidence, accident, chaos, caprice, and arbitrariness conspire to prevent true justice from being realized on earth, there is thus a clear sense in which, in the spirit of Ecclesiastes, *Snow Falling on Cedars* is infused with a certain optimism and, even, a hunger for justice, which its ostensible subject matter might not readily evince. While, on the surface, the film would appear to be a courtroom drama, whose raison d'être is to ascertain the guilt or innocence of a man charged with bludgeoning another man to death in his fishing boat late one stormy night, a closer inspection would suggest that the film is concerned more with extrapolating from our somewhat limited and defective apprehension of the whys and wherefores of the universe a deeper sense of *sedakah*. It is not the individual case that is important – indeed, for the protagonists in this film, there are wider issues concerning loss, prejudice, and identity (both personal and ethnic) that, if anything, overshadow the nuts-and-bolts issue of whether Miyamoto is guilty of murder.

In this respect, the film much resembles Sidney Lumet's courtroom thriller *The Verdict* (1982), in which what on paper would appear to comprise an open-and-shut drama concerning the culpability of the surgeons at a Boston hospital who administered the wrong anesthetic to a relatively healthy young woman while she was in the process of giving birth to her third child, thereby putting her in a permanent vegetative state, becomes a much deeper treatise on the vagaries of truth and justice, and the ability to dispense justice in a world where justice is inextricably confused with power, authority, and rhetoric. The fact that it is a disheveled, incapacitated, washed-out, ambulance-chasing lawyer, Frank Galvin (Paul Newman), who has lost all four of the cases he has fought in the previous three years, who embarks on what appears to be a futile and naïve crusade against injustice, in the form of the Catholic archdiocese that finances the hospital, adds a degree of gravitas and depth to what could so easily have been a routine, procedural legal thriller (figure 5).

Although Galvin stands to gain $70,000 in agreeing to settle out of court – which he concedes is a generous offer, and in what is his first offer of employment in 18 months – he turns the money down on the grounds that, in settling out of court, "no one will know the truth" and because he

Figure 5 Ambulance-chasing lawyer Frank Galvin (Paul Newman) embarks on a heartfelt crusade against injustice in *The Verdict* (Sidney Lumet, 1982), a film that explores the inescapable tensions between *mishpat* and *sedakah*.
Photograph: 20th Century-Fox/The Kobal Collection

wants to do "the right thing." Speaking of "the long road which has no turning," he takes the line that if he accepts the money he will be lost – "I'll just be a rich ambulance chaser. I can't do it, I can't take it" – even though, in taking this principled line, he is acting against the wishes of the patient's family, who have not even been consulted on his proposed course of action. In the course of the film, circumstances conspire against Galvin – his key witnesses all disappear, he finds out that his girlfriend, Laura Fischer (Charlotte Rampling), has betrayed his confidence as she is covertly working for the defense attorney, and the presiding magistrate is biased, leading to one pivotal courtroom scene in which an enraged Galvin, having just had his latest witness's testimony dismissed, chides Judge Hoyle (Milo O'Shea): "Your Honor, with all due respect, if you're going to try my case for me I wish you wouldn't lose it." Even when Galvin plays his trump card, in proving at the trial that the patient's admission form was doctored to cover the fact that she had eaten only an hour before her fateful operation, thereby implicating the surgeons at the St. Catherine Labouré Hospital, who should have waited a further eight hours before administering the anesthetic, his opposite number, Edward Concannon (James Mason), comes up with a legal precedent for not accepting the evidence because it is presented on a photocopied form. The judge agrees, and instructs the jury to disregard this entire testimony – to strike it from their minds and accord it no weight. In short, Galvin has put everything on the line. As he defiantly, albeit with an air of resignation, attests at one point to his confidant (and mentor), Mickey Morrisey (Jack Warden), "There are no other cases; this is *the* case."

In many respects, Galvin's understanding of justice is permeated with a strong sacramental dimension, in accordance with the discussion in chapter 1 of Niebuhr's Catholic, synthetic model of the relationship between Christ and culture, in which human culture is believed to be incomplete and in need of fulfillment from a higher, transcendent reality. Just as the likes of Anker, Greeley, and Blake have argued that there is scope for seeing in the face of a film character something of God's grace, and that the secular realm (in all its dysfunctionality) can disclose a spiritual and transcendental reality, so Galvin puts his faith – faltering and tentative though it is – in an ultimate and higher justice (that of *sedakah*, no less) that is not deflected by the vicissitudes and precariousness of human existence. Within Roman Catholicism, indeed, justice is believed to be grounded in natural law, which means that it is accessible not only to Christians but to every human being by virtue of our "nature" as "reasonable" creatures (see Lebacqz, 1998, p. 163), broken and impaired, yet created in God's image and comprising in our very essence a spark of the divine. On this basis, justice is a virtue to be cultivated (see ibid., p.169), and not a vessel for the promulgation of human-centered initiatives in the manner of the legal philosophy espoused in the film by Galvin's unctuous counterpart Ed Concannon – who is at one point categorized by Morrisey as "the prince of fucking darkness" – which is that one is not paid to do one's best, one is paid to win. We may never get to the root of truth and justice, in a world where human pride, jealousy, and materialism are inclined to thwart "natural justice," but that does not mean the human dispensation of justice should be conducted without conscience.

Rather, in keeping with the Catholic understanding that justice is a virtue to be cultivated within each person, and is fulfilled and completed by the "heavenly city" that drives earthly justice forward, Galvin's closing summation, much like that of Ned Gudmundsson in *Snow Falling on*

Cedars, amounts to an overtly theological rallying-cry, referring as it does to how so much of the time human beings are "lost" and "need God to tell us what is right, tell us what is true." In spite of the fact that, in a manner analogous to that of the "realism" of Ecclesiastes, Galvin declares there is no discernible justice in the world – "the rich win, the poor are power-less," leading us to "become weak" and to "doubt ourselves and our beliefs and institutions, and the law" – and in an age where "we are lost and need God to tell us what's right and true," he exhorts the 12 members of the jury to see the wider picture. Rejecting the province and scope of the law as merely comprising "some book," or a bunch of "lawyers," a "marble statue or the trappings of the court," which, for him, are merely "symbols of our desire to be just," Galvin beseeches them to understand that, "today, you, the jury, are the law," and that, "In my religion, they say 'act as if ye had faith, and faith will be given to you.' If we are to have faith in justice we need only to believe in ourselves, and act with justice. I believe there is justice within our hearts."

The force of this testimony is all the more remarkable when it is read (or, rather, heard) in conjunction with the equivalent scene in the novel by Barry Reed, a Boston lawyer who specialized in medical legal cases, on which *The Verdict* is based. Whereas in Lumet's film, Galvin is so convinced that he has lost the case that he has given up trying to win by appealing to evidence – there are, simply, no avenues left open to him, and his appeal to *sedakah* is sincere and authentic – in Reed's novel, first published in 1980, he is a more venal figure, and every bit the moral equal of Concannon. In lieu of the appeal to *sedakah*, in the novel Galvin is playing a legal game with the jury, appealing to their consciences as part of a skillful and calculated strategy of making his testimony more heart-felt, and the case thereby more winnable, than those of his legal counter-part. There is no appeal to transcendent or divine forces – Reed's Galvin is too enmeshed in the legal establishment and too consumed by worldly pursuits to confront the nature of his fallen self, and to want to seek redemption. In this respect, he is not a million miles away from the protagonist in Gregory Hoblit's *Primal Fear* (1996), a self-serving, publi-city-hungry, Machiavellian lawyer, Martin Vail (Richard Gere), who con-strues the courtroom as "his church, his Roman Colosseum, the arena where all his knowledge and cunning were adrenalised" (Diehl, 1992, p. 113). As William Diehl puts it, in the novel that inspired the film, "It was here he really came alive, his energy and brain fuelled by the challenge of law; to attack its canons, dogma, precepts, its very structure, as he invoked the jury to accept his concept of truth" (ibid.).

In the film version of *The Verdict*, in marked contrast, Galvin is aware of his own transgressions and sincerely beseeches God for forgiveness. In this respect, there is more than a glimmer of what Paul Giles calls "that old Catholic paradox whereby the rank black sinner, the person who is horribly aware of the awful potential of damnation, can be closer to redemptive grace than the honest citizen who has never troubled himself about anything beyond his or her own domestic affairs" (Giles, 1992, p. 332). In Reed's novel, Galvin's outlook is much more parochial, as shown when he informs the jury that "if we can't get justice in the courtroom, then we might as well give up. If we can't get it here, there's no place in the world we can get it" (Reed, 1982, p. 258). Lumet's Galvin has already given up by this stage. He genuinely believes the case is lost, and his final entreaty to the jury to "act with justice" stems from his despondency and dejection about the possibility of the instruments of earthly justice delivering a judicious verdict. Reed's Galvin, however, who is fully contaminated with, and intoxicated by, the trappings of worldly justice, may ask the right questions – "What is the value of human life? What is a good life worth?" (ibid., p. 260) – but the only reason "Galvin was on fire" and "The jury felt the heat" is because, as we learn in the novel, "he had to assess money damages," and he does not want to "lose the momentum" (ibid.). In both the novel and the film, Galvin wins his malpractice suit, but so remarkable is the verdict when it is presented in the film – Galvin is already resigned to yet another failure, yet the jury hold for the plaintiff and against the doctors, and even ask the judge to let them award more in damages than the $210,000 that had earlier been offered – that justice comes across as, if not the work of divine intervention, then surely the outpouring of divine grace.

Concluding Remarks

Although there are a number of different perspectives between Protestant and Roman Catholic theologians when it comes to questions of justice and the law – inasmuch as Catholics are inclined to lay stress on the faculties of natural law and conscience, based on the ability of human reason to arrive at ethical wisdom and knowledge, while for Protestants it is biblical texts that are the dominant framework within which justice can be fathomed – both understand justice to be grounded in "God's creating, redeeming, and sustaining acts" (Lebacqz, 1998, p. 167). If, theologically, justice is primarily determined by God, and requires humans as part of the fulfillment of the demands of relationship (and as "the human response of gratitude for these great gifts" [ibid.]) to insure that human justice should reflect divine justice, then Lumet's screen version of *The Verdict* is a prime example of a Christian understanding of *sedakah*. In Reed's novel, as well as so many cinematic courtroom thrillers, exposing the machinations of justice is the pivotal and overarching consideration, in the vein of *Jagged Edge* (Richard Marquand, 1985) – in which the all-important question is whether Jack Forrester (Jeff Bridges), a powerful San Francisco publisher, viciously murdered his wife, an heiress, and will commit the same crime against his lawyer (and girlfriend), Teddy Barnes (Glenn Close) – and *Suspect* (Peter Yates, 1987), in which Cher's crusading lawyer, Kathleen Riley, is assigned to defend a homeless, deaf, and mute Vietnam veteran who is accused of murdering a Washington legal secretary. A straight-forward dichotomy is set up between who is "good" and "bad" and who is "just" and "unjust," and it is the duty of the protagonist to ascertain the truth. In Lumet's film, however, the remit is much wider, and justice is concerned more with restoring right relationships in a way that goes beyond merely dispensing justice in accordance with a pre-established, human-oriented legal system, which, as St. Augustine put it, "is related to the enjoyment of earthly peace in the earthly city" (in Gill, 2006, p. 116). As Galvin is told at one point by his discredited "expert" witness, "Sometimes people can surprise you. Sometimes they have a great capacity to hear the truth." A film such as *The Verdict* can therefore not merely go some way toward challenging the artificial sacred–secular divide, but disclose more about theological perspectives on justice than we can learn from theological texts alone. Perhaps Sidney Lumet could even be said to possess a no less rigorous understanding than Augustine of how to delineate the dispensation (or lack thereof) of justice in a defective and fallen world.

Notes

1   A more recent example would, of course, be the terrorist attacks on the Twin Towers of the World Trade Center on September 11, 2001.
2   An excellent discussion of these two interpretations of justice can be found in Karen Lebacqz's chapter in Bernard Hoose's *Christian Ethics: An Introduction* (1998), pp. 163–72.

Dark Beauty: Theological Perspectives on War as Cinematic Mythology

> I learned early on that war forms its own culture. It is peddled by mythmakers –
> historians, war correspondents, filmmakers, novelists and the state – all of
> whom endow it with qualities it often does possess: excitement, exoticism,
> power, chances to rise above our small stations in life, and a bizarre and fantastic
> universe that has a grotesque and dark beauty.
>
> Hedges, 2002, p. 3

This chapter begins with an attempt to define the genre of the war film; because it is such a ubiquitous aspect of popular film, there are different ways of categorizing it. But a question to engage our thinking when addressing this genre is: what makes a war film also a film about peace? Are the two inextricable as concepts, as the title of the eponymous Tolstoy novel suggests, or can we have a film about war that completely excludes any possible reading of peace? Are there, conversely, films about peace that in their style and theme have nothing to say about the nature of war?

There are other thoughts that come to mind when considering the war film: how does film portray changes in the ideology of war? Films that bring a contemporary spin to wars of the past present us with the question of authenticity and fictionalization of historical events. Have Vietnam war films created a cinematic legacy for filmmakers who attempt to portray the Gulf/Iraq wars of the past two decades? With Hollywood's propensity for delineating fanaticism, fundamentalism, and jingoism, has there been

 Gaye Ortiz

a shift in emphasis in popular film since the events of September 11 from the "old-fashioned" war to the "war on terror"? What part does the resurgence of documentary filmmaking play in this?

More questions surface, couched in theological terms. What religious baggage do we carry with us when we watch war films, and how do we assess the contribution that religion and theology have made to the waging of war in today's world? Has there been a shift in the Christian perception of the "just war," the philosophical justification for Christians to wage war famously articulated by St. Augustine? How does the world react to the recent Islamist fundamentalist declarations of a "holy war"? How do films about war and peace affect our thinking about the morality or necessity of war, and do they help us visualize a peaceful world or only obsess about violence and death?

Genre

This chapter can only refer to a tiny percentage of war films; there have been many films about war but, in addition to being about war, they belong to many other genres as well. For example, the silent film *The General* (Clyde Bruckman and Buster Keaton, 1927) is not only a film about the American Civil War; additionally it is a love story and a comedy. *The Great Dictator* (Charles Chaplin, 1940), *M*A*S*H* (Robert Altman, 1970), and *Good Morning, Vietnam* (Barry Levinson, 1987) also fall into the comedy genre. As discussed later in this chapter, the documentary genre has found fertile ground in the conflicts of the Middle East of the past two decades. Neil Sinyard offers the definitive characteristics of the genre: "The great war films seem to be those which express a hatred of war, and pity for the young men whose lives will be sacrificed" (Sinyard, 1985, p. 99). He gives two examples, *All Quiet on the Western Front* (Lewis Milestone, 1930) and *Ashes and Diamonds* (Andrej Wajda, 1958, from his "Trilogy," 1955–8). Clint Eastwood, with his companion films *Flags of Our Fathers* and *Letters from Iwo Jima* (both 2006), adds to this body of work, asking tough questions that pertain to all wars about the nature of heroism and the sacrifice of young lives for political ends.

And even as we recognize the genre's enduring themes of heroism, sacrifice, and suffering, the role of satire in reminding us of the futility and waste of human life of waging war should not be forgotten, in such films as *How I Won the War* (Richard Lester, 1967) and *Dr. Strangelove Or: How I Learned to Stop Worrying and Love the Bomb* (Stanley Kubrick, 1964).

Science fiction has also relied on war as a vehicle, recently in the Tom Cruise remake of *The War of the Worlds* (Steven Spielberg, 2005); the lack of understanding between aliens and humans inevitably, it seems, culminates in these films with a battle to dominate Planet Earth (or the galaxy, universe, etc.). Popular anime films, such as *Howl's Moving Castle* (Hayao Miyazaki, 2004) and especially the poignant *Grave of the Fireflies* (Isao Takahata, 1988), demonstrate a cinematic sensitivity to the cost of war in terms of human lives and the planet itself.

Alan MacDonald says,

> War films raise important questions that come into sharp focus where human life is at stake. What is a person worth? Do widely accepted moral values still apply under conditions of war? If so, how do we know what's right and wrong? The veneer of civilized society is stripped away to reveal what humankind is like under the skin. Then are we left with an animal, a killing machine or a human being with a moral instinct that is a reflection of our Creator?
>
> (MacDonald, 1975, p. 76)

We could draw up a list of more specific themes of war films, and included in it might be the following:

- the ethics of killing;
- patriotism;
- dehumanization of war;
- post-9/11 reality/terrorism;
- torture and detention;
- desire/conditions for peace and non-violence;
- economy of war;
- anti-war black comedy.

Another way of categorizing the war film genre is chronologically. Peter Malone, when writing in the Vietnam war era about war films, commented that the contemporary attitude to war had changed since the nineteenth century, when wars were local and reflected the "remnants of chivalrous fighting" (Malone, 1971, p. 121). The world wars of the twentieth century were notable for films that boosted morale or promoted propagandist attitudes in an entertaining way. Films during the Cold War, Malone suggests, got "wider, longer and louder" (ibid., p. 125), perhaps to reinforce the message that World War II was worth the sacrifice and also to remind audiences that there remained a threat from the Soviet Union to hard-fought-for freedoms. The threat of nuclear annihilation became part of Western consciousness in the 1960s: one notable documentary, *The War Game* (Peter Watkins, 1965), shocked audiences with its blunt warning about the threat of a nuclear blast to Western civilization. Black comedy or satirical films also began to be popular in the 1960s, with the release of Stanley Kubrick's *Dr. Strangelove*. The anti-war sentiments of films like *M*A*S*H* and *Catch-22* (Mike Nichols, 1970) indicate for Malone a sea-change in the cinematic portrayal of war, "not as respectable as it once was" (ibid., p. 127).

Peace

Don Thompson claims that "if popular films have dealt with issues of peace, they have often done so within the context of war films" (Thompson, 2004). Suggesting that *Apocalypse Now* (Francis Ford Coppola, 1979) and *Platoon* (Oliver Stone, 1986) are two good examples of this, in their ability to use violence to promote the desire for peace, Thompson nevertheless accuses filmmakers Coppola and Stone of being addicted to violence as a dramatic device. They are adept, he says, at using violent images to "critique the unrelenting tendency of war to dehumanize" (ibid.) rather than to glamorize war. Thompson recalls the scene in *Apocalypse Now* when Kurtz (Marlon Brando), the renegade officer who "has become both superhuman and subhuman simultaneously" and who hides out in his jungle kingdom dispensing justice, drops a decapitated head into the lap of Willard (Martin Sheen), who is "horrified to the core and shaken by the brutality of the act" (ibid.). The transformation of Willard into Kurtz's executioner confirms for the audience the heroism present in those soldiers who maintain their moral bearings in the face of unimaginable horrors. These soldiers deny, through their righteousness, the description Chris Hedges gives of war's "grotesque and dark beauty" (Hedges, 2002, p. 3). This steadfastness reminds us that war should be the exception and peace the norm, that people are sometimes called to do extraordinary things in times of war to help peace prevail once again.

Gareth Higgins offers the opinion that we could be said to prefer the state of war rather than work actively for peace: "Humanity has found itself unable to make peace, not because it has exhausted diplomacy or discovered that nonviolent means fail, but because it has decided that the cost of peace in terms of changing our own lifestyle is too high" (Higgins, 2003, p. 234). Rosemary Radford Ruether alludes to the rationale for an unspoken acceptance in the West that sometimes war is necessary in order to sustain our lifestyle when she writes about how "the Western dream of infinitely expanding power and wealth defies the actual finitude of ourselves and the world and conceals the exploitative use of other people's resources" (Ruether, 1986, p. 67). Certainly the accusation that the Gulf and Iraq wars waged by Bush father and son were based upon the reliance of the West on Middle Eastern oil dovetails neatly with this scenario.

However, Christianity – despite the theology of the just war – has a clear lead from Jesus's blessing of the peacemakers; and many Christian theologians, even of the evangelical persuasion, have been vocal in their opposition to George W. Bush's "theology of war," particularly since his identification in 2002 of Iran, North Korea, and Iraq as the "axis of evil." According to a statement issued by Fuller Theological Seminary professors, entitled "Confessing Christ in a World of Violence," Bush's declaration sets up a "righteous" United States and "leads to a crusade in which Christians think the Christian thing to do is support war-making against an allegedly unrighteous enemy" (cited in Ekklesia, 2004). The statement, issued during the 2004 election season, urges followers of Jesus to reject the notion, saying that "such crude distinctions, especially when used by Christians, are expressions of the Manichaean heresy, in which the world is divided into forces of absolute good and absolute evil" (ibid.). It declares that "Christ commits Christians to a strong presumption against war" (ibid.) and reiterates the need for peacemaking to be the vocation for all Christians.

The Mythology of War

Films that deal with the Iraq wars, whether fictional or documentary in style, both acknowledge and surpass earlier war films in their cinematic sophistication; of course, modern-day technology allows us to have bigger, better, and more realistic special effects, but there is also an increased willingness to portray the psychological and spiritual turmoil existing in the society that sends its young people to war without what many regard as a solid reason for fighting. To some extent this ambivalent feeling is also present in many Vietnam war films, certainly in *Coming Home* (Hal Ashby, 1978), *The Deer Hunter* (Michael Cimino, 1978), and *Born on the Fourth of July* (Oliver Stone, 1989); however, those were made after the fact, while the Iraq war is being represented as the conflict actually occurs.

Jarhead (Sam Mendes, 2005) is a cinematic example of Chris Hedges's assertion that "the enduring attraction of war is this: even with its destruction and carnage it can give us what we long for in life. It can

Figure 6 "War is an exciting elixir" (Chris Hedges). Jake Gyllenhaal as marine Anthony Swofford in *Jarhead* (Sam Mendes, 2005).
Photograph: Universal/The Kobal Collection

give us purpose, meaning, a reason for living...and war is an exciting elixir (figure 6). It gives us resolve, a cause. It allows us to be noble" (Hedges, 2002, p. 3). Young marine Anthony Swofford (Jake Gyllenhaal) aspires to becoming a scout sniper and is urged on to this calling by his superiors. In one scene the troops watch what they might consider to be the Vietnam era's ultimate feel-good film, *Apocalypse Now*; they cheer as the helicopters strafe villagers and sing lustily with Wagner's *Ride of the Valkyries*. Chris Hedges explains the allure of these images for those going off to war: "The potency of myth is that it allows us to make sense of mayhem and violent death" (Hedges, 2002, p. 23). The mythology of war – that the cavalry will come riding in to save the innocent and uphold liberty – is seductive indeed for these young recruits, who all too quickly are called to be the cavalry in Operation Desert Shield.

The film's title refers to a marine whose shaven head is an empty vessel, ready to be filled with the knowledge of how to be an excellent warrior. The staff sergeant invokes the Judeo-Christian commandment "Thou shalt not kill," only to reject it by declaring, "Fuck that shit!" The irony is, however, that when engagement in battle is imminent, the high-tech air war that is ordered by higher-ups frustrates the foot soldiers, whose honed expertise with the rifle is passed over in favor of precision bombing – these young men are outdated figures of warfare, doomed to identify with and pine for the desert long after they return home, unable to adjust to "ordinary" life. The film tellingly opens with these words: "A man fires a rifle for many years, and he goes to war. And afterward he turns the rifle in at the armory, and he believes he's finished with the rifle. But no matter what else he might do with his hands, love a woman, build a house, change his son's diaper; his hands remember the rifle."

The film might suggest that those battlefield novices who, arriving in the Middle Eastern oilfields, morph so readily into the guise of desert warrior do so because they lack a sense of belonging to or identity in the American society they so readily volunteer to defend with their lives. As Hedges recalls,

> Aristotle said that only two living entities are capable of complete solitude and complete separateness: God and beast. Because of this the most acute form of suffering for human beings is loneliness. The isolated individual can never be adequately human. And many of war's most fervent adherents are those atomized individuals who, before the war came, were profoundly alone and unloved. They found fulfilment in war, perhaps because it was the closest they came to love.
>
> (Hedges, 2002, p. 161)

Back home from the war, the last line Swofford speaks in the film is: "We are still in the desert."

The suggestion that soldiers home from war cannot but be forever changed by the experiences they have had is the premise behind other films about other wars, most notably Vietnam. Alan MacDonald writes that "The best of the Vietnam films... are trying to comprehend the experience of war, not glorify it" (MacDonald, 1975, p. 75). *Jacob's Ladder* (Adrian Lyne, 1990) stars Tim Robbins as a Vietnam veteran who seeks an answer to increasingly violent hallucinations that threaten his sanity. His quest for an answer involves the possibility of a secret drug that was used on soldiers as part of an army experiment (perhaps as likely a cause as post-traumatic stress disorder for hallucinatory experiences). Probably the best-known portrayal of this lack of adjustment to life after the Vietnam war is Christopher Walken's tragic character Nick in *The Deer Hunter*. Roger Ebert says that the film, a story of three buddies from a small Pennsylvania steel-mill town who adjust to life at home with varying degrees of success after a horrendous period of captivity at the hands of the Vietcong, "evokes the agony of the Vietnam time" (Ebert, 1979b). In his review Ebert claims that *The Deer Hunter* demands that we never forget the war; the final scene is of characters gathered together singing "God Bless America," and Ebert says "the lyrics of 'God Bless America' have never before seemed to me to contain such an infinity of possible meanings, some tragic, some unspeakably sad, some few still defiantly hopeful" (ibid.).

Chris Hedges alludes to the weight that Vietnam-era soldiers bore when they realized the futility of their engagement in a war that many Americans tried to forget: "The violence of war is random. It does not make sense. Many of the soldiers who fought in Vietnam must grapple with the realization that there was no higher purpose to the war, that the sacrifice was a waste. It is easier to believe the myth that makes such loss noble and necessary, despite the glaring contradictions" (Hedges, 2002, p. 134). When soldiers cannot persist in believing the myth, then films like *Jarhead* and *The Deer Hunter* seem to say that they suffer because they cannot have closure that helps to validate their actions.

Documentary: The Search for Truth

Documentary is a style of filmmaking that has burst once again onto the screen in the past five or so years, drawing record audiences (Michael Moore's *Fahrenheit 9/11* [2004] was the largest-grossing documentary ever) as more theaters warm to the idea that documentaries are not just for arthouse cinemas anymore.[1] Of course, the tradition of narrative (fiction) versus documentary (non-fiction) – two seemingly mutually exclusive perspectives on filmmaking – stretches back to the pioneering days of French cinema. Georges Méliès was known for his cinematic trickery and special effects (e.g. *A Trip to the Moon*, 1902), while the Lumière brothers were masters of actuality, using scenes from everyday life untouched by deceptive camerawork.

There has been a steady stream of feature documentaries about the Iraq war in addition to Moore's, whose distinctive contribution to the group, according to Don Thompson, is in "trying to take the responsibility of the Kurtzes of the world back to their origins: the leaders that create them" (Thompson, 2004). But Eugene Jarecki is also in search of the origins of the "forces that drive us to fight against an ever-changing enemy" (Sony Classics, 2005) in his 2005 film *Why We Fight*: "It is a real challenge to make a film without a villain . . . too often the villain you choose is really a proxy for a system that itself needs repair" (ibid.). This film (whose title recalls Frank Capra's patriotic World War II films of the same name) traces the beginnings of the US military-industrial complex, which President Eisenhower warned against as he was leaving office in 1961. In asking whether Eisenhower's fears have been realized, Jarecki wanted audiences to take away a sense of urgency from the film that might drive them to make real change in "how they are governed and what their society represents" (ibid.).

The decision by the American government to wage war in Iraq in 2003 was supported by many loyal Americans like Wilton Sekzer, a Vietnam veteran and a New York City cop for 35 years. He suffered the tragic loss of his son in Tower One of the World Trade Center on September 11. In *Why We Fight*, Sekzer recounts his campaign to get US armed forces to put his son's name on one of the bombs dropped on Iraq, a symbolic gesture similar to what troops did in naming bombs during the Vietnam War. Sekser did this, he said, because he believed what George W. Bush said about Saddam Hussein being responsible for the 9/11 terrorist attack. He was shocked when the Bush administration later denied that they had ever made that connection, and he agreed to participate in the filming of this documentary to show his disgust at being misled (even accompanying the film to its Sundance premiere).

When real people like Sekzer are shown in such a sympathetic light, documentaries show their strength of form. Although there has been a public debate about the veracity of documentary film – even by animal lovers regarding *March of the Penguins* (Luc Jacquet, 2005), but especially by conservatives who tot up the inaccuracies or "lies" that appear in *Fahrenheit 9/11* – the search for truth is what drives a filmmaker, especially in times of war, to bring a subject before the public for debate and dialogue. Chris Hedges says that "reconciliation, self-awareness and finally the humility that makes peace probable come only when culture no longer serves a cause or a myth but the most precious and elusive of all human narratives – truth" (Hedges, 2002, p. 82). Telling the truth about a conflict that has taken many lives is a process that has yet to play itself out fully in the context of the Iraq war, and Jarecki says that it is crucial to ask "Why are we doing what we are doing? What is it doing to others? And what is it doing to us?" (Sony Classics, 2005).

The outrage at the US government's shift in rationale for the Iraq war is also the impetus for another documentary, Robert Greenwald's *Uncovered: The War on Iraq* (2004). Greenwald makes careful and sometimes intricate connections between the US government build-up to the war and the veracity of evidence used to justify it. He structures the film in chapter form so as to provide a narrative within which the experts – various diplomats, politicians, government officials, CIA employees – methodically refute the administration's evidence of weapons of mass destruction (WMDs) and state-supported terrorism, especially the link with the 9/11 attacks.

The film also provides many examples of the naiveté and gullibility of the American media. Other arguments in the build-up to war, including the evidence proffered in Colin Powell's address to the United Nations, are carefully analyzed and rejected.

In the film's eighth chapter there is a shift from the talking-head style to a still photography montage of explosions and victims, including images of American military funerals, the poignancy of which is underscored with a stirring soundtrack. This emotional charge is unexpected and gives the audience a punch in the face. The cinematic style then reverts to the previous technique of White House officials declaring that the cost of war will not be a burden (however, each official contradicts the previous one in the amounts of money they predict will be needed for the war). A lengthy interview with David Kay, the chief UN weapons inspector, confirms that there was no evidence of WMDs in Iraq and therefore the government was wrong in its assumptions. The film concludes with a profile of Washington's neo-conservative stronghold, the Office of Special Plans, where American interests are the primary goal of all foreign policy. It is suggested that the Office's work is not yet done.

Greenwald deliberately sought interviews with those within the halls of power; no ordinary characters like *Why We Fight*'s Wilton Sekzer grace the screen, only those who can provide solid evidence of the mistakes made and misleading information disseminated by the White House. Greenwald says that he wanted to keep his personal feelings out of the film, although the film was produced with help from MoveOn.org, a political grassroots internet organization that launched a web-based campaign against the war in Iraq. The film was put together in only a few months, with researchers and production staff working shifts to get it finished. Resulting reviews treated this documentary in a kinder manner overall than they did Moore's *Fahrenheit 9/11*. One reviewer commented: "Unlike the indulgent Moore, Greenwald here dispenses with manipulation, theatrics and tricks, and lets his often-angry experts wax convincingly" (Toumarkine, 2004); another says, "Basically preaching to the choir, of course, but that doesn't mean that the sermon isn't one that needs to be heard" (Swietek, 2004).

American angst over the Iraq war has driven the making of some interesting and arresting films, but the Iraqi perspective is missing from most of them. *The Dreams of Sparrows* (Hayder Mousa Daffar, 2005) builds into a crescendo of desperation as Iraqi citizens attempt to correct perceptions of Iraq by explaining what their lives are like (the filming took place in 2003). Upfront in acknowledging major technical problems, due to lack of quality equipment and funding, Daffar assembled a small crew, who unexpectedly play a central role at the climax of the film. Part One begins with the capture of Saddam Hussein and the resulting celebrations among Iraqis. The consequences of the regime's downfall are made apparent: Palestinians formerly given housing by Saddam are made homeless when he is overthrown; black-market vendors take advantage of the gas shortage in this oil-rich country; and taxi drivers speak about the breakdown of essential services in society. As the extent of the Abu Ghraib prison scandal is becoming known, the segment ends with a debate between Iraqi supporters of American troops, who see them as liberators, and those who say they are terrorists.

Part Two focuses on Fallujah, with moving testimony of the American bombing campaign from survivors and images of the burial of victims. Any hope of showing Iraqis bravely coping with chaos and violence evaporates in the film when one of the production team, Sa'ad Fakher, is killed, a victim of the upsurge in random murder, prompting the director in his voiceover to declare in frustration, "Baghdad is hell."[2] What gives this film an undisputed air of authenticity is the filming, rough and amateurish at times; the soundtrack consists of traditional instruments such as the oud, its sad tone reflecting the despair and tragedy facing the people of Iraq. *The Dreams of Sparrows* is optimistically described as the first Iraq Eye group collaboration between Iraqi and American filmmakers. The film is truthful in a way that Chris Hedges defines as that of a successful anti-war film: "one that eschew(s) battle scenes and focus(es) on the heartbreak of violence and slaughter" (Hedges, 2002, p. 91).

One observation we might make with the upsurge in documentary filmmaking concerning the war in Iraq is that the search for truth never stops. As Paul Tillich pointed out, for human beings there is an overarching concern, a central conviction, that everyone has at the centre of their lives: whether it be more basic needs for survival or the more abstract but equally important values of love, beauty, truth, or justice, "something makes an unconditional claim upon us, and we organize our lives and all of our other values in accordance with it" (Cobb, 2005, p. 103). For many of us, telling the truth – as opposed to lying – is behavior that we expect from those who lead us and determine our future. The search for truth is laudable, but some might say it is only the first step – after the truth is discovered, what then? By the fall elections of 2006 in the United States it had become evident that the reasons given by the administration for going into the war in Iraq were misleading at best and lies at worst. The truth sought by many Americans and allies about the path to war, resulting in thousands of deaths of military and civilians, has now been revealed.

Whether these lives were taken in vain or worth the sacrifice, and how to move forward past conflict to peace, is the next step.

Filmmakers who choose war as their subject may wish to learn from the occasionally vicious response from right-wing supporters of the Bush White House's war on Iraq, who charged that, because Moore's documentary was not made up totally of facts but also contained political rhetoric, this then discredited the entire film. The definition of a documentary film given by John Grierson, who is basically responsible for the development of the documentary as we know it in the Western world, involves "using a whole range of creative skills to fashion the 'fragments of reality' into an artifact that has a specific social impact" (John Izod and Richard Kilborn in Hill and Gibson, 1998, p. 426). Of course, this definition problematizes the function of documentary, but surely no one expects a filmmaker not to construct, to some extent, his or her own view of the world, determined by the perceptions and preconceptions of the documentarist and the selection and editing of materials.

Theologian Hans Kung urges the world to find a way "from wars and ideologies, which scorn the divine in every human being" (Kung, 1991, p. 68), and that necessarily entails a fundamental adjustment of the military mindset and a rethink of the industrial nature of militarism. Most importantly, he urges us to find "a way from a situation in which military intervention or the threat of military intervention seems necessary to preserve or implement human rights" (ibid., p. 68). The review of *Fahrenheit 9/11* by Frederic and Mary Ann Brussat for the website Spirituality and Practice says that "Moore wants this muckraking film to wake up citizens who have been lulled into complacency by the media or beaten down over the years by the powerful interests aligned behind the administration" (Brussat and Brussat, 2004). When documentaries serve to seek the truth about war, they may help us in rethinking our impulse to war and may instead give us hope for peace.

Terror and Freedom

George W. Bush speaks of the "war on terror" as a necessary response to the threat to the free world since 9/11. One film that certainly predates 9/11 but chillingly foreshadows the terror tactics of insurgency and bombing of civilian targets is *The Battle of Algiers* (Gilles Pontecorvo, 1966). Described by film critic Christopher Tookey as "anti-colonialist propaganda" (Tookey, 1994, p. 56), *The Battle of Algiers* tells the story of the French–Algerian conflict in a prophetic tone during the very period when the United States was itself becoming mired in Vietnam. France's decline as a colonial power came on the heels of its humiliation in Indochina in 1954, and the Algerian resistance movement began that same year. There was an absence of films about the colonial wars in the decade that followed, and *The Battle of Algiers*, an Italian-Algerian co-production, attempted to portray the Algerian struggle through a naturalistic, pseudo-documentary, but passionate style. Pauline Kael remarked that "Pontecorvo's inflammatory passion works directly on your feelings. He's the most dangerous kind of Marxist, a Marxist poet" (ibid.). The film's aesthetic effectiveness in the skillful marrying of image and music is due to the genius of composer Ennio Morricone. Although the shooting of the film is in a quite dispassionate, documentary style, the musical cues add evocatively to the buildup of tension as the bombing campaign is carried out.

The Battle of Algiers suggests that the refusal of the French government to entertain suggestions of granting independence, let alone to consider Algeria anything more than a possession, led to the eruption of guerilla warfare. The escalation in violent tactics is unswervingly portrayed, and the decision by stoic Algerian women to take on the task of planting bombs in public places frequented by the French ruling class is particularly noteworthy: because they of all Algerians are invisible in the public eye, being the housekeepers and maids of the colonial (and patriarchal) society, they can pass almost unnoticed through checkpoints with their deadly packages. The unwavering resolve of the Algerians in waging this terrorist campaign resulted eventually in the granting of independence by France.

Films like *The Battle of Algiers*, portraying the fight for freedom from occupying powers – whether they be set in Northern Ireland (*In the Name of the Father* [Jim Sheridan, 1993]) or South Africa (*Cry Freedom* [Richard Attenborough, 1987]) – are important because they bring to the fore issues of oppression, self-determination, liberty, and solidarity with people who suffer and respect for human rights. Jurgen Moltmann is one theologian who has spoken out strongly for the human dignity and rights of people who live and suffer in unjust societies:

> International solidarity in overcoming the horror of starvation and the threat of world military crises has, [. . .] because of the rights of humanity, a precedence over loyalty to one's own people, to one's own class, race, or nation. Individual communities and states have human duties in the face of the rights of the whole of humanity to life, freedom, and community. Therefore human rights point to a universal community in which alone they can be realized.
>
> (Moltmann, 1976)

The Christian dedication to freedom, as a result of being in covenant with God, consists of fulfilling human destiny in the historical movement toward the Kingdom of God – in short, it means pledging solidarity with people whose human dignity has been denied. Moltmann says:

> Christianity understands itself as witness to the three-in-one God who liberates human beings from inward and outward inhumanity, who allows them to live in his covenant, and leads them to the glory of his kingdom. Christians therefore stand up for the dignity of human beings out of which emerge their rights and duties. For the sake of God they will stand up with all means at their disposal, acting as well as suffering, for the dignity of human beings and their rights as the image of God.
>
> (ibid.)

New Testament scholar Richard B. Hays calls attention today to the choice the American government has made to spend billions on war, saying "we are putting our trust in swords and chariots and guns to somehow secure our well-being. It goes completely against the grain of what Jesus taught" (Hays, 2005, p. 3). Pointing out that the Church is called to love its enemies, Hays asks, "what would happen if we devoted anything like the same level of economic resources, energies, imagination and commitment to efforts seeking reconciliation and feeding the poor and hungry around the world[?] I wonder if that wouldn't do a lot more to protect us from terrorism than what we have, in fact, done" (ibid.).

It seems that the challenge, not only to Christians but to all who care about the dignity of human beings, is to see past the violence of war and terror – not to condone it, but to understand its root causes and commit themselves to work toward peace and justice. One film that goes some way toward explaining the rationale behind the decision to become a suicide martyr is *Paradise Now* (Hany Abu-Assad, 2005). In it we meet close friends Khaled and Said, young Palestinian men living in Nablus, involved with an underground cell violently resisting Israeli occupation. The two are notified that they are the next volunteers to carry out a suicide bombing in Tel Aviv; one of the cell members tells them, "Death is better than inferiority." They spend a final night at home with their families; Said sneaks away to visit Suha, the daughter of a martyr revered by the resistance fighters. Rather than following in her father's footsteps, she runs a human rights organization that is scorned by the resistance. The next day the process of carrying out the operation begins: Khaled and Said make the requisite martyr videos, and then have haircuts, shaves, and ritual baths and are dressed in suits, the explosives strapped onto their chests. This scene is filmed without dialogue but with prayers recited in the background. The two men are instructed to stagger their detonations so as to maximize the casualties, and the choice they must make is which one will go first: whoever it is, they are told, the second one must not watch the first one die. As they are driven to the rendezvous spot at the border with Israel, they ask what will happen to them after they die in the bombing. "Two angels will pick you up," they are told. "Are you sure?" they ask. "Absolutely. You will see."

But the hand-off to a driver across the border is bungled, and the friends lose track of each other. Khaled returns to the group, but Said cannot be found and it is feared that he has betrayed them. Khaled goes off in search of Said and finds Suha, who realizes that the men have become involved in a suicide mission. The scene between Suha and Khaled as they drive around the settlement in search of Said is tense, as she asks why they are doing this; she sees some hope with the human rights group that it will prevent the Israelis from having an excuse to keep on killing. Khaled replies that there can be no freedom without struggle and that their deaths are a sacrifice. Suha replies, "That's not sacrifice, that's revenge. If you kill there's no difference between victim and occupier." She disputes Khaled's certainty that paradise awaits him, saying it exists only in his head. Khaled says he would rather have paradise in his head than continue living "in this hell." Suha asks him what his actions do for those who remain, because the bombings give Israel an excuse to carry on their oppression. She says it is necessary to turn the conflict instead into a moral war.

Khaled finds Said, who vows to carry on with the plan. The cell prepares again and the two friends make the drop-off into Israel. As they await the next stage in the plan, Khaled, having reflected upon Suha's words, tries to talk Said out of the bombing. Said argues, "We do what we have to do. God decides the rest." Khaled responds, "But God says, 'Think first.' We kill and are killed and nothing changes." He tells Said there are other ways to liberate and change the world, but with his mind firmly made up, Said only says, "Perhaps for others."

In his article "Salvation and Suicide: What Does Islamic Theology Say?" Munawar A. Anees examines the fundamentals of Islamic faith and says that, for Muslims, salvation is founded upon "good deeds and God's mercy" (Anees, 2006, p. 275). The "violent culture of martyrdom" (ibid., p. 277) that has increased in the past five or so years sees salvation erroneously as coming with multitudes of virgins in paradise, Anees says; far from there being any Qur'anic evidence to support this vision, the

Qur'an specifically condemns suicide terrorists to hell. Neither is there any evidence that the Prophet Muhammad would have encouraged or permitted this type of act to be done in the name of Islam. Anees says that this theology "plays upon the young vulnerable psyche that yearns for leading a purposeful life" (ibid., p. 278), but he warns against dismissing the seemingly unending supply of suicide martyrs as simply an "aberration in Muslim society" (ibid., p. 277). "One needs to look much deeper into the causative factors, including widespread poverty, foreign occupation, lack of democratic freedom, absence of opportunities for personal growth and fulfilment, among others" (ibid., p. 278). Those who recruit suicide terrorists exploit their religious sentiments methodically by "invoking eternal salvation" (ibid.). Anees concludes his article by stating:

> At one time or other, all nations have transgressed the rules of war. What distinguishes the war waged by the suicide terrorist from the rest is that the combatant serves as a metaphor for a grotesque vision of Islamic doctrine of human salvation. The commission of sin by suicide and the vengeful murder of innocents notwithstanding, this is the ultimate debasement of Islamic ideals.
>
> (ibid., p. 279)

Referring to the rash of suicide bombings in the Middle Eastern terror campaigns, as well as the Al-Qaeda attacks since September 11, 2001, Ronald Kraybill, who as an expert in conflict studies has worked across four continents to provide training in conflict resolution, says that when people feel humiliated and helpless their rage can result in irrational actions such as suicide bombings: "Suicide bombers are a symptom of an underlying disease. Unfortunately, our ability to understand conflicts at this moment in history is probably as limited as our ability to understand disease was a century or two ago. We have leadership and broad populations investing enormous energy responding at the level of the symptoms who are totally clueless about the causes" (Kraybill, 2004, p. 1). He urges government leaders to develop a strategy to deal with terrorists that will "drain the swamps of human misery that breed the crocodiles of terror. Right now we're all worried about killing crocodiles. The strategies that we're using are going to multiply the crocodiles over the long term" (ibid., p. 2). Echoing Moltmann's call to stand up for the dignity of human beings, Kraybill suggests economic development, health care, education, employment, and housing for those people who are helpless and humiliated: "all the things that give people meaning and a sense of coherency in the world are bound up in this" (ibid., p. 2). The

Christian tradition calls its followers to respond to inequities and suffering; in this situation, this means Christians need to build human understandings between Christianity and Islam, Kraybill asserts, adding that "draining the swamps of misery is a requirement of our faith ... we are called to care for the world we live in and to work for its healing" (ibid., p. 3).

Conclusion

Even early war films like Buster Keaton's *The General*, Michael Curtiz's *The Charge of the Light Brigade* (1936), and Jean Renoir's *Grand Illusion* (1937) offered audiences sobering reflections on the tragic absurdity of war. Contemporary filmmakers are doing much the same thing through the diverse conventions of science fiction, anime, and documentary. There is no doubt that war involves great sacrifice and heroism, as many films about World War II showed us, but in the twenty-first century, when the "rules" of war seem to have shifted dramatically and the rationale for going to war has become a contentious political issue in many democracies, people of faith might ask whether, as Walter Wink has argued, the "just war" teaching of Augustine has gone in the wrong direction. Augustine had no hesitation in finding scriptural references to support the use of war against the Roman Empire, but appealing to his reasoning for a just war today may lead Christians to ignore the strong non-violent tradition of Jesus and the early Church. As Vardy and Grosch succinctly put it,

> The idea that wars are sometimes necessary is an odd idea in the moral arena. Ethics demands free choice and yet necessity denies free choice – there may be reasons for waging war but, Wink maintains, they can never be just reasons as justice is defined by applying fairness and bringing about equality on both sides – and war certainly does not do this.
> (Vardy & Grosch, 1994, p. 185)

Indeed, Peter Malone identifies the change of mood on war after 1945 as stemming from "the disillusionment of the aftermath of wars" (Malone, 1971, p. 122). The soul-searching that went on in American society after the Vietnam war and the political fallout from the war in Iraq might suggest that the seductive but illusory qualities of Chris Hedges's "bizarre and fantastic universe that has a grotesque and dark beauty" (Hedges, 2002, p. 3) are recognized too late by those in whose name war is waged. Don Thompson remarks on the success of *Fahrenheit 9/11* as a film whose success might indicate that "American society ... may be beginning to look inside of itself to find the root causes of its obsession with war, violence and domination" (Thompson, 2004). Helping audiences to question war in a way that exposes underlying religious and cultural attitudes may be one way in which films can promote peace. The examination of fine moral and ethical distinctions within not only the theology of war but also the holy war may provide inspiration for many more films to come.

Notes

1 As of this writing, it is the highest-grossing documentary in film history. In its first two days it reached a larger audience than Moore's previous film, *Bowling for Columbine* (2002), did in nine months. *Fahrenheit 9/11* gained more viewers for its opening weekend than *Star Wars: Episode VI – Return of the Jedi* (1983) and it broke *Rocky III*'s (Sylvester Stallone, 1982) record for the highest gross for an opening of under 1,000 theaters. It also achieved second place in the contest for the all-time record for the highest per screen audience of any major American film release (Niman, 2004).

2 A survey of the number of Iraqi civilian war casualties during the filming period of March–July 2003 estimated two thousand dead, four thousand injured (Jarrar, 2003).

Heaven, Hell, and the Sweet Hereafter: Theological Perspectives on Eschatology and Film

In much the same way as the previous chapter asked whether, and to what extent, a war film can also be construed as a film about peace, and the chapter before that questioned the distinction between the categories of justice and violence, so this chapter takes it as apparent that the theme of eschatology cannot be seen to lie in a vacuum. As has already been suggested in relation to the dispensation of justice in *Pale Rider* (Clint Eastwood, 1985) and *Unforgiven* (Clint Eastwood, 1992), in an imperfect world human beings characteristically yearn for the administration of some kind of justice, often at the cost of immense suffering and sacrifice, to the extent that the boundaries between justice, violence, vigilantism, and vengeance become blurred. And, in relation to such legal dramas as *The Verdict* (Sidney Lumet, 1982) and *Snow Falling on Cedars* (Scott Hicks, 1999), it has been observed that because of the fissure, in Augustinian terms, between the earthly and the heavenly cities there is an innate problem in reconciling divine justice with the partial and parochial orbit of human justice, where avarice, rhetoric, prejudice, manipulation, subterfuge, and the quest for power tend to hold sway. When it comes to the question of eschatology, it is similarly the case that a very fine line exists between the finality of human existence and such (aforementioned) themes as justice, violence, and warfare. For example, although he is writing in the specific context of the principle of vengeance in relation to

Chris Deacy

St. Paul's epistles and Clint Eastwood's film *Pale Rider*, Robert Jewett points out that in a world where injustice and violence is the norm, and "people have suffered at the hands of thieves and murderers," it is hardly surprising that religious adherents have come, throughout history, to formulate doctrines and tenets of belief along the lines that "such evil will someday be overcome," not least in the manner of "elaborate systems of belief in the final judgment, when all accounts will be paid in full" (Jewett, 1993, p. 127). On this basis, there is a necessary and inextricable link between justice and eschatology, in the respect that, in a Pauline sense at any rate, since "human beings yearn for some kind of justice" (ibid.) but it is not the prerogative of humans to carry out personal acts of vengeance or be a judge in one's own cause – "Behold, never avenge yourselves, but leave it to the wrath of God" (Romans 12:19) – only a future hope can properly insure that those who perpetrate acts of injustice will receive their just desserts. In keeping with St. Paul's view that there is an ontological difference between the old age, which he identifies as comprising "the works of darkness" (Romans 13:12), and the new age ("the age of light" – Romans 13:12) that enables us to "cast off the works of darkness and put on the armour of light" (Romans 13:12), only an eschatological hope can do justice to Paul's appeal for Christians to renounce regeneration through violence and lay emphasis instead on the future reign of Christ – the only forum through which all principalities and powers will be vanquished.

Problems of Definition

However, despite the integral role that eschatology plays, this is one of the most complex areas to navigate in modern theology. No matter how certain St. Paul may have been that there will be a future life, and that, as he wrote in Galatians 6:8, "the one who sows to the Spirit will from the Spirit reap eternal life," there is precious little consistency in his writings concerning the nature of the process. In Romans 8:24, for instance, Paul suggests that salvation is not merely a future event but something that has *already* happened in the *past*: "For in this hope we were saved." Conversely, in 1 Corinthians 1:18, Paul identifies eschatology as a *present* phenomenon: "For the word of the cross is folly to those who are perishing, but to us who are being saved it is the power of God." Paul was also unclear as to the timescale involved. In 1 Corinthians 15, it is clear from his treatise on the resurrection of the dead that Paul anticipated that, at the end of this space-time order, God would bring about a final resurrection of the dead as a prelude to final judgment. Using apocalyptic terminology, Paul explained that this transformation – which will vindicate the evil and suffering to which Christians are presently being subjected – will take place "in a moment, at the twinkling of an eye, at the last trumpet" (1 Corinthians 15:52). As illustrated by his conviction that "We shall not all sleep" (1 Corinthians 15:51), Paul understood that this eschatological event would occur during his own lifetime. In his later writings, however, he expressed an uncertainty as to whether he could expect to be among those who are still living at the time of the Parousia (the Second Coming of Christ in glory), or whether he would have died before that moment arrives. In his letter to the Philippians, for instance, he wrote of his desire "to depart and be with Christ" while also acknowledging his obligations in this life, "in the flesh," to the church at Philippi (Philippians 1:23–4). There is also uncertainty in Paul's mind concerning whether salvation is universal or whether only a select group of Christians can expect to be saved. Whereas in Romans 5:18 he argues that as original sin resulted in the fall of the entire human race so Christ's "righteousness leads to acquittal and life for all men," in Romans 8:29 Paul refers to those who are "predestined to be conformed to the image of his Son."

Before we can even begin, therefore, to undertake a critical conversation between theology and film vis-à-vis the question of eschatology, it is clear that there are a number of disputed definitional boundaries. The problem is further exacerbated when one considers that it is not even sufficient to posit that, in Willard G. Oxtoby's words, "To be saved, for the traditional Christian, is in its simplest terms to be saved for heaven and to be saved from hell" (Oxtoby, 1973, p. 27). Since the Enlightenment in particular, there has been a significant re-orientation of beliefs concerning eschatology, away from a traditional emphasis upon a future judgment, heaven, and hell, in the direction of an interpretation that accords a more prominent role to the ability of a person to undergo a salvific experience within the present dimensions of existence in the "here and now." Although it has traditionally been assumed that the eschatological drama entails the human individual or community being at some point "lifted out of the tears and sweat and dirt" of our present lives into "a serene empyrean where the gritty quality of our ordinary daily life is left far behind and can be forgotten" (Williams, 1972, p. 10), Don Cupitt argues that "in the modern period we have come more and more to explain events in this world in this-worldly terms," such that we "no longer seem to require the old idea that there is an invisible world of supernatural beings lying behind this world" (Cupitt, 1984, p. 34). In everyday human life, for example, Rudolf Bultmann has pointed out that modern men and women have "recourse to physicians" when they are ill and to "the results of psychological, social, economic and political sciences" (Bultmann, 1958, p. 36) in the course of their daily affairs, and so will acknowledge as reality "only such phenomena or events as are comprehensible within the framework of the rational order of the universe" (ibid., p. 37). In like manner, according to Søren Kierkegaard, all talk concerning what is to come after death must be understood solely in terms of the way in which it bears upon the will in the here and now – "Immortality is not a life indefinitely prolonged, nor even a life somehow prolonged into eternity" (in Cupitt, 1984, p. 262). Rather, it is in the present moment that the believer has passed through judgment and entered upon eternal life. Accordingly, when the Synoptic Gospels suggest that there will be a dramatic intervention, or cosmic catastrophe, in the immediate future by God, which will bring history to a conclusion, whereupon "sin, suffering and death" (Bultmann, 1953, p. 2) will be abolished – thereby reversing Adam's original disobedience – and the believer will be resurrected and proceed to enjoy communion with God upon the coming of the Parousia, this cannot be the most viable model in the modern world for understanding the vexed issue of eschatology. In Kantian terms, indeed, since metaphysical speculations concerning God and immortality are beyond the remit of human reason, we can assume nothing about the future and so ought not to look beyond our present existence on earth, to the point that, in John Macquarrie's words, "the traditional eschatology" seems like "a remnant of mythology" (Macquarrie, 1978, p. 94).

In short, therefore, there would appear to be a substantial basis to Max Weber's claim that "the most elementary forms of behavior motivated by religious . . . factors are oriented to *this* world" (Weber, 1965, p. 1). It may be the case that much early Christian literature bears witness to the contrast between "this fleeting and wretched world below in which we must spend our brief lives and the eternal heavenly world above which is the soul's true home" (Cupitt, 1984, p. 260), but, as Margaret Miles attests, "religion is first and foremost a way of managing *this* world, the only world we know," to the effect that "even the most explicitly other-worldly religious orientations are primarily responses to the exigencies of *this* life" (M. Miles, 1985, p. 1). In contrast to the pre-scientific and mythological cosmology within which the Gospel writers were functioning, which pictured the universe in spatial terms as a "three-storied structure" (Bultmann, 1953, p. 1) containing heaven above, hell beneath, and the earth – to which both God from on high and demons from below have access – somewhere in the middle, Cupitt rightly points out that "in the Christian tradition at least, religious meanings cannot be transmitted unchanged" (Cupitt, 1984, p. 16) and that "[b]y and large, people have found that scientific explanations are better explanations than the old explanations in terms of spirit-agencies" (ibid., p. 34). Significantly, the New Testament itself provides the key to this process. For, although the Synoptic Gospels speak largely of a future eschatology, there is a wide body of textual evidence to indicate that, in Emil Brunner's words, "the imminent expectation of the Parousia in the whole of the New Testament pales into insignificance before the belief that in Jesus Christ the New Age had *already* dawned" (Brunner, 1954, p. 2).

Indeed, despite Jesus's claim, as reported in the Fourth Gospel, that "the hour is coming when the dead who are in the tombs will hear his voice and come forth, those who have done good, to the resurrection of life, and those who have done evil, to the resurrection of judgment" (John 5:29), Jesus is also said to have proclaimed that "he who hears my word and believes him who sent me has eternal life," and has *already* "passed from death to life" (John 5:24). The Fourth Evangelist makes it clear that Jesus *is* the "bread of life" (John 6:35), and that the water he can offer is the "living water" (John 4:10). Not even the intervention of physical death can destroy the bond that is established once the believer has accepted that "Jesus is the Christ, the Son of God" and thereby *has* "life in his name" (John 20:31). Those who believe need not therefore wait until some future age in order to receive the benefits of salvation, for the apocalyptic and supernatural Day of Judgment "is pushed to the margins of discussion" (Bailey, 1979, p. 94). With these considerations in mind, it is not surprising that the Doctrine Commission of the Church of England felt the need to acknowledge in 1995 that "in the twentieth-century West, across a whole spectrum of types of Christianity, there seems to be a fairly consistent emphasis on salvation here and now rather than after death" (Doctrine Commission, 1995, p. 29). According to Cupitt, moreover, this can even be justified theologically, for the thought of a life after death could be construed as a symptom of a *lack* of faith inasmuch as "the whole mentality of preparing for death, of sitting around brooding over the unfortunate shortage of evidence of life after death, poisons *life*" (Cupitt, 1984, p. 263). In terms that would not be an anathema to the likes of Sigmund Freud, Karl Marx, and Richard Dawkins, Cupitt argues that to offer solutions to the problems of this life, such as poverty and injustice, by promising metaphysical consolations "is worse than useless," not least because it merely confirms our "state of impotence and illusion" (ibid., p. 272).

Filmic Depictions of a Traditional Eschatological Vision

In a number of contemporary films, however, remnants of the traditional, future-oriented eschatological vision can be seen to flourish. *What Dreams May Come* (Vincent Ward, 1998) is a case in point. This is a movie in which Robin Williams plays a children's doctor who dies in a car accident four years after his two young children were killed in a similar manner. Unable to cope with her loss, his wife, played by Annabella Sciorra, commits suicide and, like her husband, finds herself in an afterlife – only, whereas he ends up in a paradisiacal, heavenly realm more beautiful than anything he had ever imagined on earth, she journeys to a very different plane of existence, namely, a hellish environment where she is perennially punished for her violation of the natural order of things and her failure to honor the sanctity of life. Similar motifs can be seen to lie in *Defending Your Life* (Albert Brooks, 1991), in which a business executive, played by Albert Brooks, is also killed in a car crash and finds himself in a purgatorial site called Judgment City, effectively a waiting room for the afterlife, which resembles a Disneyland theme park with fantasy hotels and shuttle buses, in which his next (and final) destination depends upon the outcome of a trial in which he must defend his actions and behavior on earth.

Other recent examples include the slapstick comedy *Little Nicky* (Steven Brill, 2000), in which Adam Sandler plays the inept son of the Devil, who is sent on a mission to "save" his errant father, and the romantic comedy *Ghost* (Jerry Zucker, 1990), in which Patrick Swayze's character, Sam Wheat, is caught in the intersection between the earthly and heavenly worlds and sets about avenging evil deeds committed by those on earth. The film bears witness to a very traditional dualistic framework whereby those on earth who carry out good deeds are rewarded with a future in heaven (which they attain by literally ascending a tunnel of light that reaches into the sky) while those who perpetrate evil acts can expect, like the duplicitous, homicidal Carl Bruner (Tony Goldwyn), to be dragged (quite literally in this film) off to hell for all eternity by a pack of ravaging demons. *Ghost* suggests hell is a very real place, thereby underscoring the sense that divine justice lies at the very heart of the universe. Glimpses of a traditional eschatological picture can also be seen in Cameron Crowe's *Vanilla Sky* (2001), a film referred to by one reviewer as a "mind-bending excursion across genres – a warped fairy tale that dabbles in romance, mythology, horror, mystery, and science fiction," in which there are "plenty of philosophical musings on the difference between dreams and reality, and numerous occasions in which the film dares us to tell them apart" (Berardinelli, 2001). Although it would be too much to see the film, in which Tom Cruise's character, the spoiled, playboy son of a wealthy tycoon who increasingly becomes unable to differentiate between reality and fantasy, real life and an artificial dreamscape, as an explicit outworking of Christian eschatological motifs, the film does nevertheless raise the possibility that the protagonist has died and gone to heaven – even if it does not go quite so far as to suggest that he is thereby caused to reflect on what he has achieved in his past life and to consider whether there is any scope for him to make amends and atone for his transgressions.

Filmic Depictions of a This-Worldly Eschatology

While there are certainly remnants of traditional Christian eschatology in these pictures, it is significant that, in all these cases, the filmmakers are using earthly realities as the point of departure and choose to depict the transcendent through the lens of this-worldly phenomena. There are indubitably elements of transcendence or "beyondness," including the positing of the existence of another world beyond that of our senses, but the supernatural tends to take a back seat to the primary aim of utilizing death as a vehicle for addressing issues that pertain to the exigencies and vicissitudes of *this* life, such as the transcendent power of love. Indeed, it is no mere coincidence that most of the aforementioned films contain heavy romantic sub-plots, where *agape* between two individuals has the capacity to make amends for any past indiscretions or transgressions and/or in which celestial beings act as intermediaries between earth and heaven (or hell in the case of *Little Nicky*) in order to bring two "lost" souls into everlasting union. Robert Ellis even goes so far as to argue, in his contribution to *Flickering Images: Theology and Film in Dialogue*, that in such films the filmmakers have chosen to "portray a form of human fulfilment" from which traces of the transcendent "have been excised, and all is suffused in a warm glow of human satisfaction and non-value-laden existence," to the point, indeed, that "We are back nearer ancient immortality than Christian heaven, with a few guardian angels thrown in for good luck" (Ellis, 2005, p. 20).

Such is the emphasis upon *human* fulfillment that, Ellis continues, "No more does Saint Peter meet the newly deceased at the gates, and any hint of judgement or a personal deity is gone" (ibid.). Where the transcendent is delineated, it is often employed – as in the case of *Little Nicky* and *Bedazzled* (Harold Ramis, 2000) – for comedic purposes. Indeed, *Ghost* and *What Dreams May Come* are certainly full of references to post-mortem judgment, and the existence of a life after death is treated as a given, even if specific references to God, Jesus, or the Devil are conspicuously absent, but, for the most part, where transcendental, supernatural beings are portrayed, they invariably tend to take on distinctively human characteristics. In the case of *Bedazzled*, for example, Elizabeth Hurley plays a vampish and sexualized version of Lucifer who invites a socially incompetent computer operator to sell his soul to the Devil, in an updated version of Christopher Marlowe's Elizabethan play *Doctor Faustus*, in return for granting him seven wishes. In other instances, Death itself is anthropomorphized, such as in Ingmar Bergman's *The Seventh Seal* (1957), in which, during the Black Death, a Knight played by Max von Sydow seeks answers to the eternal questions of life, death, and the existence of God while playing a game of chess with the Grim Reaper. A similar motif is utilized in the more recent *Meet Joe Black* (Martin Brest, 1998), in which a media tycoon played by Anthony Hopkins, who is about to celebrate his sixty-fifth birthday, is visited by Death, who appears in the form of a young man in a business suit (Brad Pitt). Hopkins's character, William Parrish, ends up taking Death on a guided tour of life on earth before Death eventually releases him from this mortal coil.

On the whole, therefore, there are discernible parallels between "realized" trends in Christian theology and the way in which, even in films that outwardly appear to embrace a traditional future eschatology, salvation in the modern day is less and less a question of eternal life and increasingly a matter of personal fulfillment and human agency in *this* life on earth. This especially comes to the fore in movies that wrestle with the apocalyptic and dystopian vision of the end of the world. Traditionally, the term "apocalypticism," which is derived from the Greek for "uncovering" or "revealing" (*apokalypsis*), comprises, to quote from the Society of Biblical Literature's 1979 seminar on the apocalyptic, "A genre of revelatory literature with a narrative framework in which a revelation is mediated by an otherworldly being to a recipient, disclosing a transcendent reality which is both temporal, insofar as it envisages eschatological salvation, and spatial, insofar as it involves another, supernatural world" (qtd in Scott, 1994, p. 194). When a number of biblical texts speak of the imminent end of the world, such as the prophecies in 1 Peter 4:7 that "The end of all things is at hand," and Matthew 24:6–8, which speaks of nation rising against nation "and kingdom against kingdom" and the coming of famines and earthquakes, as well as, in the Hebrew Bible, the prediction in Deutero-Isaiah that "the heavens will vanish like smoke, the earth will wear out like a garment" and its inhabitants "will die like gnats" (Isaiah 51:6), there is never any doubt that such events are the result of divine, cataclysmic forces, completely determined and enacted by the Almighty God. In such a sacred context, in which, as Ostwalt sees it, there is a dichotomy between "the transcendent realm and the world," it makes sense that there should be a "cosmic cataclysm initiated from another realm to destroy the world ...it is almost inevitable" (Ostwalt, 1998, ¶20). However, in a contemporary secular culture where "we have difficulty conceptualizing world destruction from the hands of a sovereign God" (ibid.), it is significant that in the place of divine intervention and judgment it is characteristically the case that humanity has, through its technological and scientific skills and capabilities, managed to "supplant cosmic forces as the initiators of the apocalypse" (Ostwalt, 1998, ¶5) and been raised "to the sovereign level" (ibid., ¶20).

In *The Terminator* (James Cameron, 1984), for example, the present-day, seemingly innocuous building of computers is shown to result in the creation of sophisticated machines that, in the apocalyptic world of the future, have managed to surpass the physical and even intellectual strength of humans, and subsequently rebel and set about obliterating their creators. In the case of the sequel, *Terminator 2: Judgment Day* (James Cameron, 1991), this realized reworking of traditional eschatological ideas is even taken to a more extreme dimension, as illustrated by Fred Pfeil's contention that "here already, before the bomb falls," the apocalypse has already taken root, as manifested in the film's presentation of a "sadistically panoptical mental hospital, the gleaming surfaces and security systems of the soulless corporation" where the machines are being built, and the "massively armed and equipped, anonymous police" (Pfeil, 1993, p. 244) who patrol the city streets. This understanding of a realized hell is also a mainstay of a number of contemporary war movies, as the title of Francis Ford Coppola's seminal dissection of the chaos of the Vietnam war, *Apocalypse Now* (1979), so vividly indicates. In this instance, Vietnam is used as the setting for an examination of how the forces of order, cohesion, and control have broken down, thereby accentuating the horror, madness, and apocalyptic gloom of contemporary warfare. In a film that is largely devoid of a plot and narrative structure, the images of the jungle of Vietnam as a paranoid, schizophrenic, and hallucinatory realm, and the war itself as "a disorganized, futile exercise moving to the beat of Wagner and hard rock" (Hagen, 1983, p. 232), clearly delineate an image of hell on earth. The weaponry and military technology – machines and tools of humankind's own creation, just as in the *Terminator* series – are seemingly used arbitrarily, and are both physically and psychologically savaging "hearts, minds and bodies" (Kolker, 1988, p. 243).

Rather than progressive, *Apocalypse Now* suggests that humankind has the capacity to be irrational and even regressive; the film thereby parallels Joseph Conrad's novel *Heart of Darkness* (published 1902), on which it is loosely based. There, Conrad evokes a permanently treacherous and ominous universe, a world "so hopeless and so dark, so impenetrable to human thought, so pitiless of human weakness" (Auster and Quart, 1988, p. 65), and in which the possibility of regression from civilization to savagery is starkly illustrated. With such considerations in mind, it is not surprising that, as Hans Küng wrote in 1984, there is a widespread perception among many people today "that they have come to the end of their way," and that they are "living in an end-time, drifting increasingly rapidly towards a possibly disastrous end brought about by human failure" (Küng, 1984, p. 253). Signs of a global holocaust are beginning to appear, and, in Küng's words, "the apocalyptic vision of the end of the world is approaching," in the form of "natural disasters, atomic wars, overpopulation or environment-destruction" (ibid., pp. 253–4).

Desacralizing Salvation: From the Divine to the Human

However, just as the apocalypse is human- rather than God-initiated, so there has been a noticeable trend, particularly in the last decade, for many films to replace, or at least tone down, the pessimism that imbues traditional understandings of the apocalypse, and to delineate instead the idea that the cataclysm can be *prevented* as a direct result of human ingenuity, scientific advance, and the heroism of a human Messiah. In keeping with realized eschatology, the apocalypse has not disappeared from the radar altogether. Indeed, as Conrad Ostwalt puts it, the "popular eschatological imagination is a secular one that cannot quite let go of traditional imagery and symbol borrowed often from Jewish and Christian apocalyptic drama" (Ostwalt, 2000, ¶2). The divine may no longer be present, but religious language, vocabulary, and symbolism are nonetheless implicit, to the extent that, according to Ostwalt, "popular cultural forms have become significant, if not more effective, purveyors of our culture's eschatological consciousness" (ibid., ¶3). Despite the palpable threat that the end of the world is impending, rarely does this threat materialize, making the likes of *Apocalypse Now* the exception rather than the rule. Instead of humanity's annihilation, many films today posit the *salvation* of the human race – and by the means, moreover, not of divine intervention but of human action that has *supplanted* cosmic forces. In Frances Flannery-Dailey's words, "The divine is nowhere in view" (Flannery-Dailey, 2000 ¶16). In an article entitled "Bruce Willis as the Messiah: Human Effort, Salvation and Apocalypticism in *Twelve Monkeys*," Flannery-Dailey argues that apocalypticism has been desacralized and relocated by filmmakers "entirely within the sphere of human activity and concern" (Flannery-Dailey, 2000, ¶1). In place of a cosmic battle between God and the forces of darkness, the focus of films such as *Outbreak* (Wolfgang Petersen, 1995), *Waterworld* (Kevin Reynolds, 1995), *Twelve Monkeys* (Terry Gilliam, 1995), *Independence Day* (Roland Emmerich, 1996), and *Armageddon* (Michael Bay, 1998) is on killer viruses, alien invasions, meteors, machines, or environmental catastrophes.

In the case of *Waterworld*, for example, the greenhouse effect has caused the polar icecaps to melt and the earth to be covered with water; the film thereby reflects contemporary secular rather than overtly sacred concerns in its depiction of ecological catastrophe. At the end of the film, however, the apocalyptic threat is averted, for dry land has been discovered, complete with fresh water and vegetation. Similarly, in *Armageddon*, it is the human sacrifice and heroism of the Bruce Willis character that manage to offset world destruction, in the form of a comet that is heading toward our planet. In such films, the *eschaton* has become dependent not on the grace of God but on the ultimate power and knowledge employed by resourceful human beings, and, in Flannery-Dailey's words, "If the scientists are successful, the locus of future bliss is not heaven, but an earth purified through human effort and the power of science" (Flannery-Dailey, 2000, ¶21). It is not surprising, therefore, if, at the end of such pictures – and Ostwalt cites *Contact* (Robert Zemeckis, 1997) and *Deep Impact* (Mimi Leder, 1998) as prime examples – the "threat of the end tends to bring people together in a unified stand against annihilation, evolving out of a deep faith in the powers of scientific ingenuity and human ability" (Ostwalt, 2000, ¶7). Whereas in traditional Jewish and Christian apocalyptic dramas the impotence of humanity when confronted with a divinely programmed cosmic catastrophe tends to be a defining characteristic, in the filmic apocalypse "Angelic armies and beasts no longer suffice to usher in the end" (ibid., ¶11) and "The message is clear: together we can beat this thing" (ibid., ¶7).

Across a whole range of eschatologically themed films, therefore, a realized, this-worldly, and anthropocentric dimension, in which human agency and endeavor supplant divine activity, can be seen to prevail. There is, however, a strong theological basis to such a shift in the direction of the efficacy of the human, not least in light of the fact that, as I have argued elsewhere, there has been an increased tendency among many theologians, especially over recent centuries, to change the orientation and scope of the concept of redemption from one that construes Christ as the ultimate, and exclusive, redemptive figure to one that accords a more prominent emphasis to the role of the human individual in the redemptive process (see Deacy, 2001, p. 70). In other words, humans need to be proactive in the search for redemption, along the lines of Friedrich Schleiermacher's conviction that Christ cannot simply be construed as a detached, alien, and external figure but, in order to be meaningful to us today, consideration must be given to the individual Christian's *experience* of Christ's redemptive work – in relation, in other words, "to our own self-consciousness" (in ibid., p. 74). John Hick, likewise, has spoken of the fact that the redemptive process only makes sense when construed in terms of the manner in which Christ's resurrection impacts upon our lives in the here and now. Rather than see salvation as a merely "juridical and metaphysical idea" (Hick, 1977, p. 74) that pertains to what happened at Calvary some two thousand years ago, Hick proposes that "the meaning of our present earthly life" (ibid., p. 87) can be seen to lie in the struggle in which all humans are engaged with the problem of evil *within present human existence*. Indeed, if we are to advance or grow as humans, then what is important is not that we are saved from an apocalyptic-type scenario by the hand of God, but that we are equipped with the necessary faculties and strengths for character-building and person-making within and through this present life on earth. If human agency were not important, then it would not be possible, as a consequence of Christ's death on the Cross, for redemption to be achieved in turn by those who hear and have responded to Christ's message. While, as Paul Badham makes clear, it is entirely possible to believe in the "redemption wrought by Christ as an event wholly unique to him and entailing no consequences for the rest of humanity" (Badham, 1986, p. 126), without there being an anthropocentric dimension to the eschatological process it is hard to see why the New Testament story should retain any contemporary significance aside from merely historical interest.

Cinematic Interpretations of
a Mind-Dependent World

Even in films where traditional eschatological ideas are in evidence, it is notable that there is often an underlying assumption that heaven (and hell) is less of an objective, trans-worldly dimension of existence, and more a subjective, almost personal, realm, in which human agency plays an integral role in shaping and structuring the post-mortem environment. In the case of *What Dreams May Come*, although Chris Nielsen (Robin Williams) is in "heaven" after his untimely death, the environment in which he finds himself exists in a state of flux. It is explained to him at one point by an enigmatic spirit guide that each soul in the afterlife creates his or her own subjective paradise, which would thus explain why Nielsen spends the bulk of the movie in a landscape that resembles one of the oil paintings done by his wife, Annie, of the time (on earth) when they first met, many years earlier, in Switzerland. All boundaries between physical, exterior reality and inner, subjective reality are fissured in this film, with the suggestion that heaven is simply a mental projection of whatever one imagines. It is made clear at one point that there is a distinction between our minds and our bodies, and that thought is real but the physical is an illusion, so that what makes us human is that "essential" part of ourselves (presumably our souls) that is not equivalent to the brain or organic flesh.

In *Vanilla Sky*, also, there is a strong suggestion that the world that David Aames (Tom Cruise) is inhabiting is not a physical world as such but a mind-dependent, post-mortem dream world that is being fashioned and induced, while his physical body has been cryogenically frozen for the past 150 years, by the memories and fantasies (as well as, it transpires – albeit inadvertently – the traumas) of his earthly existence. It is even explained at one point in the film that, although his body may be comatose and inert, medical advances have enabled him to be "resurrected to continue your own life as you know it now," wherein:

> Upon resurrection, you will continue in an ageless state, preserved, but living in the present with a future of your choosing. Your death will be wiped from your memory. Your life will continue as a realistic work of art painted by you minute to minute, and you'll live it with the romantic abandon of a summer day with the feeling of a great movie, or a pop song you've always loved. With no memory of how it occurred, save for the knowledge that everything simply improved . . . The day after tomorrow, another chapter begins seamlessly. A living dream . . . Life Part Two . . .

This may not correspond to most people's traditional expectations of what heaven (or for that matter hell) will be like, but, significantly, this is not at all at odds with certain trends in modern liberal theology toward revising the traditional eschatological notion of a future, bodily resurrection and replacing it with a formulation that takes on board the concept of the immortality of the soul. From the second century of the Christian era onward, personal survival was believed by most of the early Fathers to be contingent upon direct physical continuity between the earthly and the heavenly bodies. According to article four of the Church of England's 39 articles of faith, "Christ did truly rise again from death, and took again his body, with flesh, bones, and all things pertaining to the perfection of Man's nature" (qtd in Badham, 1976, p. 47). As a corollary of this, it was likewise expected that the particles that constitute the flesh of each individual human being were to be reassembled after bodily death, and the identical structure that death has destroyed was to be restored. However, in the modern day, in which our cosmology does not allow for our bodies to be relocated after death above the earth in the sky, and heaven is no longer associated with the spatial environment above us, Paul Badham is a leading proponent of the idea that the point of contact between our mortal and immortal existence cannot be physical, and that it is more tenable to propose that we will receive new and quite different types of bodies that will serve as vehicles for the way we exist in heaven. The link between this and the next world must thus lie in the same identical ego (see also Harris, 1983, p. 126) – best encapsulated, perhaps, by the term *spiritual body* – rather than in the material or physical continuation of this flesh. Indeed, Badham has affirmed in his *Christian Beliefs about Life after Death* that it is not inconceivable that "the mind could enjoy any kind of personal life without a bodily frame to give expression to its will, and to provide it with the sensory stimuli for its consciousness" (Badham, 1976, p. 133). We should not be speaking, therefore, of our flesh surviving but of the survival (or immortality) of our spirit, soul, or personality. Elsewhere, Badham has written that "A survey of modern Christian writing on the future hope shows that this remains the most commonly accepted understanding of resurrection today" (Badham and Badham, 1982, p. 26), and he quotes the Archbishop's Commission on Doctrine in the Church of England, published in 1938, which postulated that "in the life of the world to come the soul or spirit will still have its appropriate organ of expression and activity" (qtd in ibid.). There is thus a potential correlation between the thoroughly realized eschatological tendencies in films such as *What Dreams May Come* and *Vanilla Sky* and the manner in which contemporary theologians make sense of the concept of immortality (figure 7).

Figure 7 *What Dreams May Come* (Vincent Ward, 1998) is one of a number of recent filmic attempts to visualize the afterlife through the lens of this-worldly phenomena, in a manner which tallies with H. H. Price's understanding of a mind-dependent universe.
Photograph: Polygram/The Kobal Collection

The British philosopher and parapsychologist Henry H. Price took this line of thinking even further forward in his address in 1952 to the Society for Psychical Research on the concept of a mind-dependent universe, entitled "Survival and the Idea of 'Another World.'" Difficult though it may be for us to envisage a disembodied future life in which "the supply of sensory stimuli is perforce cut off" and "the supposed experient has no sense organs and no nervous system" (Price, 1973, p. 23), Price refuted the idea that without any sense perception one "has no means of being aware of material objects any longer" (ibid.) as well as the claim that "it is hard to see how one could have any emotions or wishes either" since "all the emotions and wishes we have in this present life are concerned directly or indirectly with material objects" (ibid.). Despite the common assumption that "one could only be said to have experiences at all if one is aware of some sort of a *world*" (ibid., p. 24), Price thought it was quite conceivable that experiences could occur even if they were not causally connected with a physical organism. When we dream, for instance, "sensory stimuli are cut off ... [b]ut we still manage to have experiences" (ibid.). For some people, moreover, "the mental images they experience when awake are more interesting – more attention-absorbing – than the physical objects they perceive" (Price, 1992, p. 217). Accordingly, just as we do not require physical organs in order to dream, Price contended that we cannot rule out that a disembodied survivor could also engage in mental experiences. When we dream, we do not normally doubt that what we are dreaming about is actually taking place, and, no matter how unusual or peculiar the things about which we dream may happen to be, "it does not at all disconcert us at the time, and our personal identity is not broken" (Price, 1973, p. 25). On this basis, Price concluded that there are good grounds for supposing that the afterlife will be akin to the world of our dreams. In his words: "If we retain our memories and desires after death (and there can be no personal survival unless we do) these memories and desires may continue to manifest themselves by means of mental images, as they do in this present life when we are dreaming" (Price, 1972, p. 105). To give an example, Price thought that "We can quite well image to ourselves what it feels like to be in a warm bath, even when we are not actually in one," and that "a person who has been crippled can image what it felt like to climb a mountain" (Price, 1973, p. 28). Personal identity need not, then, be broken by physical death, provided that "there are images after death which sufficiently resemble the organic sensations one had before" (ibid., p. 30). The analogy is thus akin to "what happens when one falls asleep and begins dreaming" (ibid.), the only fundamental difference being that "life after death on this view would be a kind of dream from which we never wake up" (Price, 1972, p. 105).

When, in *Vanilla Sky*, David Aames repeatedly hears a female voice telling him to "Open your eyes," and characters inexplicably swap identities and manage to appear and disappear from one moment to the next, there is a discernible link with Price's idea that the post-mortem world is an environment composed of and forged by memories and mental imaging derived from our mortal existence. Reading the film through the lens of Price's model, Aames's tendency to flit between different states of consciousness and to appear to travel backward and forward in time makes sense if we interpret that which seems to be happening not within the spatial, geographical environment of New York c.2001 but within a mental, or mind-dependent, realm. The images of his two lovers, a model played by Cameron Diaz and a Spanish dancer played by Penélope Cruz, whose identities blur, and who constantly cross-reference and shadow one another – to the point that it is unclear whether they are separate individuals or comprise two separate archetypes of his febrile imagination, thereby making it impossible for the audience to determine which, if either, of the two he is supposedly responsible for murdering at one point in the narrative – thus tally with how, for Price, the things about which we dream have the semblance of being spatially related to one another, but in reality "are not at any distance nor in any direction" (in Badham, 1976, p. 136) from where our physical bodies happen to lie. In Aames's case, he has spent the previous century and a half in earth time lying in a comatose state as a client of the mysterious Life Extension Corporation, which peddles in the trade of selling Lucid Dreams, yet so inextricably linked are the "real world" and the "dream world" that, as Xan Brooks puts it in his review of *Vanilla Sky*, the film comprises "a portrait of two parallel unrealities that reflect and inform each other to such a degree that you can barely see the join," a portrait whose skill lies "in making you wonder if there's really much difference between the two" (Brooks, 2002, p. 64). Like Chris Nielsen in *What Dreams May Come*, Aames is able to travel from one "place" to another on the basis of having what Price would construe as a vivid and detailed set of images of two different places, such that, in Penelhum's words, "the wish to be at a certain place might be followed by the images of that place" (Penelhum, 1970, p. 50). Rather than an actual movement in space, however, the different experiences Aames undergoes in the film arise from changes in consciousness, in which, to quote Price, "perception ceases and imaging replaces it" (Price, 1973, p. 33). The fact that Aames spends the movie confusing two girlfriends could be construed as evidence that the laws that operate in this mind-dependent world are not physical, as in the case of our present physical world, but are more akin to those of Freudian or Jungian psychology. This is certainly compatible with how, for Price, in the absence of a "real" environment, the survivor's imagination might be predisposed to create its own private one, by means of wishes and desires.

To forge too great a connection between a cultural product, such as the film *Vanilla Sky*, and the rudiments of a Christian understanding of eschatology would, however, be injudicious, and fall into the trap of trying to read theological language into a film that *per se* does not countenance it. Indeed, listening to the DVD commentary of *Vanilla Sky*, it is apparent that the director, Cameron Crowe, has deliberately kept all options open as to the film's meaning, and, while he concedes that the idea that Aames is dreaming is a persuasive one, at no point does the concept of a mind-dependent world appear to have caught the attention of the filmmakers. That said, though, in juxtaposing the film with Price's theory, it is apparent that the film presents a version of a mind-dependent world that, if anything, resolves one of the problems that frustrates the theory. For one of the problems with Price's model, as he himself conceded, is that it is difficult to posit whether the mind-dependent world would be entirely solipsistic in form, that is, it would be made up entirely of our own memories and desires (so that we would, in effect, be alone), or whether "it would be the joint-product of a group of telepathically-interacting minds and public to all of them" (Price, 1973, p. 37), so that there would be a communal and corporate dimension to this dreamscape. Rather than directly address this problem, however, Price appears to be trying to hold together both of these alternative renderings at the same time, so that in order to address the fact that the traditional Christian picture posits a common hope whereby we will, in the afterlife, be reunited with our loved ones from earth (on the grounds, indeed, that we are, at root, social beings), Price suggested that there would be *multiple* individual mind-dependent worlds, "a different one for each group of like-minded personalities" (Price, 1973, p. 37).

This is a perspective that is taken even further by John Hick, who envisages the existence of one, single, common world, whose character is made up of the "emotions, desires and memories of the entire human race" (Hick, 1985, p. 272). For Hick, it would exist "in its totality in the divine consciousness" (ibid., p. 275) while different parts of it are imparted to the minds of different individuals, and so would in many respects be remarkably akin to our present life on earth in that, to paraphrase Badham, although we would not have "bodies" as such, we would nevertheless have *image*-bodies that could be the vehicle of expression of our personalities (Badham, 1976, p. 140). In the film, however, the model that is being posited is an unequivocally solipsistic dreamscape, dependent exclusively on the memories and desires of, and only of, David Aames. This approach also happens to be very similar in kind to Badham's preferred model, according to which, although it is a private image-world (and so by definition solipsistic), there is no reason why, in such a world, the agent should not be able to form *images* of other persons (Badham, 1976, p. 144). Other persons – such as, in terms of the film, Sofia (Penélope Cruz) and Julianna (Cameron Diaz) – may appear to the agent, but they have no objective essence. Although Badham elaborates upon this position by positing, in a way the film does not, the possibility of a form of telepathic communication between minds, thereby fulfilling the expectation that we will be reunited in heaven with those persons we used to know on earth – as well as overcoming the problem that would invariably apply in the case of objective images, namely, that we would have difficulty recognizing those friends or relatives who lived longer on earth than we did and who would have aged, possibly beyond recognition, since we last saw them (ibid.) – there is a remarkable congruence between Price and

Badham's positions and the dreamscape delineated in *Vanilla Sky*. For, despite not living in a shared environment (wherein telepathic communication is not an option), Aames is nevertheless able to fashion a communal world out of his memories and desires and is capable of a form of social interaction.

There is a further important theological angle here, in that although Aames's world is inescapably subjective in nature – he is, literally, inhabiting a kind of dream world that has been molded by the experiences, hopes, and fears of his life on earth – there is also a certain objectivity to his mind-dependent environment, as, being shaped by his character, he is required to experience this world *whether he likes it or not*. At the very end of the picture, Aames chooses to sever all ties with Life Extension Corporation, a choice visually represented by his decision to plummet to his "death" by jumping from the roof of a high building; this fits in with Price's argument that a mind-dependent world is consistent with the Christian idea that we reap what we sow and that we will be confronted in the afterlife with ourselves *as we really are* (cf. Price, 1973, p. 45). Rather than a world that is too good to be true, the guilt-ridden, paranoid and alienated world Aames finds himself in in *Vanilla Sky* is, to paraphrase Price, too *bad* to be true (Price, 1973, p. 41). Much as Aames may want to seek integration and harmony, his inability to reconcile his conflicting feelings for the two women in his life, and the guilt he feels at having (metaphorically or literally, the film allows for either reading) killed one (or maybe both!) of them, have thus permeated – and defined – the fabric of the world in which he resides. In keeping with Robert Jewett's reading of *Groundhog Day* (Harold Ramis, 1993), identified in chapter 1, in which the disposition of Phil Connors (Bill Murray), in Pauline terms, to "sow to the flesh" and "reap the corruption of emptiness" is the precursor to self-transformation and enlightenment, so David Aames's "pampered playboy lifestyle" (Brooks, 2002, p. 63) becomes too dispiriting and facile for him to want to relive for an eternity, to the extent that (in the reverse of the choice made by Connors to *stay* in Punxsutawney) Aames finally chooses annihilation from the cycle of life.

Although, for much of the film, Aames is unable to differentiate between his mind-dependent dreamscape and his former life on earth, which is fueling and sustaining his post-mortem memories and experiences – and to this end we can draw parallels with what John Hick says in relation to evidence drawn from some aspects of Western spiritualist literature pertaining to psychic correspondence, namely that for many people who die the (first phase at least of the) next life "may be so like earth that they do not at first realize that they have died" (Hick, 1985, p. 404) – by the film's denouement, Aames sees his condition as anything but "an experience of delightful wish-fulfilment" (ibid., p. 405). Instead, Aames's plight is closer in essence to what one alleged spiritualist communication[1] has referred to as that of "[t]he cold selfish man in Illusion-land" who dwells "in darkness" (cited in Hick, 1985, p. 405). Yet whereas for Price there may be positive value here, in that we may become dissatisfied with the kind of world we have made for ourselves and so attempt to alter our character (see Price, 1973, p. 45) – to the extent of hungering and thirsting after righteousness (cf. Matthew 5:6) – Aames's redemptive journey, if we can call it that, has come to an end.

Conclusion

Although it has not been the aim of this discussion to suggest that Hollywood films have a predilection for bearing witness to specifically Christian eschatological motifs – at the end of the day, filmmakers themselves are often hesitant to broach specifically theological questions – it has become apparent that a critical theological conversation carried out between the theologian and filmic texts can be a rewarding one. It is a conversation, moreover, that, in a manner akin to Lynch's revised correlational model (itself a refinement of Niebuhr's fourth, dualist approach to the relationship between Christ and culture), "values a complex conversation between the questions and insights of both religious tradition and popular culture, and allows for the possibility that both religious tradition and popular culture can be usefully challenged and transformed through this process" (Lynch, 2005, p. 105). Cameron Crowe's *Vanilla Sky* and H. H. Price's mind-dependent world can thus be seen as two vital conversation-partners that shed light on and inform one another in a mutually enlightening way. In his monograph *A History of Heaven*, Jeffrey Burton Russell begins by arguing that we may not be able to describe heaven itself, but it is nevertheless possible to list the attributes of the *human* concept of heaven (Russell, 1997, p. 3). For example, he indicates that some see heaven as the epitome of a place that is not dull, static, or monochrome, but, rather, "an endless dynamic of joy" (ibid.) where one's potential for love, understanding, and wisdom can be realized. There may be diverse and diffuse questions concerning the make-up of heaven – for example, pertaining to how many people will go there, and what will be their gender, age, and appearance (ibid., p. 4) – but, ultimately, heaven is something "ineffable, beyond words" (ibid., p. 6), which can only be spoken of in *human* categories, such as being "up there" as opposed to "down there" and as being a place of incandescent light, as opposed to darkness, where goodness, perfection, and perfect judgment ultimately prevail.

This can be seen to apply to the question of eschatology more generally. Although I referred earlier in this chapter to some of the more traditional uses by filmmakers of Christian eschatological motifs (such as the disjuncture between the earthly and heavenly realms evinced in *Ghost*), it is apparent that realized trends in post-Enlightenment theology have also worked their way into filmic texts. So, in the film *Working Girl* (Mike Nicholls, 1988), for example, the New Jerusalem no longer has any specific anchorage in Old Testament salvation history, but is now used to evoke the fulfillment of the American Dream. When Tess McGill (Melanie Griffith) climbs the corporate ladder and achieves financial and personal success by overcoming her working-class origins, Carly Simon's song "Let the River Run," which invokes the "New Jerusalem," underscores McGill's trajectory in this film: those who work hard and play by the rules are rewarded in an eschatologically fulfilling manner (cf. Scott, 1994, p. 138) and have inaugurated on earth the vision of the Old Testament prophets. In *The Shawshank Redemption* (Frank Darabont, 1994), too, the achievement of "redemption" is correlated with a vision of paradise on earth, namely, the "new world of sun, beach, and water" (Reinhartz, 2003, p. 141) in which two institutionalized prison inmates are enabled to spend their remaining years. As Reinhartz puts it, "The Mexican beach represents an eschatological vision as foreign to the realities of modern North American life as it is to Shawshank Prison" (ibid.), and so in this respect Red (Morgan Freeman) and Andy (Tim Robbins) are afforded an opportunity to taste a new life in another world, as dichotomous from their former life on earth as heaven is from earth in traditional Christian interpretation. Both film and Christianity can thus be seen to be involved in a related journey: one in which salvation and redemption can be apprehended at the very cusp, and at the very fulfillment, of a distinctly human process of transformation, enlightenment, and evolution.

Note

1   The source concerned is a communication, professing to be from the psychical researcher F. W. H. Myers following his death, through the medium Geraldine Cummins, which is cited in Hick, 1985, p. 405. The full extract reads: "The

cold selfish man in Illusion-land may dwell in darkness, for it is not within the power of his ego to throw itself outward, to express itself in the fantasy of fulfilled desires. He is thrown more than ever inward by the shock of death. He believes that he has lost everything. He loses contact with all except the sense of his own thinking substance. A nightmare of darkness prevails for a time, prevails as long as he lives within his morbid sense of loss, within his desire, which is merely to gratify himself without any regard for others. There may be only night in Illusion-land for the abnormally selfish man."

Conclusion: Theological Perspectives on Cinematic Storytelling

> We play the creator every time we speak. We reshape the world every time we say what something means.
>
> Paden, 1992, p. 9

Having surveyed a variety of theological perspectives and filmic themes, ranging from violence to feminism, the environment to war, and justice to eschatology, it is apparent that a two-way dialogical process between the film text and the theologian has the capacity not simply to demonstrate that we can find traces of theology *in* film, but that the cinematic medium itself is a prime and fertile repository for theological encounter and exchange. Along the lines of Aichele and Walsh's *Screening Scripture* and Gordon Lynch's revised correlational model, it is our contention that a film can (and should) challenge our reading of theology just as theology can (and should) challenge our reading of films. In accordance, moreover, with the discussion generated in chapter 1 around H. Richard Niebuhr's five models of Christ and culture, and Dietrich Bonhoeffer's understanding of "religionless Christianity," it is apparent that the line of demarcation between the sacred and the secular is never other than a thin, broken, and permeable one, so that a conversation between theology and film is not only recommended but is integral to any proper and balanced account of the role of religion and society in the modern world.

 Gaye Ortiz with Chris Deacy

In this final chapter, we will survey the fruits of the exploration to date, with a particular focus on the cinematic narrative. With few exceptions, the story is the driving force behind a film. But this observation does not justify the hallowing of the narrative to the detriment of attention to the way a film is shot and edited, the performance of the actors, etc. Theologians who teach and write about film have been criticized, often quite rightly – not least by Steve Nolan (2005, pp. 26–7) and Melanie J. Wright (2007, pp. 21–2) – for ignoring the other elements of film-making to zero in on the story, upon which oftentimes they heap their own confessional interpretations. The beauty of a film is that all the parts come together to create an unforgettable whole, a cinematic experience that is said to be felt long before it is understood. This is not to say, however, that the story cannot, or should not, be central to making sense of the sensory overload that is the film-watching experience.

The early forms of moving pictures were meant to entertain, amusing vignettes viewed in seconds among other penny-arcade attractions. Yet when the narrative was integrated into the film it linked movies to the long list of storytelling media, from epic poems to the Bible and Greek drama. Oral, visual, and written narratives are integral to the story of human existence, whether they were invented to entertain, educate, or memorialize. As film narrative became a cinematic fixture in the early twentieth century it established the need for scriptwriters, writers who used the language of film to tell stories. Silent film, even with its intertitles, was able to create wonderful narratives (*Broken Blossoms* [D. W. Griffith, 1919]; *Sunrise* [F. W. Murnau, 1927]; *The Passion of Joan of Arc* [Carl Theodor Dreyer, 1928]), but the effect of the enhancement of sound in the late 1920s on the development of richer dialogue and intricate character-ization was significant. As Corrigan and White put it, the development of sound allowed for the creation of "more intricate characters, whose often rich dialogue and vocal intonations signaled new psychological and social dimensions. More intricate characters could, in turn, propel more complex movie plots through the 1920s and thereafter" (Corrigan & White, 2004, p. 223).

The Quest for Meaning

David Jasper is right to warn, however, against the uncritical appro-priation by theologians of a filmic text. In the penultimate chapter of *Explorations in Theology and Film* (1997), Jasper, professor in literature and theology at the University of Glasgow, tossed many balls into the air. His contention was that there is an ontological difference between the business of film and the business of theology, since the former is a commercial medium that revolves around "money and profit...in which the stars are paid enormous sums of money, and all too often fall from their dizzy heights as dramatically as they climb to fame" (Jasper, 1997, p. 235), while theological reflection is necessarily "two-edged, ironic, difficult and ambiguous," and so cinema's "house of illusions" is not in the same league (ibid., p. 244). From the outset, therefore, caution must be exercised before we uncritically endorse Ernest Ferlita's claim that "film appears to be the most suitable art for supporting our continued or renewed quest for meaning" (Ferlita, 1982, p. 117). Rather, as Jasper sees it, cinema – or Hollywood at any rate – "is there to help us through the tedium of inactivity, and is supremely an art of illusion" (Jasper, 1997, p. 235) and can do no more than emulate, or "mimic" (ibid., p. 237), theology, through the discernment, say, of Christ-figure motifs.

In response to Jasper, however, it is apparent that some films are more readily amenable to a theological conversation than such a unilateral portrait might suggest. Even Jasper concedes, for example, that the cinema of Martin Scorsese "sustains a consistently 'theological' possibility, by continually deflecting the aspirations and anticipations of the viewer in complex visions which both confuse and prompt attempts at systematization out of the threat of chaos" (Jasper, 1997, p. 243). In other words, where films are capable of critiquing and challenging the very conventions on which escapism rests, and of transgressing the demands of the audience who ostensibly expect to be served up frothy and escapist entertainment, it is not inconceivable that films can lend themselves to creative theological encounter. The onus is also on the viewer to insure that, even if a film is not in itself particularly demanding or intrinsically open to a theological reading, it is not thereby dismissed as having no theological function. Sometimes, indeed, it is a film's underlying ideological position that might be germane to the theologian, rather than any specific "religious" content. The way a film mirrors (or subverts) a culture's norms and values, along the lines of the discussion of war films earlier in this volume, is a case in point. A comedy such as *Liar Liar* (Tom Shadyac, 1997) unmistakably serves up escapist entertainment, but its premise – that a lawyer is unable to speak any untruths for 24 hours following his son's birthday wish – also plays a potentially educative role. As Johnston says in relation to *Liar Liar*: "To the degree that a movie appeals to popular culture, it is entertaining. To the degree that it seeks to portray some aspect of truth, beauty, and/or goodness, it is educating" (R. Johnston, 2000, p. 89).

Formulaic and crass though much of Hollywood's output may be, Johnston is right to attest that "Film has the power to disturb and enlighten, to make us aware of both who we are and what our relationship with others could be. It can even usher us into the presence of the holy" (ibid., p. 87). Before we dismiss Hollywood cinema, therefore, it may first be worth considering the possibility that, as Gerard Loughlin puts it, "we should ask more of ourselves as viewers, demand more of the films we watch. For when we ask more, we may find that the films have more to give, that their writers and directors have given us more than we first think" (Loughlin, 2005, p. 2). Rob Johnston similarly counsels that "to the degree that a film, whether through fantasy or realism, and even when primarily entertainment, succeeds artistically in depicting life, it engages our lives. As it does, it educates, inviting our response as whole persons, including our religious convictions" (R. Johnston, 2000, p. 90). As we have argued in this book, film in a holistic sense discourages us from thinking in a way that dissects the sacred/spiritual from the secular.

Film stories can therefore help in our quest for human meaning and fulfillment. In writing about the human search for answers to the question "Why are we here?" Ferlita suggests that Vicktor Frankl's theory of logotherapy is instructive: "we can discover meaning in our lives in three different ways: 1) by doing a deed 2) by experiencing a value 3) by suffering" (Ferlita, 1982, p. 118). It is not difficult to identify these three themes when trawling through the decades of films, but the themes do vary according to the culture and values of the times. As Jeff Stein observes, the quest in 1960s American films was linked to the awakening of people to the need to do right, with a film such as *The Graduate* (Mike Nichols, 1967) seeking meaning in challenging society (J. Stein, 2006). The themes are also more suited to particular filmic genres. These ways of discovering meaning may be portrayed very personally, as in *Being There* (Hal Ashby, 1979) or *Secrets and Lies* (Mike Leigh, 1996), or in the larger-than-life arena of the blockbuster epic (*Star Wars* [George Lucas, 1977], *Star Trek* [Gene Roddenberry, 1966], *Lord of the Rings* [Peter Jackson, 2001]), in relation to which John Izod comments:

> While a true epic is a narrative which may well have a large number of characters in it, the fundamental point is that its action should be on a grand scale, its themes involving the fate of an entire people...Nothing inhibits the presentation of large heroes and villains with strongly marked personalities, but such characters should in some way further the noble

purposes of the epic as leaders of a people, or their all-too-threatening enemies. Characters are likely to be used as vehicles to convey substantial moral statements, whether by words or deeds.

(Izod, 2001, p. 187)

Whatever form it may take, in theological terms Ferlita says that this search for meaning "is deeply related to hope . . . (fundamental) hope is the wellspring of all vitality . . . It has to do . . . with the salvation of the human person . . . Fundamental hope asserts itself most tellingly only when all our hopes collapse and lose their meaning" (Ferlita, 1982, p. 121). In other words, when we are unexpectedly faced with a complete reversal of fortune and the lack of a moral compass, that is the time when we begin to make our own meaning. The situation is not wholly different from what Paul Giles calls "that old Catholic paradox whereby the rank black sinner, the person who is horribly aware of the awful potential of damnation, can be closer to redemptive grace than the honest citizen who has never troubled himself about anything beyond his or her own domestic affairs" (Giles, 1992, p. 332; and see the reference to this above, chapter 6).

Moreover, this kind of narrative can be very powerful in terms of a filmic experience. David Dark, writing about the contemporary alienation from life that film characters like Neo (in *The Matrix*, Andy and Larry Wachowski, 1999) and Truman (in *The Truman Show*, Peter Weir, 1998) experience, says that the search for meaning is something that many of us can identify with in a culture where real choice and freedom seem out of reach: "*The Matrix* and *The Truman Show* are for many the most convincing metanarratives of our own culture . . . films whose protagonists discover themselves in carefully scripted, immersive environments that create the illusion of freedom while using inhabitants to fuel their own machinery" (Dark, 2002, p. 81). However, John Izod warns us against identifying too closely with these fictional characters, because the analogy can only go so far: "From their earliest lessons in scriptwriting, novice writers learn that fictional characters are not people. They are goal-driven. Their function is to try to fulfill the overriding purpose that (whether they know it or not) is their object" (Izod, 2001, p. 206). Accordingly, although we may feel connected to characters because they are facing a challenge that we may find familiar, no character can ever have the complexity of a human existence; she or he exists on screen for the simple purpose of telling a good story. As Jasper says in relation to *The Terminator* films (James Cameron, 1984, 1991), for instance, "As long

204

as Sarah Connor is around we know that humanity will defeat the machine nightmare," and in the absence of depth and complexity "in the end [these movies] are just good entertainment within both myth and an environment (the cinema) that is ultimately reassuring and safe" (Jasper, 1997, p. 238).

Still, in any good story that ultimately reunites a character with the world, with family or friends or, most importantly, with his or her soul, we learn again the lesson of life described by Ernest Ferlita: "The personal dimension of that search addresses the issue of man's alienation from self: it impels him to a sense of his own worth. We are not born with that sense, and in this world of ours we never perfectly achieve it: we are always on the way, on a pilgrimage towards self-realization" (Ferlita, 1982, pp. 123–4). According to Ferlita, this pilgrimage "is marked by three essential experiences: 1) by trusting and mastering the world around us 2) by being loved and 3) by loving" (ibid.). It is the opening of ourselves to the experience of narrative, which is propelled toward us at 24 frames per second in a rich mix of sight and sound, that Ferlita declares to be a redemptive and transforming personal experience: "The image of journey resonates with that attitude of mind; the experience of film at its deepest level prompts that response... with that attitude of mind the quest for meaning never truly begins and never rightly ends" (ibid., p. 131).

The History of the Hero's Journey

In the 1970s, the film world had its first taste of a mythic journey in outer space that drew explicitly upon academic studies of heroes who set off on a quest for meaning. Many students of theology and film are familiar with Joseph Campbell's hero's journey and the call to adventure, especially since it was the inspiration for George Lucas in his *Star Wars* creation. However, according to Robert Segal, the study of hero myths dates back at least to 1871. In his *Theorizing about Myth*, Segal cites the English anthropologist Edward Tylor, for whom many hero myths follow a uniform plot or pattern, whereby the hero is exposed at birth, is saved by other humans or animals, and grows up to become a national hero (Segal, 1999, p. 117). Segal discusses the contributions made by Johann Georg von Hahn, Vladimir Popp, Lord Raglan, Otto Rank, and Joseph Campbell to the study of myth. Although he identifies Jungian and Freudian emphases in much of the more recent theory, Segal observes that Campbell is not a

Jungian, differing most with Jung over the origins and function of myth.[1] From this, it is easy to understand why the cinema has a literally universal storytelling appeal. In Segal's words: "The contents of myth – called archetypal simply because they are similar worldwide – emerge from the imprint of either recurrent or traumatic experiences. In all of these cases each society creates its own myths – whatever the source of the material it uses" (ibid., p. 119).

Joseph Campbell succinctly draws the picture of the hero's journey as consisting of a separation from everyday life with five stages: (1) the call to adventure, (2) the refusal of the call, (3) supernatural aid, (4) the crossing of the first threshold, and (5) the belly of the whale. The first stage of departure is followed by a series of trials and victories of initiation; that process of surviving tests and ordeals, often of a magical nature, is followed by a return to and reintegration with society (see Campbell, 1988, p. 36). Rather than being spirited away to a new and better world, the hero finds that he is reintegrated with his former existence and, in fact, finds that he has been imbued all along with the powers that he so bravely fought to obtain on his journey. Segal describes this transformation in terms of self-perception:

> Having managed to break free of the secure, everyday world and go off to a dangerous new one, Campbell's hero, to complete his journey, must in turn break free of the new world, in which he has become ensconced, and return to the everyday one ... Campbell's hero returns and remains home not only because he finds the new world back home but also because he wants selflessly to save others.
>
> (Segal, 1999, pp. 127–8)

Campbell articulates this transformative act as "symbolical of that divine and redemptive image which is hidden within us all, only waiting to be known and rendered into life" (Campbell, 1988, p. 39). The identification of the audience with Luke Skywalker, Indiana Jones, E. T., Butch Cassidy, or even Wallace and Gromit can be a manifestation of the desire in each of us to find that hero quality, as Campbell suggests, within our own lives. Irrespective of whether these films are inevitably escapist in orientation, they can nevertheless serve a deep mythological – if not, in terms of Jasper's reservations, a strictly theological – function.

If, as Campbell suggests, the struggle for identity is universal, perhaps we might all be united in that search and transcend the things that divide and alienate us one from another. Segal insists that Campbell is an "uncompromising world ecumenist," quoting him as wanting, in the preface to

The Hero with a Thousand Faces, "to demonstrate that all myths are one in order to demonstrate that all people are one. In *The Power of Myth*...he continues to say that we still 'need myths that will identify the individual not with his local group but with the planet'" (Segal, 1999, p. 135, citing Campbell, 1988, p. 24).

Genres

Segal declares that "Campbell's work is an important introduction to myth. It is simply not the last word" (Segal, 1999, p. 141). He ignores, however, the vital contribution to the cinematic understanding of the hero that Campbell has made. Although the best-known example of Campbell's influence on film comes from the science fiction genre, there are many heroes in a range of genres who follow Campbell's hero's journey. Stuart Voytilla is one film scholar who applies the structure of the hero's journey to film genres such as Western, horror, action adventure, war, and science fiction. In his case studies, Voytilla details both the stages of the journey undertaken by the hero and the archetypes or roles that filmic characters play, such as hero, mentor, trickster, and threshold guardian. One of the genres that Voytilla finds illuminating in the understanding of mythical heroes is the Western. He calls the Western film "American mythology," where "as our nation's identity changes with each decade, with each generation, and with domestic and world pressures, these shifts are reflected in the stories we tell" (Voytilla, 1999, p. 48). Some of the films he discusses are clearly supportive of his claim: *High Noon* (Fred Zinnemann, 1952), *The Searchers* (John Ford, 1956), *Dances with Wolves* (Kevin Costner, 1990), and *Unforgiven* (Clint Eastwood, 1992). Although both *High Noon* and *Unforgiven* articulate moral tales of good and bad, the heroes are vastly different in their understandings of personal integrity. In particular, the romanticization of the hero changes dramatically in the 40 years that separate the films. What remains the same is that the Western landscape is as important as the characters inhabiting it (Voytilla, 1999, p. 52).

John Izod suggests, in his 2001 publication *Myth, Mind and the Screen*, that *2001: A Space Odyssey* (Stanley Kubrick, 1968) offers audiences a hero in the science fiction genre. Izod echoes Campbell's understanding of the hero's journey as universal in consequence, in solidarity with the struggle of humanity to grow and progress through eons of time. The science fiction theme of exploration into the unknown and unknowable universe is a fruitful one for the hero's quest. Writing about astronaut Dave Bowman's "journey through rainbow light" Izod says:

> Dave's odyssey, which he carries out for all humanity, is a voyage of discovery – an exploration of the unknown which deliberately extends the realm of consciousness by penetrating the mysteries. The further it progresses, the more Dave's journey becomes a dynamic image of the self as evolving, progressing, recurring through the generations. It is that great journey, characteristic of the human experience, to the very edge of the unknown, looking into the unknown, which is here couched in terms exactly right for our age.
>
> (Izod, 2001, p. 195)

This journey is illustrated through the magnificence of Stanley Kubrick's cinematography, as Bowman is catapulted forward into spectacular light shows as "supernovae explode, galaxies wheel and plasma streams from stars" (ibid., p. 194). Izod observes that the cycle of life, in which the Star Child is born as Bowman dies, is specific to this twentieth-century human's development and yet "thoroughly grounded in the old mythological forms" (ibid., p. 198) of reborn hero-gods. Izod links Bowman's rebirth to the Jungian idea of the god within us, the finding of the authentic self that, for Campbell, is the fulfillment of the journey.

We can find many other genres that lend themselves to telling the story of the hero's journey. A recent drama, *The World's Fastest Indian* (Roger Donaldson, 2005), builds upon the real-life story of Burt Munro, an eccentric New Zealander who spends years tinkering with a 1920 Indian motorcycle, which he then takes to America in order to set the land-speed world record at Utah's Bonneville Salt Flats in 1967. It is the arduous journey, which – as in David Lynch's *The Straight Story* (1999) – involves an older man in an impetuous late-in-life, do-or-die ordeal, that sets the standard of storytelling for the audience at its highest level. For hero Munro, the Joseph Campbell-like assortment of encounters along the journey only strengthen his resolve to attain the victory. Munro, played by Anthony Hopkins, duly returns to his modest abode in his homeland to be hailed as a hero by the townsfolk, his true worth now recognized and appreciated. The dramatic theme of this and many other films that tell the story of overcoming adversity often rests on the ability of the hero to cope with unforeseen obstacles. In *The World's Fastest Indian*, Munro is helped by the kindness of strangers but also his innate friendliness and equanimity, personal qualities that become critical for both his survival and transformation into a hero.

The Silence of the Lambs (Jonathan Demme, 1991) is a film within the crime/horror/thriller genre with a heroine on a similar quest. FBI agent Clarice Starling (Jodie Foster), accompanied by shadow-mentor Hannibal Lecter (Anthony Hopkins), takes a psychological and physical journey that is as much a rite of passage through her childhood ordeal as it is a descent into the present hell of the Buffalo Bill serial murder case (as described in Voytilla, 1999, pp. 96–8). Stuart Voytilla points to the crucial moment in the film when Starling physically touches "death" (Lecter), as she grabs a file from the killer's hand: this is the only time the two characters touch, and through this Lecter becomes her liberator – he lifts her into resurrection (because by her survival of the encounter with Lecter she is able to solve the case). This is a good illustration of how films do more than peddle in illusions. As Lyden puts it, "We willingly enter another world in the cinema, one that we realize is not the empirical world, but one that has power over us nonetheless" (Lyden, 2003, p. 52). Filmgoers may know that a filmic "text" is fictional, but this is not to say that the narrative and experience concerned cannot convey or generate authentic truths that impinge upon empirical reality.

Conclusion

Cinematic fiction, with its gift of image, narrative, and sound, can tell a story like no other human art form yet invented. Part of the magic of film for spectators is that they can be drawn into a story that is not theirs but that they can experience and even live, vicariously, for a hundred or so minutes of reel time. V. F. Perkins insists that this is something to be treasured about film, thereby rebuffing the criticism of writers such as Ivor Montagu and the poet Cecil Day-Lewis (see Perkins, 1972, pp. 134–57) who denigrate film as "day-dreaming" or a "drug" that distracts people from real life and allows for escapist behavior:

> The screen between ourselves and the film's world allows us to enjoy experiences which would be insupportable in reality. We can indulge desires and impulses which we would not allow ourselves outside this privileged area. In Jung's words, "the cinema...makes it possible to experience without danger all the excitement, passion and desirousness which must be repressed in a humanitarian ordering of life." Our involvement is a game as well as a dream: literally, a game of make-believe.
>
> (Perkins, 1972, p. 144)

Storytelling certainly can be a boon to our mental and spiritual health, whether it is through a book, play, or film. Film-watching can not only take on cultural significance but can help filmgoers to explore and construct their approaches to living, and in so doing can function theologically and challenge the artificial sacred–secular divide. Gerard Loughlin is quite right to exercise caution at this juncture, in his attestation that, no matter how eager we may be for conversation and interchange between theology and film, we should bear in mind that "except when discourses on theology and film are reports of actual conversations between film-makers and theologians, such dialogues are nearly always acts of ventriloquism, since film itself is a cultural product about which we may talk, but which is not itself a conversing partner" (Loughlin, 2005, p. 3). Indeed, whereas theology is an academic discipline, being conducted by academic practitioners, a film is a commercial and entertainment product that can only be appropriated – some might say hijacked – unilaterally by the theologian.

A balance must be struck, therefore, between the academic penchant for setting up typologies in order to systematize and categorize the theology–film interface, along the lines of H. Richard Niebuhr's *Christ and Culture*, which provided the foundation for chapter 1 of this volume, and allowing a film to be heard (and seen) in its own voice. What is important is that the zeal of the theologian is not unduly brought to bear on the interchange, so that we do not have the situation where a film itself is distorted in order to "fit in" with a particular theological paradigm – in the form, for instance, of much of the Christ-figure literature. As a corollary of this, it may of course be the case that some films will ultimately prove to be less adequate dialogue-partners with theology than their initial subject matter might suggest. For example, as the application of Niebuhr's *Christ and Culture in Paradox* model to a number of debates on violence and justice has suggested, it is not improbable that a revenge-based Western such as *Unforgiven* should offer more fertile ground for theological reflection than the more overtly theological *The Passion of the Christ* (Mel Gibson, 2004), not least because of the former's accumulation of images that, as Sara Anson Vaux sees it, "foreground the fragility of the human condition" (Vaux, 1998, p. 445). There may be no exultant or exuberant "resurrection" motif as in the case of the latter, but in the place of *The Passion*'s black-and-white, good-versus-evil trajectory, a more nuanced reading, as facilitated by Niebuhr's fourth category, suggests that a film character does not need to be what Vaux calls "a blameless hero" on the one hand or "a seamless villain" (ibid.) on the other in order to be theologically valuable. The fact that Clint Eastwood's protagonist constitutes a "deeply conflicted person such as we are" (ibid.), striving to reconcile the tensions between his ethical or religious values on the one hand and the realities of the empirical world of everyday reality, with all its contradictions, doubts, and discontinuities, on the other, makes for a challenging, if uncertain, theological adventure.

Provided that the theologian does not come to the table with a pre-set pattern or model of how films can illuminate or bear witness to theological themes, but is prepared to be challenged by film *qua* film – in both its low and high manifestations – and is prepared to acknowledge (in the way that Robert Jewett, for example, is not quite prepared to do) that no typology ever yields unambiguous or certain results, then we are in a position to conclude that filmmakers, as modern-day storytellers, are fulfilling the roles of priests, shamans, and healers for our contemporary culture. Long may the journey continue!

Note

1 Segal also offers a comparison of Rank, Campbell, and Raglan, saying that for Campbell, myth transcends religion (Segal, 1999, p. 134).

Bibliography

Acker, Ally (1993) *Reel Women*, New York: Continuum.

Adam, David (2006) "Earthshakers: The Top 100 Green Campaigners of All Time." *Guardian*, November 28, http://environment.guardian.co.uk/climate-change/story/0,,1958602,00.html.

Agajanian, Rowana (2000) " 'Peace on Earth, Goodwill to All Men': The Depiction of Christmas in Modern Hollywood Films." In: Mark Connelly (ed.) *Christmas at the Movies: Images of Christmas in American, British and European Cinema*, London: I. B. Taurus, pp. 143–64.

Aichele, George (2002) "Foreword." In: Larry Kreitzer, *Gospel Images in Fiction and Film: On Reversing the Hermeneutical Flow*, London: Sheffield Academic Press, pp. 7–10.

Aichele, George and Walsh, Richard (eds.) (2002) *Screening Scripture: Intertextual Connections Between Scripture and Film*, Harrisburg, PA: Trinity Press International.

Aitken, Tom, Christianson, Eric, Francis, Peter, et al. (2005) "Table Talk: Reflections on *The Passion of the Christ*." In: Eric Christianson, Peter Francis, and William Telford (eds.) *Cinéma Divinité: Readings in Film and Theology*, London: SCM, pp. 311–30.

Alexander, Louis (1999) "Hollywood Often Puts Environment Out on a Limb." *Business Review* (Albany), September 3, www.bizjournals.com/albany/stories/1999/09/06/smallb2.html?t=printable.

Anees, Munawar A. (2006) "Salvation and Suicide: What Does Islamic Theology Say?" *Dialog: A Journal of Theology*, 45/3, Fall, pp. 275–9.

Anker, Roy M. (2004) *Catching Light: Looking for God in the Movies*, Grand Rapids, MI: Eerdmans.

Arendt, Paul (2006) Review of *Poseidon*. BBC Movies, June 1, www.bbc.co.uk/films/2006/05/16/poseidon_2006_review.shtml.

Bibliography

Auster, Albert and Quart, Leonard (1988) *How the War was Remembered: Hollywood and Vietnam*, New York: Praeger.

Austin, Guy (1996) *Contemporary French Cinema*, Manchester: Manchester University Press.

Bach, Alice (ed.) (1996) *Biblical Glamour and Hollywood Glitz. Semeia* 74. Atlanta: Scholar's Press.

Badham, Paul (1976) *Christian Beliefs about Life after Death*, London: SPCK.

Badham, Paul (1986) "In Search of Heaven." In: Tony Moss (ed.) *In Search of Christianity*, London: Firethorn Press, pp. 124–36.

Badham, Paul and Badham, Linda (1982) *Immortality or Extinction?* 2nd edn., London: SPCK.

Bailey, Lloyd R. (1979) *Biblical Perspectives on Death*, Philadelphia: Fortress Press.

Barth, Karl (1967) *The Humanity of God*, London: Collins.

Barth, Karl (2004) "Church Dogmatics, Vol. 2: The Doctrine of God." In: Gesa Elsbeth Thiessen (ed.) *Theological Aesthetics: A Reader*, London: SCM, pp. 315–19.

Bauckham, Richard (2005) "Jürgen Moltmann." In: David Ford with Rachel Muers (eds.) *The Modern Theologians*, 3rd edn., Oxford: Blackwell, pp. 147–62.

Baugh, Lloyd (1997) *Imaging the Divine: Jesus and Christ-Figures in Film*, Kansas City: Sheed and Ward.

BBC News (1999a) "Sir Cliff Left Off Radio 2 Playlist." *BBC News*, November 3, http://news.bbc.co.uk/1/hi/entertainment/503675.stm.

BBC News (1999b) "Michael Brands Cliff Campaign 'Vile.'" *BBC News*, December 10, http://news.bbc.co.uk/1/hi/entertainment/558321.stm.

BBC News (1999c) "Mel C Lashes Out at *Millennium Prayer*." *BBC News*, December 13, http://news.bbc.co.uk/1/hi/entertainment/562955.stm.

BBC News (2005) "Imax 'Shuns Films on Evolution'." *BBC News*, March 20, http://news.bbc.co.uk/1/hi/entertainment/film/4365999.stm.

Bedborough, Sally (2005) "Taking the Waves by 'Surprise': *Master and Commander*." In: Anthony J. Clarke and Paul S. Fiddes (eds.) *Flickering Images: Theology and Film in Dialogue*, Oxford: Regent's Park College, pp. 123–35.

Bennett (2006) "Now Playing." In: Susan Wolpert and Raymond Lesser (eds.) *Funny Times*, 21/11, November, Cleveland, OH: Funny Times Inc., p. 19.

Berardinelli, James (2001) Review of *Vanilla Sky*. James Berardinelli's Reelviews, www.reelviews.net/movies/v/vanilla_sky.html.

Berenbaum, Michael and Landres, J. Shawn (2004) "Introduction." In: J. Shawn Landres and Michael Berenbaum (eds.) *After The Passion Is Gone: American Religious Consequences*, Walnut Creek, CA: AltaMira Press, pp. 1–17.

Berger, John (1972) *Ways of Seeing*, London: Penguin.

Bertrand, Ina (2005) Review of David Ingram's *Green Screen: Environmentalism and Hollywood Cinema. Screening the Past*, July 19, www.latrobe.edu.au/screeningthepast/reviews/rev_18/IB2br18a.html.

Bird, Michael (1982) "Film as Hierophany." In: John R. May and Michael Bird (eds.) *Religion in Film*, Knoxville: University of Tennessee Press, pp. 3–22.

Blake, Richard A. (2000) *AfterImage: The Indelible Catholic Imagination of Six American Filmmakers*, Chicago: Loyola Press.

Boff, Leonardo (2004) "Liberating Grace." In: Gesa Elsbeth Thiessen (ed.) *Theological Aesthetics: A Reader*, London: SCM, pp. 284–5.

Bonhoeffer, Dietrich (1963) *Letters and Papers from Prison*, London: Fontana.

Borg, Marcus (1994) *Meeting Jesus Again for the First Time: The Historical Jesus and the Heart of Contemporary Faith*, San Francisco: HarperSanFrancisco.

Bradshaw, Tim (2005) "All-Consuming Holiday Snaps: *Open Water*." In: Anthony J. Clarke and Paul S. Fiddes (eds.) *Flickering Images: Theology and Film in Dialogue*, Oxford: Regent's Park College, pp. 163–74.

Brandon, S. G. F. (1967) *Jesus and the Zealots: A Study of the Political Factor in Primitive Christianity*, Manchester: Manchester University Press.

Brooke, Michael (n.d.) www.imdb.com/name/nm0000247/bio.

Brooks, Xan (2002) Review of *Vanilla Sky*. *Sight and Sound*, 12/2, February, pp. 63–4.

Brown, Stephen (1997) "Optimism, Hope, and Feelgood Movies: The Capra Connection." In: Clive Marsh and Gaye Ortiz (eds.) *Explorations in Theology and Film: Movies and Meaning*, Oxford: Blackwell, pp. 219–32.

Brunner, Emil (1954) *Eternal Hope*, London: Lutterworth Press.

Brussat, Frederic and Brussat, Mary Ann (2003) Review of *Something's Gotta Give*. Spirituality and Practice, www.spiritualityandpractice.com/films/films.php? id=6826.

Brussat, Frederic and Brussat, Mary Ann (2004) Review of *Fahrenheit 9/11*. Spirituality and Practice, www.spiritualityandpractice.com/films/films.php? id=8568.

Bryant, M. Darroll (1982) "Cinema, Religion and Popular Culture." In: John R. May and Michael Bird (eds.) *Religion in Film*, Knoxville: University of Tennessee Press, pp. 101–14.

Bultmann, Rudolf (1953) "New Testament and Mythology." In: Hans-Werner Bartsch (ed.) *Kerygma and Myth*, vol. 1, London: SPCK, pp. 1–44.

Bultmann, Rudolf (1958) *Jesus Christ and Mythology*, New York: Charles Scribner's Sons.

Burns, Charlene P. E. (2004) "*Mystic River*: A Parable of Christianity's Dark Side." *Journal of Religion and Film*, 8/1, April, http://avalon.unomaha.edu/jrf/Vol8No1/MysticBody.htm.

Butler, Alison (2002) *Women's Cinema*, London: Wallflower.

Caldecott, Léonie (2005) "Transcending the Cave: Fantasy Film as Spiritual and Philosophical Reflection." In: Anthony J. Clarke and Paul S. Fiddes (eds.) *Flickering Images: Theology and Film in Dialogue*, Oxford: Regent's Park College, pp. 49–57.

Campbell, Joseph (1988) *The Hero with a Thousand Faces*, London: Paladin.

Campbell, Joseph and Moyers, Bill (1988) *The Power of Myth*, New York: Doubleday.

Canto, Monique (1986) "The Politics of Women's Bodies." In: Susan Rubin Suleiman (ed.) *The Female Body in Western Culture*, Cambridge, MA: Harvard University Press.

Bibliography

Carmody, Denise Lardner (1994) *Responses to 101 Questions about Feminism*, London: Geoffrey Chapman.

Carson, Rachel (1962) *Silent Spring*, New York: Crest Books.

Casselman, Anne (2006) "Climate-Changing Sci Fi: How Global Warming is Turning a Genre Once Filled with Pipe Dreams into a Pipeline of Ideas." *Seed Magazine*, October 16, www.seedmagazine.com/news/2006/10/climate_changing_scifi.php.

Chadwick, Benjamin (2005) "L.A. Environmental: Hollywood's Best and Worst 'Green' Movies." *E Magazine*, XVI/5, September/October, www.emagazine.com/view/?2861.

Christianson, Eric (2005) "An Ethic You Can't Refuse?: Assessing *The Godfather* Trilogy." In: William Telford, Eric Christianson, and Peter Francis (eds.) *Cinéma Divinité: Readings in Film and Theology*, London: SCM, pp. 110–23.

Christianson, Eric, Francis, Peter, and Telford, William (eds.) (2005) *Cinéma Divinité: Readings in Film and Theology*, London: SCM.

Clarke, Anthony J. (2005) "Gaining Fresh Insights: Film and Theological Reflection in a Pastoral Setting." In: Anthony J. Clarke and Paul S. Fiddes (eds.) *Flickering Images: Theology and Film in Dialogue*, Oxford: Regent's Park College, pp. 59–79.

Clarke, Anthony J. and Fiddes, Paul S. (eds.) (2005) *Flickering Images: Theology and Film in Dialogue*, Oxford: Regent's Park College.

Cobb, Kelton (2005) *The Blackwell Guide to Theology and Popular Culture*, Oxford: Blackwell.

Cohn-Sherbok, Dan and Cohn-Sherbok, Lavinia (1994) *A Short History of Judaism*, Oxford: Oneworld.

Conrad, Joseph (1987) *Heart of Darkness*, New York: Chelsea House.

Cork, William J. (2004) "Passionate Blogging: Interfaith Controversy and the Internet." In: J. Shawn Landres and Michael Berenbaum (eds.) *After The Passion Is Gone: American Religious Consequences*, Walnut Creek, CA: AltaMira Press, pp. 35–46.

Corrigan, Timothy and White, Patricia (2004) *The Film Experience*, Boston: Bedford St. Martin's.

Cox, Harvey (1966) *The Secular City*, New York: Macmillan.

Cox, Harvey (2004) "The Seduction of the Spirit: The Use and Misuse of People's Religion." In: Gesa Elsbeth Thiessen (ed.) *Theological Aesthetics: A Reader*, London: SCM, pp. 253–55.

Crichton, Michael (1994) *Disclosure*, London: Arrow Books.

Cupitt, Don (1984) *The Sea of Faith*, London: BBC.

Daly, Mary (1994) "Sisterhood as Cosmic Covenant." In: Charlene Spretnak (ed.) *The Politics of Women's Spirituality*, New York: Anchor, pp. 351–61.

Dark, David (2002) *Everyday Apocalypse*, Grand Rapids, MI: Brazos.

Deacy, Christopher (2001) *Screen Christologies: Redemption and the Medium of Film*, Cardiff: University of Wales Press.

Bibliography

Deacy, Christopher (2005) *Faith in Film: Religious Themes in Contemporary Cinema*, Aldershot: Ashgate.

Deacy, Christopher (2007) "From Bultmann to Burton, Demythologizing the Big Fish: The Contribution of Modern Christian Theologians to the Theology–Film Conversation." In: Robert Johnston (ed.) *Re-Viewing Theology and Film: Moving the Discipline Forward*, Grand Rapids, MI: Baker Academic.

De Hirsch, Storm and Clarke, Shirley (1977) "A Conversation." In: Karyn Kay and Gerald Peary (eds.) *Women and the Cinema*, New York: E. P. Dutton, pp. 231–42.

Demers, Patricia (1992) *Women as Interpreters of the Bible*, Mahwah, NJ: Paulist.

Diehl, William (1992) *Primal Fear*, London: Arrow Books.

Doctrine Commission of the Church of England (1995) *The Mystery of Salvation*, London: Church House.

Dönmez-Colin, Gönül (2004) *Women, Islam and Cinema*, London: Reaktion Books.

Dougan, Andy (1997) *Martin Scorsese: The Making of His Movies*, London: Orion Media.

Dowell, Susan and Hurcombe, Linda (1981) *Dispossessed Daughters of Eve*, London: SCM.

Downs, Douglas (1999) Review of *The Omega Code*. Christian Spotlight on the Movies, www.christiananswers.net/spotlight/movies/pre2000/theomegacode.html.

Ebert, Roger (1979a) Review of *The China Syndrome*. Chicago Sun-Times, January 1, http://rogerebert.suntimes.com/apps/pbcs.dll/article?AID=/19790101/REVIEWS/901010309/1023.

Ebert, Roger (1979b) Review of *The Deer Hunter*. Chicago Sun-Times, March 9, http://rogerebert.suntimes.com/apps/pbcs.dll/article?AID=/19790309/REVIEWS/903090301/1023

Ebert, Roger (1994) Review of *Pulp Fiction* (a). Chicago Sun-Times, October 14, http://rogerebert.suntimes.com/apps/pbcs.dll/article?AID=/19941014/REVIEWS/410140304/1023.

Ebert, Roger (2001) Review of *Pulp Fiction* (b). Chicago Sun-Times, June 10, http://rogerebert.suntimes.com/apps/pbcs.dll/article?AID=/20010610/REVIEWS08/106100301/1023.

Ebert, Roger (2002) Review of *Unforgiven*. Chicago Sun-Times, July 21, http://rogerebert.suntimes.com/apps/pbcs.dll/article?AID=/20020721/REVIEWS08/207210301/1023.

Ebert, Roger (2004a) Review of *The Passion of the Christ*. Chicago Sun-Times, February 24, http://rogerebert.suntimes.com/apps/pbcs.dll/article?AID=/20040224/REVIEWS/402240301/1023.

Ebert, Roger (2004b) Review of *Spider-Man 2*. In: Chicago Sun-Times, June 30, http://rogerebert.suntimes.com/apps/pbcs.dll/article?AID=/20040629/REVIEWS/406300301/1023.

Ebert, Roger (2006) Review of *An Inconvenient Truth*. Chicago Sun-Times, June 2, http://rogerebert.suntimes.com/apps/pbcs.dll/article?AID=/20060601/REVIEWS/60517002/1023.

Bibliography

Eco, Umberto (2004) *The Name of the Rose*, London: Vintage/Random House.

Ekklesia (2004) "Evangelicals Slam Bush for His 'Theology of War'." *Ekklesia –* A New Way of Thinking, www.ekklesia.co.uk/content/news_syndication/article_041012bsh.shtml.

Elcott, David M. (2004) "Five Introspective Challenges." In: J. Shawn Landres and Michael Berenbaum (eds.) *After* The Passion *Is Gone: American Religious Consequences*, Walnut Creek, CA: AltaMira Press, pp. 229–42.

Eller, Cynthia (2003) *Am I a Woman?* Boston: Beacon Press.

Ellis, Robert (2005) "Movies and Meaning: An Introduction to Reading Films." In: Anthony J. Clarke and Paul S. Fiddes (eds.) *Flickering Images: Theology and Film in Dialogue*, Oxford: Regent's Park College, pp. 7–23.

Exum, J. Cheryl (1996). *Plotted, Shot and Painted: Cultural Representations of Biblical Women*, Sheffield: Academic Press.

Ferlita, Ernest (1982) "Film and the Quest for Meaning." In: John R. May and Michael Bird (eds.) *Religion in Film*, Knoxville: University of Tennessee Press, pp. 115–31.

Ferré, John P. (2003) "The Media of Popular Piety." In: Jolyon Mitchell and Sophia Marriage (eds.) *Mediating Religion: Conversations in Media, Religion and Culture*, London: Continuum, pp. 83–92.

Fiddes, Paul S. (2005) "When Text Becomes Voice: *You've Got Mail*." In: Anthony J. Clarke and Paul S. Fiddes (eds.) *Flickering Images: Theology and Film in Dialogue*, Oxford: Regent's Park College, pp. 97–111.

Fitch, John, III (2005) "Archetypes on Screen: Odysseus, St. Paul, Christ and the American Cinematic Hero and Anti-Hero." *Journal of Religion and Film*, 9/1, April, www.unomaha.edu/jrf/Vol9No1/FitchArchetypes.htm.

Flannery-Dailey, Frances (2000) "Bruce Willis as the Messiah: Human Effort, Salvation and Apocalypticism in *Twelve Monkeys*." *Journal of Religion and Film*, 4/1, April, www.unomaha.edu/jrf/Messiah.htm.

Floyd, Wayne Whitson (2005) "Dietrich Bonhoeffer." In: David Ford with Rachel Muers (eds.) *The Modern Theologians*, 3rd edn., Oxford: Blackwell, pp. 43–61.

Foster, Gwendolyn Audrey (1995) *Women Film Directors: An International Biocritical Dictionary*, Westport, CT: Greenwood.

Francis, Peter (2005) "Clint Eastwood Westerns: Promised Land and Real Men." In: Eric Christianson, Peter Francis, and William Telford (eds.) *Cinéma Divinité: Readings in Film and Theology*, London: SCM, pp. 182–98.

Frederick, Jenn (n.d.) "Breaking the Waves: Continuities and Discontinuities Between Second and Third Wave Feminism." Thesis, http://home.comcast.net/~theennead/bean/conclusion.htm.

Fredriksen, Paula (2003) "The Gospel According to Gibson: Mad Mel." *New Republic*, July 22, www.moviecitynews.com/notepad/2003/030722b_tue.html.

French, Philip (2006) Review of *Poseidon*. *Observer*, June 4, http://film.guardian.co.uk/News_Story/Critic_Review/Observer_review/0,,1789840,00.html.

Gallagher, Margaret (1992) "Women and Men in the Media." *Communication Research Trends*, 12/1, pp. 7–9.

Gibson, E. C. S. (1902) *The Thirty-Nine Articles of the Church of England*, London: Methuen.

Giles, Paul (1992) *American Catholic Arts and Fictions: Culture, Ideology, Aesthetics*, Cambridge: Cambridge University Press.

Gilkey, Langdon (2004) "Can Art Fill the Vacuum?" In: Gesa Elsbeth Thiessen (ed.) *Theological Aesthetics: A Reader*, London: SCM, pp. 263–6.

Gill, Robin (2006) *A Textbook of Christian Ethics*, 3rd edn., London: T&T Clark.

Girard, René (1977) *Violence and the Sacred*, London: Johns Hopkins University Press.

Glanzer, Perry L. (2003) "Christ and the Heavy Metal Subculture: Applying Qualitative Analysis to the Contemporary Debate about H. Richard Niebuhr's *Christ and Culture*." *Journal of Religion and Society*, 5, http://moses.creighton.edu/jrs/2003/2003–7.html.

Graham, David John (1997) "Redeeming Violence in the Films of Martin Scorsese." In: Clive Marsh and Gaye Ortiz (eds.) *Explorations in Theology and Film: Movies and Meaning*, Oxford: Blackwell, pp. 87–95.

Grant, Myrna R. (2003) "Christ and the Media: Considerations on the Negotiation of Meaning in Religious Television." In: Jolyon Mitchell and Sophia Marriage (eds.) *Mediating Religion: Conversations in Media, Religion and Culture*, London: Continuum, pp. 121–30.

Greeley, Andrew (1988) *God in Popular Culture*, Chicago: Thomas More.

Greenville Advocate (2001) "Medved Indicts Films and TV for Lying." *Greenville Advocate*, March 21, www.greenville.edu/backup/publications/news/medved321.shtml.

Grey, Mary (1989) *Redeeming the Dream*, London: SPCK.

Gu, B.(1994) "Fertility Declined Most Rapidly Between 1970 and 1981 from a Birth Rate of 33.59 to 20.91/1000 and from a Fertility Rate of 5.8 to 2.6 Children," www.ncbi.nlm.nih.gov/entrez/query.fcgi?cmd=Retrieve&db=PubMed&list_uids=12319286&dopt=Abstract.

Guterson, David (1995) *Snow Falling on Cedars*, London: Bloomsbury.

Hagen, William M. (1983) "*Apocalypse Now* (1979): Joseph Conrad and the Television War." In: Peter C. Rollins (ed.) *Hollywood as Historian: American Film in Cultural Context*, Lexington: University Press of Kentucky, pp. 230–45.

Harries, Richard (2004) "Art and the Beauty of Good." In: Gesa Elsbeth Thiessen (ed.) *Theological Aesthetics: A Reader*, London: SCM, pp. 351–4.

Harris, Murray (1983) *Raised Immortal: Resurrection and Immortality in the New Testament*, London: Marshall, Morgan and Scott.

Hays, Richard B. (2005) "U.S. Seeks Salvation through Violence." *Vital Theology*, 2/1, March 15, p. 3.

Hedges, Chris (2002) *War is a Force that Gives Us Meaning*, New York: Public Affairs.

Bibliography

Henderson, Paul (2006) "Feelin' Movie." Grist, www.grist.org/advice/books/2006/03/15/henderson.

Herrmann, Jörg (2003) "From Popular to Arthouse: An Analysis of Love and Nature as Religious Motifs in Recent Cinema." In: Jolyon Mitchell and Sophia Marriage (eds.) *Mediating Religion: Conversations in Media, Religion and Culture*, London: Continuum, pp. 189–99.

Heschel, Susannah (2004) "Theological Bulimia: Christianity and its DeJudaization." In: J. Shawn Landres and Michael Berenbaum (eds.) *After* The Passion *Is Gone: American Religious Consequences*, Walnut Creek, CA: AltaMira Press, pp. 177–92.

Hick, John (1977) *The Centre of Christianity*, London: SCM.

Hick, John (1985) *Death and Eternal Life*, Basingstoke: Macmillan.

Higgins, Gareth (2003) *How Movies Helped Save My Soul*, Lake Mary, FL: Relevant Books.

Hill, John and Church Gibson, Pamela (eds.) (1998) *The Oxford Guide to Film Studies*, Oxford: Oxford University Press.

Hinton, Rosalind (2002) "A Legacy of Inclusion: An Interview with Rosemary Radford Ruether." Crosscurrents, www.crosscurrents.org/Ruetherspring2002.htm.

Hollows, Joanne and Jancovich, Mark (eds.) (1995) *Approaches to Popular Film*, Manchester: Manchester University Press.

Holmlund, Chris (2002) *Impossible Bodies*, New York: Routledge.

Hoose, Bernard (ed.) (1998) *Christian Ethics: An Introduction*, London: Cassell.

Horsfield, Peter (2003) "Electronic Media and the Past-Future of Christianity." In: Jolyon Mitchell and Sophia Marriage (eds.) *Mediating Religion: Conversations in Media, Religion and Culture*, London: Continuum, pp. 271–82.

Hurley, Neil (1970) *Theology Through Film*, New York: Harper and Row.

Hurley, Neil (1982a) "Alfred Hitchcock." In: John R. May and Michael Bird (eds.) *Religion in Film*, Knoxville: University of Tennessee Press, pp. 177–81.

Hurley, Neil (1982b) "Cinematic Transfigurations of Jesus." In: John R. May and Michael Bird (eds.) *Religion in Film*, Knoxville: University of Tennessee Press, pp. 61–78.

Ingram, David (2004) *Green Screen: Environmentalism and Hollywood Cinema*, Exeter: University of Exeter.

"Inside Story" (2005) "The Minds Boggle." *Media Guardian*, May 16, p. 4.

IPL (Interfaith Power and Light) (2006a) "Global Warming and Religious Values." IPL Media Kit.

IPL (Interfaith Power and Light) (2006b) "A Religious Response to Global Warming." IPL Flyer.

Izod, John (2001) *Myth, Mind and the Screen*, Cambridge: Cambridge University Press.

Izod, John and Kilborn, Richard (1998) "The Documentary." In: John Hill and Pamela Church Gibson (eds.) *The Oxford Guide to Film Studies*, Oxford: Oxford University Press, pp. 426–33.

Jarrar, Raed (2003) "Iraqi Civilian War Casualties," http://civilians.info/iraq.

Bibliography

Jasper, David (1997) "On Systematizing the Unsystematic: A Response." In: Clive Marsh and Gaye Ortiz (eds.) *Explorations in Theology and Film: Movies and Meaning*, Oxford: Blackwell, pp. 235–44.

Jewett, Robert (1993) *Saint Paul at the Movies: The Apostle's Dialogue with American Culture*, Louisville: Westminster/John Knox Press.

Jewett, Robert (1999) *Saint Paul Returns to the Movies: Triumph over Shame*, Cambridge: Eerdmans.

Johnston, Claire (1977) "Myths of Women in the Cinema." In: Karyn Kay and Gerald Peary (eds.) *Women and the Cinema*, New York: E. P. Dutton, pp. 407–11.

Johnston, Robert (2000) *Reel Spirituality: Theology and Film in Dialogue*, Grand Rapids, MI: Baker Academic.

Johnston, Robert (2004) *Useless Beauty: Ecclesiastes through the Lens of Contemporary Film*, Grand Rapids, MI: Baker Academic.

Joseph, Mark (1999) *The Rock & Roll Rebellion: Why People of Faith Abandoned Rock Music and Why They're Coming Back*, Nashville: Broadman and Holman.

Juergensmeyer, Mark (2004) "Afterword: The Passion of War." In: J. Shawn Landres and Michael Berenbaum (eds.) *After The Passion Is Gone: American Religious Consequences*, Walnut Creek, CA: AltaMira Press, pp. 279–87.

Juhasz, Alexandra (ed.) (2001) *Women of Vision*, Minneapolis: University of Minnesota Press.

Kaplan, Ann (1997) *Looking for the Other: Feminism, Film and the Imperial Gaze*, New York: Routledge.

Kay, Karyn and Peary, Gerald (eds.) (1977) *Women and the Cinema*, New York: E. P. Dutton.

Kelsey, David H (2005) "Paul Tillich." In: David Ford with Rachel Muers (eds.) *The Modern Theologians*, 3rd edn., Oxford: Blackwell, pp. 62–75.

King, Ursula (1993) *Women and Spirituality*, London: Macmillan.

Kolker, Robert P. (1988) *A Cinema of Loneliness*, Oxford: Oxford University Press.

Kolker, Robert P. (1998) "The Film Text and Film Form." In: John Hill and Pamela Church Gibson (eds.) *The Oxford Guide to Film Studies*, Oxford: Oxford University Press, pp. 11–23.

Kozlovic, Anton Karl (2004) "The Structural Characteristics of the Cinematic Christ-Figure." *Journal of Religion and Popular Culture*, VIII (Fall), www.usask.ca/relst/jrpc/art8-cinematicchrist.html.

Kraemer, Christine Hoff (2004) "From Theological to Cinematic Criticism: Extricating the Study of Religion and Film from Theology." *Religious Studies Review*, 30/4, October, pp. 243–50.

Kraybill, Ronald (2004) "Humiliation, Helplessness Propel Outbreak of Suicide Bomber Attacks." *Vital Theology*, I/11, September 30, p. 1.

Kreitzer, Larry J. (1999) *Pauline Images in Fiction and Film: On Reversing the Hermeneutical Flow*, Sheffield: Sheffield Academic Press.

Kreitzer, Larry (2002) *Gospel Images in Fiction and Film: On Reversing the Hermeneutical Flow*, London: Sheffield Academic Press.

Küng, Hans (1984) *Eternal Life?* London: Collins.

Küng, Hans (1991) *Global Responsibility*, London: SCM.

Kwok Pui-Lan (2002) "Feminist Theology as Intercultural Discourse." In: Susan Frank Parsons (ed.) *The Cambridge Companion to Feminist Theology*, Cambridge: Cambridge University Press, pp. 23–39.

Lacugna, Catherine (1993) *Freeing Theology*, New York: HarperCollins.

Landres, J. Shawn and Berenbaum, Michael (eds.) (2004) *After The Passion Is Gone: American Religious Consequences*, Walnut Creek, CA: AltaMira Press.

Lauzen, Martha (2006) "The Celluloid Ceiling." Report, Moviesbywomen.com, www.moviesbywomen.com/marthalauzenphd/stats2005.html.

Lay, Anna (2004) "Kiss Me Quick Draws Film Censors Ire." *Qantara.de*, September 7, www.qantara.de/webcom/show_article.php/_c-310/_nr-101/_p-1/i.html.

Lebacqz, Karen (1998) "Justice." In: Bernard Hoose (ed.) *Christian Ethics: An Introduction*, London: Cassell, pp. 163–72.

Loades, Ann (1987) *Searching for Lost Coins*, London: SPCK.

Loughlin, Gerard (2005) "Cinéma Divinité: A Theological Introduction." In: Eric Christianson, Peter Francis, and William Telford (eds.) *Cinéma Divinité: Readings in Film and Theology*, London: SCM, pp. 1–12.

Lyden, John C. (2003) *Film as Religion: Myths, Morals and Rituals*, New York: New York University Press.

Lynch, Gordon (2005) *Understanding Theology and Popular Culture*, Oxford: Blackwell.

MacDonald, Alan (1975) *Films in Close-up*, Leicester: Frameworks.

Macquarrie, John (1978) *Christian Hope*, Oxford: Mowbray.

Mahon, Jim (1996) *CAW-TCA Canada Newsletter*, 4/8, August, www.caw.ca/whatwedo/healthandsafety/newsletter/4.8.aug96.asp#xtocid110768.

Makhmalbaf Film House (n.d.) Interview with Marziyeh Meshkini, www.makhmalbaf.com/articles.php?a=335.

Malone, Peter (1971) *Films and Values*, Melbourne: Chevalier Press.

Maritain, Jacques (2004) "Art and Scholasticism." In: Gesa Elsbeth Thiessen (ed.) *Theological Aesthetics: A Reader*, London: SCM, pp. 326–9.

Marsh, Clive (1997) "Film and Theologies of Culture." In: Clive Marsh and Gaye Ortiz (eds.) *Explorations in Theology and Film: Movies and Meaning*, Oxford: Blackwell, pp. 21–34.

Marsh, Clive (1998) "Religion, Theology and Film in a Postmodern Age: A Response to John Lyden." *Journal of Religion and Film*, 2/1, April, http://avalon.unomaha.edu/jrf/marshrel.htm.

Marsh, Clive (2004) *Cinema and Sentiment: Film's Challenge to Theology*, Carlisle: Paternoster Press.

Marsh, Clive and Ortiz, Gaye W. (eds.) (1997a) *Explorations in Theology and Film*, Oxford: Blackwell.

Marsh, Clive and Ortiz, Gaye (1997b) "Introduction." In: Clive Marsh and Gaye Ortiz (eds.) *Explorations in Theology and Film: Movies and Meaning*, Oxford: Blackwell, pp. 1–6.

Marsh, Clive and Ortiz, Gaye (1997c) "Theology Beyond the Modern and the Postmodern: A Future Agenda for Theology and Film." In: Clive Marsh and Gaye Ortiz (eds.) *Explorations in Theology and Film: Movies and Meaning*, Oxford: Blackwell, pp. 245–55.

Matthews, Peter (1998) Review of Clive Marsh and Gaye Ortiz (eds.) *Explorations in Theology and Film: Movies and Meaning*. *Sight and Sound*, 8/2, p. 30.

Matthews, Peter (1999) "Divining the Real." *Sight and Sound*, 9/8, pp. 22–5.

May, John R. (ed.) (1992) *Image and Likeness: Religious Visions in American Film Classics*, Mahwah, NJ: Paulist.

May, John R. (ed.) (1997) *New Image of Religious Film*, Kansas City: Sheed and Ward.

May, John R. and Bird, Michael (eds.) (1982) *Religion in Film*, Knoxville: University of Tennessee Press.

Mayne, Judith (2002) "Paradoxes of Spectatorship." In: Graeme Turner (ed.) *Film Cultures Reader*, London: Routledge, pp. 28–45.

McCormick, Ruth (1977) "Notes on Women's Liberation Cinema." In: Karyn Kay and Gerald Peary (eds.) *Women and the Cinema*, New York: E. P. Dutton, pp. 283–91.

McEver, Matthew (1998) "The Messianic Figure in Film: Christology Beyond the Biblical Epic." *Journal of Religion and Film*, 2/2, October, http://avalon.unomaha. edu/jrf/McEverMessiah.htm.

McGrath, Alister E. (2001) *Christian Literature: An Anthology*, Oxford: Blackwell.

McNab, Geoffrey (2004) "Sadean Woman." *Sight and Sound*, 14/12, December, pp. 20–2.

Medved, Michael (2004a) *"The Passion* and Prejudice." *Christianity Today*, www.christianitytoday.com/movies/commentaries/passion-prejudice.html.

Medved, Michael (2004b) " 'Passion' Will Inspire Other Religious Films." *USA Today*, www.usatoday.com/news/opinion/editorials/2004-03-14-medved_x.htm.

Medved, Michael (2004c) "Critics in the 'Passion' Pit." *Beliefnet*, www.beliefnet. com/story/140/story_14054_1.html.

Medved, Michael (2004d) "Gibson's Right to His 'Passion'." *Christian Science Monitor*, www.csmonitor.com/2004/0202/p09s01-cogn.html.

Medved, Michael (2004e) "Crucifying Mel Gibson." *American Enterprise Online*, www.taemag.com/issues/articleid.17815/article_detail.asp.

Medved, Michael (2005) "A Movie With Legs." MichaelMedved.com, January 27, www.michaelmedved.com/site/product?pid=20002.

Medved, Michael (2006a) Review of *Superman Returns*. Michael Medved's Movie Minute, www.michaelmedved.com/pg/jsp/eot/review.jsp?pid=2925.

Medved, Michael (2006b) Review of *The Fast and the Furious: Tokyo Drift*. Michael Medved's Movie Minute, www.michaelmedved.com/pg/jsp/eot/review.jsp? pid=2865.

Miles, Herbert (1947) *Movies and Morals*, Grand Rapids, MI: Zondervan.

Miles, Margaret R. (1985) *Image as Insight: Visual Understanding in Western Christianity and Secular Culture*, Boston: Beacon Press.

Bibliography

Miles, Rosalind (1988) *The Women's History of the World*, London: Paladin.

Miller, L. and Grenz, Stanley J. (1998) *Fortress Introduction to Contemporary Theologies*, Minneapolis: Fortress.

Mitchell, Jolyon (2005), "Theology and Film." In: David Ford with Rachel Muers (eds.) *The Modern Theologians*, 3rd edn., Oxford: Blackwell, pp. 736–59.

Moltmann, Jürgen (1976) "A Christian Declaration on Human Rights." World Alliance of Reformed Churches, http://warc.ch/dt/erl2/01a.html.

Mulvey, Laura (1977) "Visual Pleasure and Narrative Cinema." In: Karyn Kay and Gerald Peary (eds.) *Women and the Cinema*, New York: E. P. Dutton, pp. 412–28.

NASA Facts (1997) "A History of U.S. Space Stations." In: NASA Facts, June, http://spaceflight.nasa.gov/spacenews/factsheets/pdfs/history.pdf.

National Center for Biotechnology Information (1994) "Fertility in China." NCBI, www.ncbi.nlm.nih.gov/entrez/query.fcgi?cmd=Retrieveanddb=PubMedandlist_uids=12319286anddopt=Abstract.

National Resources Defense Council (1997) "The Story of *Silent Spring*." NRDC, April 16, www.nrdc.org/health/pesticides/hcarson.asp.

Niebuhr, H. Richard (1952) *Christ and Culture*, London: Faber and Faber.

Niman, Michael I. (2004) "*Fahrenheit 9/11* Sets American Politics Ablaze." *Mediastudy.com*, July 15, http://mediastudy.com/articles/av7-15-04.html.

Nolan, Steve (2005) "Understanding Films: Reading in the Gaps." In: Anthony J. Clarke and Paul S. Fiddes (eds.) *Flickering Images: Theology and Film in Dialogue*, Oxford: Regent's Park College, pp. 25–48.

Oden, Amy (1994) *In Her Words*, London: SPCK.

Ortiz, Gaye (2003) "The Catholic Church and its Attitude to Film as an Arbiter of Cultural Meaning." In: Jolyon Mitchell and Sophia Marriage (eds.) *Mediating Religion: Conversations in Media, Religion and Culture*, London: Continuum, pp. 179–88.

Ostwalt, Conrad (1998) "Visions of the End: Secular Apocalypse in Recent Hollywood Film." *Journal of Religion and Film*, 2/1, April, www.unomaha.edu/jrf/OstwaltC.htm.

Ostwalt, Conrad (2000) "*Armageddon* at the Millennial Dawn." *Journal of Religion and Film*, 4/1, April, www.unomaha.edu/jrf/armagedd.htm.

Oxtoby, Willard G. (1973) "Reflections on the Idea of Salvation." In: Eric J. Sharpe and John R. Hinnells (eds.) *Man and His Salvation: Studies in Memory of S.G.F. Brandon*, Manchester: Manchester University Press, pp. 17–37.

Paden, William E. (1992) *Interpreting the Sacred*, Boston: Beacon Press.

Papamichael, Stella (2005) Review of *What the Bleep Do We Know!?* BBC Movies, www.bbc.co.uk/films/2005/09/21/what_the_bleep_2005_dvd_review.shtml.

Park, Jacob (2006) Review of *The Day After Tomorrow*, www.carnegiecouncil.org/viewMedia.php/prmID/5043.

Parker, Rebecca and Brock, Rita Nakashima (2002) *Proverbs of Ashes*, Boston: Beacon Press.

Parsons, Susan Frank (ed.) *The Cambridge Companion to Feminist Theology*, Cambridge: Cambridge University Press.

Penelhum, Terence (1970) *Survival and Disembodied Existence*, London: Routledge and Kegan Paul.

Perkins, V. F. (1972) *Film as Film*, New York: Penguin.

Pfeil, Fred (1993) "Home Fires Burning: Family Noir in *Blue Velvet* and *Terminator 2*." In: Joan Copjec (ed.) *Shades of Noir: A Reader*, London: Verso, pp. 227–59.

Pope, Robert (2005) "Speaking of God and Donald Duck: Realism, Non-Realism and Animation." In: Eric Christianson, Peter Francis, and William Telford (eds.), *Cinéma Divinité: Readings in Film and Theology*, London: SCM, pp. 167–81.

Postman, Neil (1986) *Amusing Ourselves to Death: Public Discourse in the Age of Show Business*, Heinemann: London.

Pribram, Deidre (1988) *Female Spectators: Looking at Film and Television*, London: Verso.

Price, Henry H (1972) *Essays in the Philosophy of Religion*, Oxford: Clarendon Press.

Price, Henry H. (1973) "Survival and the Idea of 'Another World.'" In: Terence Penelhum (ed.) *Immortality*, Belmont, CA: Wadsworth, pp. 21–47.

Price, Henry H. (1992) "What Kind of Next World?" In: Paul Edwards (ed.) *Immortality*, New York: Macmillan, pp. 213–19.

Puig, Claudia (2004) "Subtle, Haunting Moments Sustain Power of *Passion*." *USA Today*, February 24, www.usatoday.com/life/movies/reviews/2004-02-24-passion_x.htm.

Quart, Leonard and Auster, Albert (1991) *American Film and Society since 1945*, London: Praeger.

Quinn, Anthony (2004) "Losing My Religion." *Independent*, March 26, http://enjoyment.independent.co.uk/film/reviews/article66016.ece.

Rahner Karl (2004) "Theology and the Arts." In: Gesa Elsbeth Thiessen (ed.) *Theological Aesthetics: A Reader*, London: SCM, pp. 218–22.

Reed, Barry (1982) *The Verdict*, St. Albans: Granada.

Régamey, Pie-Raymond (2004) "Religious Art in the Twentieth Century." In: Gesa Elsbeth Thiessen (ed.) *Theological Aesthetics: A Reader*, London: SCM, pp. 223–7.

Reinhartz, Adele (1999) "Scripture on the Silver Screen." *Journal of Religion and Film*, 3/1, April, www.unomaha.edu/jrf/scripture.htm.

Reinhartz, Adele (2003) *Scripture on the Silver Screen*, Louisville: Westminster/John Knox Press.

Rettig, Dave (1998) Review of *Pleasantville*. Christian Spotlight on the Movies, www.christiananswers.net/spotlight/movies/pre2000/i-pleasantville.html.

Riley, Robin (2003) *Film, Faith, and Cultural Conflict: The Case of Martin Scorsese's The Last Temptation of Christ*, Westport, CT: Praeger.

Robinson, B. A. (2004) "*The Passion of the Christ:* Should Children and Youths See the Film?" Religious Tolerance.org, February 28, www.religioustolerance.org/chrgibson6.htm.

Romanowski, William D. (2000) "Evangelicals and Popular Music: The Contemporary Christian Music Industry." In: Bruce David Forbes and Jeffrey H. Mahan

Bibliography

(eds.) *Religion and Popular Culture in America*, Berkeley, CA: University of California Press.

Romanowski, William D. (2001) *Eyes Wide Open: Looking for God in Popular Culture*, Grand Rapids, MI: Brazos Press.

Roncace, Mark (2002) "Paradoxical Protagonists: *Sling Blade*'s Karl and Jesus Christ." In: George Aichele and Richard Walsh (eds.) *Screening Scripture: Intertextual Connections Between Scripture and Film*, Harrisburg, PA: Trinity Press International, pp. 279–300.

Rose, Steve (2005) Review of *What the Bleep Do We Know!? Guardian*, May 20, http://film.guardian.co.uk/News_Story/Critic_Review/Guardian_review/ 0,,1487760,00.html.

Rosen, Marjorie (1973) *Popcorn Venus*, New York: Coward, McCann and Geoghegan.

Rosenthal, Daniel (ed.) (2005) *Variety International Film Guide 2005*, London: Button.

Ruether, Rosemary Radford (1986) *To Change the World*, New York: Crossroads.

Ruether, Rosemary Radford (1993) *Sexism and God-Talk*, Boston: Beacon.

Ruether, Rosemary Radford (1994) *Today's Woman in World Religions*, New York: SUNY Press.

Ruether, Rosemary Radford (1998) *Women and Redemption*, Augsburg: Fortress.

Ruether, Rosemary Radford (2001) *Christianity and the Making of the Modern Family*, Boston: Beacon.

Ruether, Rosemary Radford (2005) *Goddesses and the Divine Feminine*, Berkeley, CA: University of California.

Ruether, Rosemary Radford and Keller, Rosemary Skinner (eds.) (1995) *In Our Own Voices*, New York: HarperCollins.

Runions, Erin (2003) *How Hysterical: Identification and Resistance in the Bible and Film*. New York: Palgrave Macmillan.

Russell, Jeffrey Burton (1997) *A History of Heaven: The Singing Silence*, Princeton, NJ: Princeton University Press.

Schrader, Paul (1972) *Transcendental Style in Film: Ozu, Bresson, Dreyer*, Berkeley, CA: University of California Press.

Schulman, Mark (2004) Inaugural address to Goddard College. www.goddard. edu/about/inaug.html.

Schüssler Fiorenza, Elizabeth (1993) *Searching the Scriptures*, London: SCM.

Scott, Bernard Brandon (1994) *Hollywood Dreams and Biblical Stories*, Minneapolis: Fortress.

Segal, Robert A. (1999) *Theorizing about Myth*, Amherst: University of Massachusetts Press.

Siker, Jeffrey S. (2004) "Theologizing the Death of Jesus, Gibson's *The Passion*, and Christian Identity." In: J. Shawn Landres and Michael Berenbaum (eds.) *After* The Passion *Is Gone: American Religious Consequences*, Walnut Creek, CA: AltaMira Press, pp. 137–47.

Simmons, Marlise (2004) "Ex-Muslim Turns Her Lens on a Taboo." *New York Times*, September 27, www.religionnewsblog.com/print.php?p=8840.

Sinyard, Neil (1985) *Classic Films*, London: Chancellor Press.

Soencksen, Keith P. (2006) Review of *R.V.* Christian Spotlight on the Movies, www.christiananswers.net/spotlight/movies/2006/rv2006.html.

Sony Classics (2005) Interview with Eugene Jarecki. www.sonyclassics.com/whywefight/main/html.

Spretnak, Charlene (ed.) (1982) *The Politics of Women's Spirituality*, New York: Anchor.

Staley, Jeffrey L. (2002) "Meeting Patch Again for the First Time: Purity and Compassion in Marcus Borg, the Gospel of Mark, and *Patch Adams*." In: George Aichele and Richard Walsh (eds.) *Screening Scripture: Intertextual Connections Between Scripture and Film*, Harrisburg, PA: Trinity Press International, pp. 213–28.

Stanton, Elizabeth Cady (1993) *The Woman's Bible*, Boston: Northeastern University Press.

Stark, Rodney and Bainbridge, William Sims (1985) *The Future of Religion: Secularization, Revival and Cult Formation*, Berkeley, CA: University of California Press.

Stein, Jeff (2006) "Revelation in the Movies: Where Mythology and History Intersect." Workshop Presentation, Unitarian Universalist General Assembly, St. Louis, MO.

Stein, Ruthe (2004) Review of *What the Bleep Do We Know!? San Francisco Chronicle*, July 23, www.sfgate.com/cgi-bin/article.cgi?f=/c/a/2004/07/23/DDG257QTL41.DTL#what.

Stone, Bryan (1999) "Religion and Violence in Popular Film." *Journal of Religion and Film*, 3/1, April, www.unomaha.edu/jrf/Violence.htm.

Suleiman, Susan Rubin (1986a) "(Re)Writing the Body: The Politics and Poetics of Female Eroticism." In: Susan Rubin Suleiman (ed.) *The Female Body in Western Culture*, Cambridge, MA: Harvard University Press, pp. 7–29.

Suleiman, Susan Rubin (ed.) (1986b) *The Female Body in Western Culture*, Cambridge, MA: Harvard University Press.

Swartz, Rabbi Daniel (2006) "Religions Unite over Global Warming." Press release, October, Interfaith Power and Light.

Swietek, Frank (2004) Review of *Uncovered: The War on Iraq*. oneguysopinion.com, www.oneguysopinion.com/Review.php?ID=1431.

Taylor, Paul S. (1996) "Message from the Executive Director (Eden Communications)." ChristianAnswers.net, www.christiananswers.net/eden/purpose.html.

Telford, William R. (2005) "Through a Lens Darkly: Critical Approaches to Theology and Film." In: Eric Christianson, Peter Francis, and William Telford (eds.) *Cinéma Divinité: Readings in Film and Theology*, London: SCM, pp. 15–43.

Thiessen, Gesa Elsbeth (2004) "Theology and Modern Irish Art." In: Gesa Elsbeth Thiessen (ed.) *Theological Aesthetics: A Reader*, London: SCM, pp. 246–9.

Thompson, Don (2004) "Peace as Style." webdelsol.com, www.webdelsol.com/SolPix/sp-peace.htm.

Bibliography

Thumin, Janet (1992) *Celluloid Sisters*, London: Macmillan.

Tietjens Meyers, Diana (2002) *Gender in the Mirror*, Oxford: Oxford University Press.

Tillich, Paul (1964) *Theology of Culture* (ed. Robert C. Kimball), New York: Oxford University Press.

Tillich, Paul (2004) "Art and Ultimate Reality." In: Gesa Elsbeth Thiessen (ed.) *Theological Aesthetics: A Reader*, London: SCM, pp. 209–17.

Tookey, Christopher (1994) *The Critics' Film Guide*, London: Boxtree.

Toumarkine, Doris (2004) Review of *Uncovered: The War on Iraq*. *Film Journal International*, August 24, http://uk.rottentomatoes.com/m/uncovered_the_war_on_iraq/reviews_users_article.php?articleid=1312999.

Trible, Phyllis (1992) *Texts of Terror*, London: SCM.

Turner, Graeme (ed.) (2002) *The Film Cultures Reader*, London: Routledge.

Tuska, Jon (1984) *Dark Cinema: American Film Noir in Cultural Perspective*, London: Greenwood Press.

Updike, John (1963) *The Centaur*, Harmondsworth: Penguin.

Updike, John (1984) *The Witches of Eastwick*, New York: Knopf.

Updike, John (2006) *Terrorist*, New York: Knopf.

Vardy, Peter and Grosch, Paul (1994) *The Puzzle of Ethics*, London: Fount.

Vaux, Sara Anson (1998) "*Unforgiven*: The Sentence of Death and Radical Forgiveness." *Christianity and Literature*, 47/4 (Summer), pp. 443–58.

Vincendeau, Ginette (2001) "Sisters, Sex and Sitcom." *Sight and Sound*, 11/12, December, pp. 18–20.

Vincendeau, Ginette (2005) "Miss France." *Sight and Sound*, 15/2, February, pp. 13–15.

Voytilla, Stuart (1999) *Myth and the Movies*, Studio City, CA: Michael Wiese Productions.

Wall, James M. (1970) "Biblical Spectaculars and Secular Man." In: John C. Cooper and Carl Skrade (eds.) *Celluloid and Symbols*, Philadelphia: Fortress Press, pp. 51–60.

Walls, Jerry L. (1992) *Hell: The Logic of Damnation*, Notre Dame: University of Notre Dame Press.

Walsh, John (2003) *Are You Talking to Me? A Life Through the Movies*, London: HarperCollins.

Walsh, Richard and Aichele, George (2002) "Introduction: Scripture as Precursor." In: George Aichele and Richard Walsh (eds.) *Screening Scripture: Intertextual Connections Between Scripture and Film*, Harrisburg, PA: Trinity Press International, pp. vii–xvi.

Weber, Max (1965) *The Sociology of Religion*, London: Methuen.

Williams, Harry A. (1972) *True Resurrection*, London: Mitchell Beazley.

Willis, Brett (2004) Review of *The Passion of the Christ*. Christian Spotlight on the Movies, www.christiananswers.net/spotlight/movies/2004/thepassionofthechrist.html.

Bibliography

Wilmington, Michael (2004) Review of *The Passion of the Christ*. *Chicago Tribune*, February 25, http://metromix.chicagotribune.com/movies/mmx-040225-movies-review-mw-thepassionofthechrist,1,1280116.story.

Wood, Nicholas (2005) "Bucking the System: *One Flew Over the Cuckoo's Nest*." In: Anthony J. Clarke and Paul S. Fiddes (eds.) *Flickering Images: Theology and Film in Dialogue*, Oxford: Regent's Park College, pp. 113–22.

Wright, Melanie J. (2007) *Religion and Film: An Introduction*, London: I. B. Taurus.

Filmography

2001: A Space Odyssey, Stanley Kubrick, 1968.
About Schmidt, Alexander Payne, 2002.
The Age of Innocence, Martin Scorsese, 1993.
All Quiet on the Western Front, Lewis Milestone, 1930.
L'Amant, Jean-Jacques Annaud, 1992.
Anatomy of Hell, Catherine Breillat, 2004.
Annie Hall, Woody Allen, 1977.
Antz, Eric Darnell and Tim Johnson, 1998.
Apocalypse Now, Francis Ford Coppola, 1979.
Armageddon, Michael Bay, 1998.
Ashes and Diamonds, Andrej Wajda, 1958.
Avalanche, Corey Allen, 1978.
The Aviator, Martin Scorsese, 2004.
Awakenings, Penny Marshall, 1990.
Babe, Chris Noonan, 1995.
Baby Boom, Charles Shyer, 1987.
Batman Begins, Christopher Nolan, 2005.
The Battle of Algiers, Gilles Pontecorvo, 1966.
Bedazzled, Harold Ramis, 2000.
Being There, Hal Ashby, 1979.
The Bells of St. Mary's, Leo McCarey, 1945.
The Birds, Alfred Hitchcock, 1963.
Bonnie and Clyde, Arthur Penn, 1967.
Born on the Fourth of July, Oliver Stone, 1989.
Bowling for Columbine, Michael Moore, 2002.
Bridges of Madison County, Clint Eastwood, 1995.
Brief Encounter, David Lean, 1946.
Broken Blossoms, D. W. Griffith, 1919.

The Butterfly Effect, Eric Bress and J. Mackye Gruber, 2004.

Cabaret, Bob Fosse, 1972.

Casino, Martin Scorsese, 1995.

Catch-22, Mike Nichols, 1970.

The Chamber, James Foley, 1996.

The Charge of the Light Brigade, Michael Curtiz, 1936.

Chicken Run, Peter Lord and Nick Park, 2000.

Child's Play 3, Jack Bender, 1991.

The China Syndrome, James Bridges, 1979.

The Circle, Jafar Panahi, 2000.

Citizen Ruth, Alexander Payne, 1996.

A Civil Action, Steven Zaillian, 1998.

The Client, Joel Schumacher, 1994.

The Clutch, Sedat Semavi, 1917.

The Color Purple, Steven Spielberg, 1985.

Coming Home, Hal Ashby, 1978.

Contact, Robert Zemeckis, 1997.

Cool Hand Luke, Stuart Rosenberg, 1967.

CopLand, James Mangold, 1997.

Cosmic Voyage, Bayley Silleck, 1996.

Cry Freedom, Richard Attenborough, 1987.

The Dam Busters, Michael Anderson, 1955.

Dances with Wolves, Kevin Costner, 1990.

Daughter Rite, Michelle Citron, 1978.

The Da Vinci Code, Ron Howard, 2006.

The Day After Tomorrow, Roland Emmerich, 2004.

The Day I Became a Woman, Marziyeh Meshkini, 2000.

Dead End, William Wyler, 1937.

Dead Man Walking, Tim Robbins, 1995.

Dead Poets Society, Peter Weir, 1989.

Deep Impact, Mimi Leder, 1998.

The Deer Hunter, Michael Cimino, 1978.

Defending Your Life, Albert Brooks, 1991.

The Departed, Martin Scorsese, 2006.

Desert Hearts, Donna Deitch, 1985.

The Devil Wears Prada, David Frankel, 2006.

Die Hard, John McTiernan, 1988.

Die Hard 2: Die Harder, Renny Harlin, 1990.

Disclosure, Barry Levinson, 1994.

Dr. Strangelove Or: How I Learned to Stop Worrying and Love the Bomb, Stanley Kubrick, 1964.

Do the Right Thing, Spike Lee, 1989.

Don't Look Now, Nicolas Roeg, 1973.

The Dreams of Sparrows, Hayder Mousa Daffar, 2005.

Earthquake, Mark Robson, 1974.

East of Eden, Elia Kazan, 1955.

Edward Scissorhands, Tim Burton, 1990.

Emmanuelle, Just Jaeckin, 1974.

The End of the Affair, Neil Jordan, 1999.

Erin Brockovich, Steven Soderbergh, 2000.

E.T. The Extra Terrestrial, Steven Spielberg, 1982.

The Exorcist, William Friedkin, 1973.

Le Fabuleux destin d'Amélie Poulain, Jean-Pierre Jeunot, 2001.

Face/Off, John Woo, 1997.

Fahrenheit 451, François Truffaut, 1966.

Fahrenheit 9/11, Michael Moore, 2004.

The Fast and the Furious: Tokyo Drift, Justin Lin, 2006.

Fat Girl, Catherine Breillat, 2001.

Fatal Attraction, Adrian Lyne, 1987.

Father of the Bride, Charles Shyer, 1991.

Father of the Bride Part II, Charles Shyer, 1995.

Ferngully: The Last Rainforest, Bill Kroyer, 1992.

Field of Dreams, Phil Alden Robinson,1989.

Fight Club, David Fincher, 1999.

The Firm, Sydney Pollack, 1993.

The First Wives Club, Hugh Wilson, 1996.

Flags of Our Fathers, Clint Eastwood, 2006.

The Fog of War: Eleven Lessons from the Life of Robert S. McNamara, Errol Morris, 2003.

Galapagos: The Enchanted Voyage, David Clark and Al Giddings, 1999.

The General, Clyde Bruckman and Buster Keaton, 1927.

Ghost, Jerry Zucker, 1990.

The Girl, Márta Mészáros, 1968.

The Godfather, Francis Ford Coppola, 1972.

Good Morning, Vietnam, Barry Levinson, 1987.

The Graduate, Mike Nichols, 1967.

Grand Canyon, Lawrence Kasdan, 1991.

Grand Illusion, Jean Renoir, 1937.

Grave of the Fireflies, Isao Takahata, 1988.

The Great Dictator, Charles Chaplin, 1940.

The Green Mile, Frank Darabont, 1999.

Groundhog Day, Harold Ramis, 1993.

A Hard Day's Night, Richard Lester, 1964.

The Hidden Half, Tahmineh Milani, 2001.

High Noon, Fred Zinnemann, 1952.

Home Alone, Chris Columbus, 1990.

How I Won the War, Richard Lester, 1967.
Howl's Moving Castle, Hayao Miyazaki, 2004.
In the Name of the Father, Jim Sheridan, 1993.
An Inconvenient Truth, Davis Guggenheim, 2006.
Independence Day, Roland Emmerich, 1996.
Jacob's Ladder, Adrian Lyne, 1990.
Jagged Edge, Richard Marquand, 1985.
Jarhead, Sam Mendes, 2005.
Judgment at Nuremberg, Stanley Kramer, 1961.
Kill Bill: Vol. 2, Quentin Tarantino, 2004.
Kingdom of Heaven, Ridley Scott, 2005.
Kiss Kiss Bang Bang, Shane Black, 2005.
Kiss Me Quick, Findo Poernowo, 2004.
Klute, Alan J. Pakula, 1971.
Koyaanisqatsi, Godfrey Reggio, 1982.
Kramer versus Kramer, Robert Benton, 1979.
The Last Temptation of Christ, Martin Scorsese, 1988.
Lethal Weapon, Richard Donner, 1987.
Letters from Iwo Jima, Clint Eastwood, 2006.
Lianna, John Sayles, 1983.
Liar Liar, Tom Shadyac, 1997.
Life is Beautiful, Roberto Benigni, 1998.
Little Caesar, Mervyn LeRoy, 1931.
Little Nicky, Steven Brill, 2000.
The Long Kiss Goodnight, Renny Harlin, 1996.
Looking for Mr. Goodbar, Richard Brooks, 1977.
Lord of the Rings, Peter Jackson, 2001.
Love and Death, Woody Allen, 1975.
Manhattan, Woody Allen, 1979.
March of the Penguins, Luc Jacquet, 2005.
Marnie, Alfred Hitchcock, 1964.
$M^*A^*S^*H$, Robert Altman, 1970.
The Matrix, Andy and Larry Wachowski, 1999.
The Matrix Reloaded, Andy and Larry Wachowski, 2003.
The Matrix Revolutions, Andy and Larry Wachowski, 2003.
Mean Streets, Martin Scorsese,1973.
Meet Joe Black, Martin Brest, 1998.
Menses, Barbara Hammer, 1974.
Million Dollar Baby, Clint Eastwood, 2004.
Miss Congeniality 2: Armed and Fabulous, John Pasquin, 2005.
Mr. Holland's Opus, Stephen Herek, 1995.
Multiple Orgasm, Barbara Hammer, 1976.
Mutiny on the Bounty, Lewis Milestone, 1962.

Mystic River, Clint Eastwood, 2003.
The Name of the Rose, Jean-Jacques Annaud, 1986.
National Treasure, Jon Turteltaub, 2004.
Network, Sidney Lumet, 1976.
Norma Rae, Martin Ritt, 1979.
The Omega Code, Robert Marcarelli, 1999.
The Omen, John Moore, 2006.
One Flew Over the Cuckoo's Nest, Milos Forman, 1975.
Outbreak, Wolfgang Petersen, 1995.
The Outlaw, Howard Hughes, 1934.
Pale Rider, Clint Eastwood, 1985.
Paradise Now, Hany Abu-Assad, 2005.
The Passion of the Christ, Mel Gibson, 2004.
The Passion of Joan of Arc, Carl Theodor Dreyer, 1928.
Patch Adams, Tom Shadyac, 1998.
The Pelican Brief, Alan J. Pakula, 1993.
The Perfect Storm, Wolfgang Petersen, 2000.
Personal Best, Robert Towne, 1982.
Pirates of the Caribbean: Dead Man's Chest, Gore Verbinski, 2006.
Platoon, Oliver Stone, 1986.
Pleasantville, Gary Ross, 1998.
Pocahontas, Mike Gabriel and Eric Goldberg, 1995.
Poseidon, Wolfgang Petersen, 2006.
The Poseidon Adventure, Ronald Neame, 1972.
Priest, Antonia Bird, 1994.
Primal Fear, Gregory Hoblit, 1996.
Psycho, Alfred Hitchcock, 1960.
The Public Enemy, William A. Wellman, 1931.
Pulp Fiction, Quentin Tarantino, 1994.
Raging Bull, Martin Scorsese, 1980.
Rear Window, Alfred Hitchcock, 1954.
Rebel without a Cause, Nicholas Ray, 1955.
Robin Hood: Prince of Thieves, Kevin Reynolds, 1991.
Rocky III, Sylvester Stallone, 1982.
Romance, Catherine Breillat, 1999.
Runaway Jury, Gary Fleder, 2003.
R.V., Barry Sonnenfeld, 2006.
Sauve qui peut (la vie), Jean-Luc Godard, 1975.
Scarface, Howard Hawks, 1932.
The Sea Inside, Alejandro Amenábar, 2004.
The Searchers, John Ford, 1956.
The Second Awakening of Christa Klages, Margarethe von Trotta, 1977.
Secrets and Lies, Mike Leigh, 1996.

The Seventh Seal, Ingmar Bergman, 1957.
The Seventh Veil, Compton Bennett, 1945.
Shane, George Stevens, 1953.
The Shawshank Redemption, Frank Darabont, 1994.
The Silence of the Lambs, Jonathan Demme, 1991.
Silent Running, Douglas Trumbull, 1972.
Silkwood, Mike Nichols, 1983.
Sister Act, Emile Ardolino, 1992.
Sleeper, Woody Allen, 1973.
Sleepers, Barry Levinson, 1996.
Sling Blade, Billy Bob Thornton, 1996.
Snow Falling on Cedars, Scott Hicks, 1999.
Something's Gotta Give, Nancy Meyers, 2003.
The Sound of Music, Robert Wise, 1965.
Soylent Green, Richard Fleischer, 1973.
The Spell, Dariush Farhang, 1986.
Spider-Man, Sam Raimi, 2002.
Spider-Man 2, Sam Raimi, 2004.
Star Trek (TV), Gene Roddenberry, 1966.
Star Wars, George Lucas, 1977.
Star Wars: Episode VI – Return of the Jedi, Richard Marquand, 1983.
The Straight Story, David Lynch, 1999.
Submission Part I, Theo van Gogh, 2004.
Sunrise, F. W. Murnau, 1927.
Superman Returns, Bryan Singer, 2006.
Suspect, Peter Yates, 1987.
Taxi Driver, Martin Scorsese, 1976.
Ten, Abbas Kiarostami, 2002.
The Terminator, James Cameron, 1984.
Terminator 2: Judgment Day, James Cameron, 1991.
Them!, Gordon M. Douglas, 1954.
To Kill a Mockingbird, Robert Mulligan, 1962.
Tootsie, Sydney Pollack, 1982.
A Trip to the Moon, Georges Méliès, 1902.
True Crime, Clint Eastwood, 1998.
The Truman Show, Peter Weir, 1998.
The Turning Point, Herbert Ross, 1977.
Twelve Monkeys, Terry Gilliam, 1995.
Twister, Jan de Bont, 1996.
The Two of Them, Márta Mészáros, 1977.
Two Women, Tahmineh Milani, 1998.
Uncovered: The War on Iraq, Robert Greenwald, 2004.
Unforgiven, Clint Eastwood, 1992.

Filmography

Vanilla Sky, Cameron Crowe, 2001.
The Verdict, Sidney Lumet, 1982.
A Very Long Engagement, Jean-Pierre Jeunot, 2004.
Volcanoes of the Deep Sea, Stephen Low, 2003.
The War Game, Peter Watkins, 1965.
The War of the Worlds, Steven Spielberg, 2005.
Waterworld, Kevin Reynolds, 1995.
What Dreams May Come, Vincent Ward, 1998.
What the Bleep Do We Know!?, Mark Vicente, Betty Chasse, and William Arntz, 2004.
Why We Fight, Eugene Jarecki, 2005.
The Witches of Eastwick, George Miller, 1987.
Working Girl, Mike Nichols, 1988.
The World's Fastest Indian, Roger Donaldson, 2005.
You've Got Mail, Nora Ephron, 1998.

Index